Colin

a dullish book on a good subject

Peter.

FROM CLERGYMAN TO DON

Untitled drawing by Max Beerbohm, *c.* 1894

FROM CLERGYMAN TO DON

The Rise of the Academic
Profession in
Nineteenth-Century Oxford

A. J. ENGEL

CLARENDON PRESS · OXFORD
1983

Oxford University Press, Walton Street, Oxford OX2 6DP

London Glasgow New York Toronto
Delhi Bombay Calcutta Madras Karachi
Kuala Lumpur Singapore Hong Kong Tokyo
Nairobi Dar es Salaam Cape Town
Melbourne Auckland

and associates
Beirut Berlin Ibadan Mexico City Nicosia

OXFORD is a trade mark of Oxford University Press

Published in the United States by
Oxford University Press, New York

British Library Cataloguing in Publication Data
Engel, A.J.
From clergyman to don.
1. University of Oxford — History
2. College teachers — England — Oxford (Oxfordshire)
— History
I. Title
378'.121   LF518
ISBN 0-19-822606-3

Library of Congress Cataloging in Publication Data
Engel, A. J.
        From clergyman to don.
        Revision of thesis (Ph. D.) — Princeton
University, 1975.
        Includes bibliographical references and index.
        1. University of Oxford — Faculty — History —
19th century.   2. Education, Higher — Great Britain
— History — 19th century.   I. Title.
LF519.E53 1983   378.425'74   82-8292
ISBN 0-19-822606-3

Typeset by Hope Services, Abingdon,
Printed in Great Britain
at the University Press, Oxford
by Eric Buckley
Printer to the University

To my parents,

Henry A. Engel

and

Bertha Schaefer Engel

Acknowledgements

This study is a revised version of my dissertation (Princeton University, 1975). My intellectual debt to Professor Lawrence Stone goes far beyond conventional acknowledgements to a supervisor. I also benefited greatly from the comments of the readers, Dr James Obelkevich and Dr James McLachlan, and from discussions of professionalization with Professor Donald W. Light. In Oxford Mr Trevor Aston, Professor A. H. Halsey, and Mr A. F. Thompson were sources of both instruction and encouragement.

In revising the thesis, I was saved from factual errors and stylistic faults by Professor Hugh Trevor-Roper (Lord Dacre) and Mr John Sparrow. I owe a special obligation to Warden Sparrow, who showed me the frontispiece and has permitted me to reproduce it.

Virginia Commonwealth University   A.J.E.
Richmond, Virginia

Contents

x   *Contents*

Introduction

In the frontispiece of this volume the large clerical figure of the 'Don of the Old School' greets with surly disapproval the self-confident little 'Don of the New School'. The drawing is on the stationery of the Oxford Union Society and was made by Max Beerbohm when he was a Merton under-graduate in the early 1890s.[1] The Oxford of the 'Don of the Old School' was an overwhelmingly clerical society with virtually all dons in holy orders, with a substantial plurality of undergraduates from clerical homes and destined them-selves for careers in the Church. The new Oxford which came into being in the nineteenth century and which so offended the 'Don of the Old School' was an increasingly secular institution. The Church had been expropriated and a secular profession of university teaching and scholarship had been created with the resources of the colleges and university. To accomplish this goal, the institution had to be altered in all its functions: its educational ideals, its clientele, its recruitment patterns, its size, its social and economic roles.

This transformation could not have taken place without controversy and bitter conflict. It is this reality which can be seen in the attitudes of the two dons meeting in Max Beerbohm's drawing. The 'Don of the New School' refers contemptuously to the bad old days of 'Platitude & Port Wine'. From his perspective, reform had triumphed and entrenched corruption had been uprooted. The attitude of the 'Don of the Old School' is necessarily different. His views of the nature and role of the university had been defeated. He expresses his anger and frustration by impugning the religious convictions and social background of his successor. The traditional clerical Oxford had been destroyed to make

---

[1] See Rupert Hart-Davis, *A Catalogue of the Caricatures of Max Beerbohm* (Cambridge, Mass., 1972), no. 1932, p. 171.

way for a new secular profession. This book is a study of how this transformation took place and what differences it made for the role of the university in society.

Throughout the eighteenth and early nineteenth centuries, the University of Oxford was the object of violent and diverse public criticisms. The colleges were condemned as 'close corporations', eccentric, uncompetitive, and often corrupt, operating simply to distribute their great wealth among the members of their foundations. Their statutes were ridiculed as obsolete, though they also were censured for failing to obey statutory injunctions to prefer 'poor scholars' in awarding scholarships and fellowships. They were blamed for the idleness, immorality, and extravagance of the undergraduates. The religious tests which excluded Dissenters were strongly attacked. The contribution of the university to the advancement of learning was belittled and its examinations for degrees were denounced as meaningless rituals, emptied of all educational content.

Despite these criticisms, until 1854 Oxford continued to be governed by the statutes given by Archbishop Laud in the early seventeenth century. The examination system began to be reformed in 1800, but the structure of university and college institutions remained unchanged. The government was dominated by the heads of colleges and halls who, with the two proctors responsible for university discipline, formed the Hebdomadal Board, the executive committee of the university. All students were required to be members of a college or hall and they had to subscribe to the Thirty-nine Articles of the Church at matriculation. The colleges also dominated the educational system. Although the duties of the university professors included giving instruction through public lectures, this obligation had been allowed largely to fall into abeyance during the eighteenth century. Most professorships were in subjects outside the narrowly classical and mathematical curriculum and many chairs were of such small value that their holders were often non-resident. The result was that the entire official responsibility for teaching fell on the tutors provided by the colleges. By the Laudian statutes, the colleges became the centre of the university for the purposes of both government and instruction.

The colleges of Oxford were autonomous corporations, governed in most cases by their fellows and the heads, elected by the fellows. A fellowship entitled its holder to a share in the income derived from the property held by the college as a charitable foundation. In general these prizes were tenable for life on the condition of taking holy orders within a specified period, remaining unmarried, and not holding a Church living or other income over a certain value. Virtually all fellowships were restricted to men born in particular localities, or to those who had attended particular schools. Most colleges were also required by their statutes to prefer candidates who could prove descent from their founder.[2] The headships were generally restricted to clergymen and, in most elections, one of the fellows or former fellows was the successful candidate. The colleges also owned advowsons which gave them the right to appoint clergymen to Church livings. These livings, when they fell vacant, were offered to the fellows in holy orders in order of seniority. Teaching and administrative duties were performed by a few of the fellows, most often selected by the head, while the remainder were free to use their fellowships simply as incomes to enable them to begin their careers, generally in the Church.

The fellows of the colleges were the vast majority of the senior academic community of the university. There were about 500 fellowships divided among the 19 colleges and only about 50 other official positions in Oxford; the 24 headships of colleges and halls, the approximately 20 professorships,[3] the 8 canonries of Christ Church, and a few other university offices. These 50 posts were the only ones which could be held by married men. Some of them, notably the headships of most colleges, the canonries of Christ Church, and a few of the professorial chairs were rich prizes providing fine houses and large incomes. Many of the others, however, offered little more than an honorarium.

In the early nineteenth century, one more class was added

---

[2] On this subject, see G. D. Squibb, *Founders' Kin, Privilege and Pedigree* (Oxford, 1972).

[3] There were 19 university professorships in 1800 and 25 by 1854.

to the senior academic community: the coaches. The coaches were called into being by the reform of the examination system. The examination statutes of 1800 and 1807 established honours examinations in *Literae Humaniores* (classical studies; including history, literature, and philosophy, as well as Latin and Greek) and in science and mathematics. The ordinary 'pass' school was also altered to require some degree of knowledge. All through the eighteenth century, the examination for the BA had been a purely formal ritual of answering standard questions known in advance, and reading a 'wall-lecture', so called because the examiners would often leave while it was being read.

One unintended result of the reform of the examination system was that an increased demand for teaching was created. Collegiate instruction was conducted through 'catechetical lectures' composed of all students, regardless of attainments, studying a particular classical text for the examinations. The text would be read and translated in class, the lecturer commenting on both the language and the substance of the work. This method was ill-suited both to students whose classical preparation was weak and to those who wished to take the honours examinations. The system of coaching grew to meet their needs for more personal and intensive teaching. The coaches were outside the official body of collegiate and university instructors. For a fee of about £10 per term, they would undertake to give private instruction for three hours per week. The coaches in most cases were young graduates since the uncertainty of the income and the lack of official status made the position undesirable as a life-career.

In the early nineteenth century the Oxford don was by profession a clergyman, not a university teacher. In most cases, holy orders were a condition for holding his fellowship, and he was destined to resign this prize after about ten or fifteen years to take up the duties of a country parson. The Church was the only profession smoothly connected to the holding of a fellowship. Although in many cases a fellow could attempt to make a career in Law or Medicine, the colleges could not provide clients or patients, while they did offer Church livings. The result was that even in those colleges such as Merton, in which most fellows were not required to be in holy orders, the great majority did, in fact, choose this path. Most fellows were elected soon after receiving their BAs, took holy orders, and spent their period of waiting for a college living holding various curacies. They were generally non-resident but would come to Oxford occasionally for college meetings and elections. They might also reside if their curacy was nearby or if called upon to hold a college office. For these dons, a fellowship was a prize which provided a favourable mode of entry to a career in the Church; academic duties themselves did not constitute a life-career.[4]

By the end of the nineteenth century this career link had become the exception rather than the rule. Four important government commissions in 1850-2, 1854-8, 1871-3, and 1877-81 had resulted in innumerable revisions of college and university statutes affecting the senior members of the university. Although the outward structure of the fellowship had changed little, its function had been altered drastically. Most fellows, and virtually all the younger ones, were engaged in teaching within the colleges. Furthermore, their teaching was no longer an interlude before commencing their true career, it was their career itself. Tutorial fellows were permitted to marry and many would remain in Oxford all their lives as teachers and scholars. Even those who left often went to posts at other universities. The outlines of academic life as a profession had already been drawn.[5]

---

[4] For two late eighteenth-century diaries which show the functioning of this system, see W. N. Hargreaves-Mawdsley (ed.), *Woodforde at Oxford 1759-76* (Oxford, 1969) and G. Galbraith (ed.), *The Journal of the Rev. William Bagshaw Stevens* (Oxford, 1965). For Parson Woodforde the system worked smoothly, transporting him effortlessly from Fellow and sometime Sub-warden of New College to Rector of Weston Longeville. For Stevens a slowdown in the succession to fellowships at Magdalen meant an embittered life of disappointed collegiate expectations and uncongenial occupations.

[5] See below, Appendix 1, p. 286. Academic life was only, however, a profession for men. Women's colleges did not begin to appear in Oxford until the 1870s and did not attain full membership in the university until 1920. The problems of creating an academic profession for women in Oxford were quite different from those encountered by the male dons who are the subject of this study. The poverty of the women's colleges and their long struggle for official recognition made for some differences in the efforts of their dons to achieve professional status. The most important difference, however, was made by society's radically dichotomous conceptions of the roles of men and women. This difference affected every issue from the value of personal supervision to ideals of education and appropriate

This change was not, of course, confined to Oxford. Cambridge also had been an overwhelmingly clerical institution which was transformed in the nineteenth century to fit the needs of a secular academic profession. Many Oxford conflicts; between Church and State, Science and Religion, colleges and university, tutors and professors, teaching and research, 'liberal' and 'professional' education all had their analogues in Cambridge.[6] None the less, there were important local differences between the two universities and these also had their influence on the shape of the emerging academic profession. Probably the most important was that the university of Cambridge managed to gain considerably more power in relation to its colleges than did the University of Oxford. The need for centralized laboratories in the natural and physical sciences, in which Cambridge had stronger traditions than Oxford,[7] tended to this result. Also the fact that Cambridge had more poor colleges and only a few rich ones may have disposed the majority to favour granting more power to the university. In any case, the consequence was that the emerging academic profession was relatively more centred on the faculty boards of the university than on the fellowships of the colleges.

The new universities of the nineteenth century also saw the development of professional careers for academics. The very creation of these new institutions marked the rejection by their supporters of clerical control of university teaching.[8] Without clerical traditions and interests or powerful autonomous colleges, however, their conflicts tended to differ from

careers. From the viewpoint of the dons' struggle for professional status, the crucial expression of this dichotomy was that marriage and a professional career were considered incompatible for women while the right to marry was seen as essential for men. The result of these differences has been to make the creation of an academic profession for women in Oxford a separate story. See Annie M. H. Rogers, *Degrees by Degree* (Oxford, 1938), and Vera Brittain, *The Women at Oxford* (London, 1960).

[6] See Sheldon Rothblatt, *The Revolution of the Dons: Cambridge and Society in Victorian England* (London, 1968). On the conflict over ideals of education, see Martha McMackin Garland, *Cambridge Before Darwin: The Ideal of a Liberal Education 1800–1860* (Cambridge, 1980).

[7] The importance of this scientific tradition has been stressed by G. L. Geison in his *Michael Foster and the Cambridge School of Physiology* (Princeton, 1978), esp. 89–115.

[8] See W. H. G. Armytage, *Civic Universities* (London, 1956), chs. 8–11.

those of Oxford and Cambridge. Although they experienced the struggle between 'liberal' and 'professional' education, power was not as heavily weighted toward the former as it was in the older universities. Though teaching versus research was a common issue, the shape of this battle was altered by the fact that they were not disputing the proper uses for pre-existing endowments. The result of these differences was that the academic profession which developed in the new universities centred more on the professoriate and departmental organization than was the case in Oxford and Cambridge. Faculty autonomy was protected in the end by professional organization rather than by collegiate power.[9]

Throughout Europe and in the United States as well, academic professions were also forming in the late eighteenth and nineteenth centuries, though national variations in the organization and social role of universities, as well as in attitudes toward professionalism, resulted in important differences from the Oxford pattern.[10] The absence, in general, of celibacy restrictions, clerical control, college systems, and large endowments made for fewer obstacles to the creation of a secular academic profession and a faster pace of development. The relative eagerness of the European universities to accept government aid and direction as well as the strong historical connections between the professions and the State also had far-reaching consequences for both the role of the university and the definition of the academic profession. In Germany and France, the training of teachers for academic secondary schools provided a teaching basis for specialists in a wide range of humanistic subjects while government support for technical education and research institutes gave an analogous stimulus to the sciences.[11] In

[9] See Harold Perkin, *Key Profession: The History of the Association of University Teachers* (London, 1969).

[10] For a comparative study of England, Germany, Russia, and the United States, see the series of essays in Konrad Jarausch (ed.), *The Transformation of the Higher Learning 1860-1930* (Cologne, 1982). For a comparative study of Germany and France, see Fritz K. Ringer, *Education and Society in Modern Europe* (Bloomington and London, 1979).

[11] For France, see Robert Fox and George Weisz (eds.), *The Organization of Science and Technology in France 1808-1914* (Cambridge, 1980), George Weisz, 'The Anatomy of University Reform in France 1863-1914', in Donald Baker and

Scotland, the creation of academic careers was prompted by the large numbers of students drawn to the universities by their inexpensiveness and the fame of their professors.[12] In the United States, although the traditional clerically-controlled colleges of the East experienced obstacles similar to those of Oxford to the creation of a secular academic profession, the newer land-grant universities tended toward German and Scottish examples.[13] At various times in the nineteenth century, these foreign universities were to provide Oxford dons with both models and cautionary tales for their own emerging career aspirations: models of public service and research, but cautionary tales of superficial instruction and irreligion.

The transformation of university teaching from an aspect of a clerical career into a separate profession was also part of the larger movement toward the development and expansion of the professions in Victorian society. When R. L. Edgeworth published his *Essays on Professional Education* in 1808, he assumed the professions to consist only of the Church, the Law, Medicine, and the Army. By 1928, Carr-Saunders and Wilson, in their study of *The Professions,* listed fifteen distinct professions.[14] Even this growth does not fully indicate the

---

Patrick Harrigan (eds.), *The Making of Frenchmen, Current Directions in the History of Education in France 1679-1979* (Waterloo, Ontario, 1980), 363-79; Terry Nichols Clark, *Prophets and Patrons: The French University and the Emergence of the Social Sciences* (Cambridge, Mass., 1973); and William R. Keylor, *Academy and Community: The Foundation of the French Historical Profession* (Cambridge, Mass., 1975). For Germany, see R. Steven Turner, 'University Reformers and Professional Scholarship in Germany 1760-1806', in Lawrence Stone (ed.), *The University in Society* (Princeton, 1974) ii. 495-531 and 'The Growth of Professional Research in Prussia 1818-1848 — Causes and Context', *Historical Studies in the Physical Sciences* iii (1971), 167-82.

[12] See G. E. Davie, *The Democratic Intellect, Scotland and her Universities in the Nineteenth Century* (Edinburgh, 1961).

[13] See Laurence R. Veysey, *The Emergence of the American University* (Chicago and London, 1965) and Burton J. Bledstein, *The Culture of Professionalism: The Middle Class and the Development of Higher Education in America* (New York, 1976).

[14] See Table III, p. 507 (Barristers, Solicitors, Patent Agents, Doctors, Dentists, Veterinary Surgeons, Engineers, Chemists, Physicists, Architects, Surveyors Etc., Accountants, Actuaries, Civil Servants, Teachers).

magnitude of the change since Carr-Saunders·and Wilson refused to include many vocations whose associations, modelled
on those of the recognized professions, announced their
aspirations toward professional status. A more recent study,
which rejected this exclusion as an unwarranted value-judge-
ment, listed seventy-eight separate professions and over 100
professional organizations.[15] It was within this expanding
world of professions that academics too were able to find a
place for themselves.

The structure and values of the career which Oxford dons
succeeded in creating for themselves owed much to enduring
conceptions of the nature of professional employment. Their
goal was not merely to make university teaching into a permanent career, but rather to make it a profession, comparable
in rewards and social position to the traditional learned
professions of barrister, physician, and clergyman. None the
less, the two main structural characteristics which sociologists
have often used to define a profession seem to have only
limited connections with the conditions of academic life,
namely the application of a branch of learning or science to
a practical area of life and the existence of an association
serving to license practitioners and promulgate standards of
ethical conduct.[16] Teaching and research might be considered
to fit the first of these characteristics but the second seems to
have been entirely absent from the concerns of nineteenth-
century Oxford dons.

The reason for this omission was simply that the vital
functions performed by professional associations were
satisfied for academics by the colleges and the fellowship
system. Carr-Saunders observed that the goal of professional

[15] Geoffrey Millerson, *The Qualifying Associations: A Study in Professionalization* (London, 1964). See the lists of 'fields' having one or more 'qualifying
association', 222–45.

[16] The most influential structuralist interpretation of professionalism has been
that of Talcott Parsons. See his *The Social System* (New York, 1951) and 'The
Professions and Social Structure', in *Essays in Sociological Theory* (New York,
1954), 34–49. A ground-breaking attack on this approach, emphasizing issues
of power, status, and autonomy has been made for the American medical profession
by Eliot Freidson in an important series of articles which culminated in *The
Profession of Medicine* (New York, 1970). Magali Sarfatti Larson has made effective
use of this approach for a comparative study of the United States and England,
The Rise of Professionalism: A Sociological Analysis (Berkeley, Calif., 1977).

associations was to raise the level of attainments and the standard of professional conduct of practitioners by separating the qualified from the unqualified.[17] Professional associations served to control entry to the profession, to grant this exclusionary power to members of the profession itself, and to reduce the potential dominance which, under the ordinary rules of the market-place, would have belonged either to the employing institution or to the customer. Since dons themselves decided who was qualified and who was not, especially after 1854 when most previous restrictions of fellowships to specific localities, schools, or families were abolished and 'open competition' became the rule, they did not need professional associations to fulfil these purposes.

Oxford dons were, however, as concerned as other nascent professional men in the nineteenth century with problems of status. The new professions often expressed this concern explicitly in the charters whereby they obtained official recognition. For example, the charter of the Royal College of Veterinary Surgeons, founded in 1844, mentioned the hope that this association would 'contribute to the respectability' of the profession. Similarly, the National Union of Teachers, founded in 1870, referred in their charter to the desire of the association '[t] o raise the status of the teaching profession'.[18] Although academics in Oxford were more concerned with preserving their traditional social position than with raising it, the problems they encountered were often analogous to those experienced by other new professions in the nineteenth century.

Oxford dons were, in fact, cutting away an important element of their status position in attempting to make the position of the university teacher a permanent career, separate from that of the clergymen. The traditional social rank of the

---

[17] *Professions: Their Organization and Place in Society* (Oxford, 1928), cited in H. M. Vollmer and Donald L. Mills (eds.), *Professionalization* (Englewood Cliffs, N. J., 1966), 5–7. Carr-Saunders quoted the *Pharmaceutical Journal for 1847*: 'The Pharmaceutical Society was designed as a means of raising the qualifications of pharmaceutical chemists and placing between them and unqualified persons a line of demarcation.' (p. 5.)

[18] Both examples were cited from Carr-Saunders, in ibid. 5–7.

clergyman had served to compensate for the conspicuous lack of high status in the role of teacher itself. This was certainly true for schoolmasters, that occupation whose functions were most similar to those of the college don. Mr Riley, the worldly lawyer in George Eliot's *The Mill on the Floss*, expressed this attitude bluntly, '[A]ll the best schoolmasters are of the clergy', he insisted. 'The schoolmasters who are not clergymen, are a very low set of men generally . . . [A] clergyman is a gentleman by profession and education'.[19] Academics' insistence on the analogy between their career and the traditional 'higher professions' was an attempt to obtain a new source of assured status to take the place of their old connection with the Church. As professionals, dons could be certain they would not be viewed as a 'low set of men' by the Mr Rileys of the world.

High social position was a crucial element in Victorian people's conception of professional work. Anthony Trollope expressed succinctly this popular understanding in his definition of a profession as 'a calling by which a gentleman, not born to the inheritance of a gentleman's allowance of good things, might ingeniously obtain the same by some exercise of his abilities'.[20] To the middle and upper classes, this idea of the 'gentleman' was the most important of status distinctions. It embodied the ideal of ruling-class egalitarianism: all men certainly were not socially equal, but all gentlemen were. Fundamentally, a profession was an occupation which a gentleman could follow without losing his claim to this coveted social position.

A perceptive literary critic has noted the extreme and growing importance of the idea of the gentleman. 'The question is the burning Victorian question', V. S. Pritchett has asserted. 'What is a gentleman? It is the obsessive preoccupation of the ever-expanding middle class.'[21] Several historians of English education have remarked that the public schools and ancient universities, with their uniform and distinctive curricula and their strong sense of social community, played an important role in creating and main-

---

[19] (New York ed., 1860), Book I, ch. iii, 21.
[20] *The Bertrams* (New York ed., 1867), ch. viii, 84.
[21] *George Meridith and English Comedy* (New York, 1969), 75.

taining the solidarity of the gentleman class.[22] It has been argued that much of the impetus for the growth of nineteenth-century professions was the need to expand the opportunities for obtaining 'a gentleman's allowance of the good things' for the growing numbers receiving this type of education.[23]

Oxford dons found themselves in a situation analogous in certain ways to that of these new recruits to ruling-class values. Throughout the nineteenth century, the great majority of Oxford dons were from families of undisputed 'gentleman' status, but few possessed independent means.[24] Their social need was to obtain a life-career without endangering their position as gentlemen. The obvious solution to this dilemma, sanctioned by growing social usage, was for the don to become a professional man. Family background also may have played a role in the drive of Oxford dons toward professionalism. The late nineteenth century dons who rejected their traditional clerical position were themselves only half as likely as their predecessors to be the sons of clergymen and were twice as likely to be the sons of secular professional men.[25] The professional ideology which Oxford dons applied to their own careers may have been learned in the home as well as from the values of society at large.

Although the transformation of academic life into a secular profession has not gone unnoticed by previous historians of the university, their perspectives have differed from that of the present study. The earliest historians of the reform of Oxford in the nineteenth century regarded the redefining of the function of academics as part of the general elimination

---

[22] See T. W. Bamford, *The Rise of the Public Schools* (London, 1967) and R. H. Wilkinson, *The Prefects* (London, 1964).

[23] See F. Musgrove, 'Middle-class Education and Employment in the Nineteenth Century', *Economic History Review*, 2nd Series, xii (1959–60), 99–111.

[24] Comparing the social background of dons first appointed to college offices from 1813 to 1830 with those first appointed from 1881 to 1900, about 80 per cent in both periods were of the 'gentleman class'. Only a few, however, of the sons of 'squires/private gentlemen' and 'merchants/manufacturers' could have inherited enough private wealth to make an occupation financially unnecessary. See below, Appendix 2, p. 287.

[25] Clerical families fell from 45 per cent to 26 per cent while professional families rose from 8 per cent to 21 per cent. See ibid., compare I.a with I.d.

of corruption.[26] Depending on the individual historian's temperament, the eighteenth century was viewed with either indignation or amusement; but all were agreed in accepting contemporary denunciations at face value. Later historians have modified this view by suggesting that these attacks originated as much in political and ecclesiastical party conflict as in righteous indignation.[27] W. R. Ward has argued that the importance of the nineteenth-century reforms was that they removed Oxford from the area of politics to concentrate on its prime tasks of education and research.[28] Since these latter functions were assumed to be the proper tasks of the university, however, the importance of the issue of defining the academic profession was not systematically analysed. The present study is an attempt to demonstrate that central to the intellectual conflicts and institutional changes in nineteenth-century Oxford was the question whether the university ought to provide a career for academics and, if so, what sort of career it should be in terms of functions, status, and duties. The answers to these questions have largely determined the shape of modern Oxford.

---

[26] See A. D. Godley, *Oxford in the 18th Century* (London, 1908); A. Hamilton Gibbs, *Rowlandson's Oxford* (London, 1911); C. E. Mallet, *A History of the University of Oxford* (New York ed., 1928) iii.

[27] See W. R. Ward, *Georgian Oxford* (Oxford, 1958), also the excellent brief background chapter in V. H. H. Green, *The Young Mr. Wesley* (London, 1961) 13–40. Dame Lucy Sutherland has proposed a more positive interpretation in her Bryce Memorial Lecture, *The University of Oxford in the Eighteenth Century* (Oxford, 1973).

[28] *Victorian Oxford* (London, 1965).

Chapter 1

EMERGING CONCEPTS OF THE ACADEMIC PROFESSION 1800–1845

During the first half of the nineteenth century, and especially during the period of intense debate surrounding the appointment and proceedings of the Royal Commision of 1850, all the fundamental issues regarding academic work were first introduced. These issues continued to excite controversy in Oxford throughout the nineteenth century and many of them still remain unresolved. The conventional eighteenth-century denunciations of corruption and extravagance eventually came to be blended with more pointed criticisms relating the deficiencies of the university to its failure to provide life-careers for dons. College tutors and university professors, as well as outside critics, began to call for the acceptance of academic work as a recognized profession.

The basic problems were raised during the first half of the nineteenth century concerning the position which this new profession ought to occupy in relation to both the outside learned professions and the ecclesiastical nature of the collegiate foundations. There was strenuous debate about whether this new academic profession ought to consider teaching or scholarly research as its primary function, whether it ought to be organized in the colleges or in the university, whether the education it offered ought to be 'liberal' or 'professional', and whether its teaching methods ought to concentrate on formal lectures, small classes, or individual instruction. The intellectual conflicts of this period were to form the basis for enduring academic party alignments and also for the profound structural changes which the university was to experience in the second half of the nineteenth century.

A. Early Reform Proposals

The idea of university teaching as a profession played little or no part in the reform debates of the late eighteenth and early nineteenth centuries. Complaints about the fellowship system were concentrated on the venality of elections and the lack of a proper life of discipline and poverty for the fellows. The reformers generally confined themselves to simple denunciations, but when they did venture to suggest reforms, the suggestions ran directly counter to the encouragement of an academic profession. One writer suggested that fellowships ought to be limited to twenty years' tenure rather than held on condition of celibacy. He argued that the existing system 'occasions many persons spending their whole life in a College, without doing any the least service to their country, but to their own hurt, being generally as they advance in years, over-run with spleen or taking to sottishness'.[1] The author admitted that the twenty-year limit might be relaxed for two fellows, at the most, in each college if they had served as tutors for fifteen years; these men should be allowed their fellowships for life on the ground that since they are 'pretty much obliged to keep to academical learning they cannot so well pursue the study of some profession'.[2] The author did not indicate that any educational advantage would accrue to the student or university from this extended tenure in the tutorial office.

Even in regard to the venality of fellowship elections, the reformers did not complain that fellowships were not given to the men of the highest intellectual merit; rather, they complained that fellowships were given to rich men who did not use them as their sole means of support.

Fellowships are rarely given to Scholars of *low condition*, whatever be their Merit. Men of *Family* and *Fortune* are, now, not only ready to *accept* of them, but make great Interest to procure them. . . . *Possessed* of the Endowments, they live not in the simple, frugal Manner, so necessary to Health, and Study and Virtue, which their Founders designed they should. . . . A Founder's Endowment is no longer considered as a charitable Provision for *intire* Maintenance, or as laying any obligation upon those who accept of it to observe his Rules, but as a Branch of their Revenue in general to be spent in the manner they like best.[3]

---

[1] Anon. (attributed by E. H. Cordeaux and D. H. Merry, *A Bibliography of the Printed Works Relating to the University of Oxford* (Oxford, 1968), to the third Earl of Macclesfield) 'A Memorial Relating to the Universities', in J. Gutch (ed.), *Collectanea Curiosa* (Oxford, 1781), iii. 56.

[2] Ibid. 58.

[3] 'Supplement' Well-Wishers to the University of Oxford', *The General Evening*

Clearly, these critics had no conception of university teaching as a lifetime career or of a fellowship as providing a satisfactory stipend for a teacher.

The first criticisms of Oxford to question this idea of academic life were in the famous *Edinburgh Review* articles of 1808-10.[4] Although the main thrust of the attack was directed against the system of classical education at Oxford, the reviewer also criticized the lack of scholarly activity within the university. In discussing the classical texts published by the Clarendon Press, the reviewer observed that 'though this learned Body have occasionally availed themselves of the sagacity and erudition of Rhunken, Wyttenbach, Heyné and other *foreign* professors, they have, of late, added nothing of their own, except what they derived from the superior skill of British manufacturers, and the superior wealth of their establishment; namely, whiter paper, blacker ink, and neater types'.[5] There was no overt call in the *Review* for the university to take the advancement of learning as one of its goals, but that was the clear implication of this taunt. It was certainly taken as such by Edward Copleston of Oriel, who took upon himself the task of defending the university against these attacks:

If we send into the world an annual supply of men, whose minds are imbued with literature according to their serveral measures of capacity, impressed with what we hold to be the soundest principles of policy and religion, grounded in the elements of science and taught how they may best direct their efforts to further attainments in that line ... I think we do a greater and more solid good to the nation, than if we sought to extend over Europe the fame of a few exalted individuals or to acquire renown by exploring untrodden regions, and by holding up to the world ever ready to admire what is new, the fruits of our discovery.[6]

Post, no. 2546 (London, 11-13 Jan. 1750). Attributed by Cordeaux and Merry to R. Newton, Principal of Hart Hall, Oxford.

[4] See [John Playfair,] 'Traité de Méchanique Céleste, par P. S. LaPlace', *Edinburgh Review* xi (Jan. 1808), 249-84; [Richard Payne Knight,] 'The Oxford Edition of Strabo', *Edin. Rev.* xiv (July 1809), 429-41; [Sydney Smith,] 'Essays on Professional Education, by R. L. Edgeworth', *Edin. Rev.* xv (Oct. 1809), 40-53; 'Woodhouse's Trigonometry', *Edin. Rev.* xvii (Nov. 1810), 122-35.

[5] *Edin. Rev.* xiv (July 1809), 431.

[6] *A Reply to the Calumnies of the Edinburgh Review against Oxford containing an account of the studies pursued in the University* (Oxford, 1810), 150. The other defences of Oxford against the criticisms of the *Edinburgh Review* did not

Copleston identified the advancement of knowledge with teaching through public, professorial lectures to large classes even though no mention was made of the professorial system in the *Edinburgh* articles. Copleston noted that instruction at Oxford was 'not by solemn public lectures, delivered to a numerous class from a Professor's Chair, but by private study in their respective colleges'.[7] Collegiate lectures, he argued, were more effective as a means of instruction since the student was given more individual attention and the instructor could accommodate the teaching to the capacities and previous knowledge of each student.[8] He added: 'I would not undervalue these higher doings [public lectures] ; but we must be cautious how they lead us out of the track of plain and sober industry. A thirst for distinction may interfere with homely duties more really important to mankind. Our husbandry is truly on a large scale; but let us beware how we sacrifice, after the example of vain, ostentatious breeders, the food of some twenty or thirty, for the sake of making a proud shew of one.'[9] The advancement of knowledge and public lectures were linked for Copleston since he considered both 'more exalted' and 'higher doings' which benefited the few at the expense of the many. Likewise, teaching and collegiate lectures were bound together as 'homely duties' conducive of 'greater and more solid good'. This connection between the professorial system and the advancement of learning was to have a long history in the debate over the nature of the academic profession in nineteenth-century Oxford. The conception of professorial lectures as the 'higher' form of teaching was also to have a long life, although it would eventually be overthrown by the idealization of the tutorial system which was to replace catechetical lectures as the primary mode of Oxford teaching.

Although this controversy of 1808–10 was the beginning of the debate from which there eventually developed the idea of an academic profession, it was not until the 1830s that direct attacks were made on the existing structure of academic life.

---

go beyond simply agreeing with Copleston on every point. See 'Replies to the Calumnies against Oxford', *Quarterly Review* vii (Aug. 1810), 177–206; also 'Three Replies to the Calumnies against Oxford', *British Critic* xxxvii (1811), 346–56.

[7] Ibid. 145   [8] Ibid. 149   [9] Ibid. 145–7 and *passim.*

It was also in this period from 1800 to 1830 that the working of the new system of examinations established in 1800 began to have its effect. These new examinations put a great strain on the teaching resources of the colleges. This problem was further compounded by the sharp increase in student numbers during this period[10] which also increased tutors' incomes at the same time as it decreased their effectiveness.[11] It was discovered that richly endowed colleges with from ten to forty MAs on their foundations were unable to provide adequate instruction to enable their students to pass the new examinations. The inadequacy of collegiate tuition was made up by the development of private coaching. Although sometimes condemned as mere crammers, by the 1830s they had become an important, though embarrassing, element in the academic system.[12] This situation inevitably stimulated both a greater emphasis on the teaching function of the colleges and a serious questioning of the institutions and mechanisms by which these inadequate collegiate teachers were selected and supported.

---

[10] Annual admissions rose from an average of 236 p.a. during the period 1800–9 to 410 p.a. in 1820–9 and 384 p.a. in 1830–9. See Lawrence Stone, 'The Size and Composition of the Oxford Student Body 1500–1909', Table 1A, 91, in Lawrence Stone (ed.), *The University in Society* (Princeton, 1974) i.

[11] Since the tuition fees generally were divided among the tutors, there was a strong financial incentive not to increase their number despite rising student admisssions. At Lincoln, for example, undergraduates increased from 19 in 1813 (of whom only 6 were commoners paying full fees, the others being scholars, exhibitioners, and bible clerks) to 51 in 1827–8 (of whom 40 were commoners). The result was that the incomes of the two college tutors rose from £156 to £282 exclusive of their fellowships. See Lincoln MS Day Books. The series is very incomplete before 1813 and has some gaps until 1851–2. At a more fashionable college, such as University College, the two tutorships, which had been worth only £188 in 1812 had risen to £433 by 1827. See University College MS Bursar's Ledgers. The series begins in 1810 but has many gaps until 1837–8.

[12] An Oxford Student guidebook of 1837 complains of the growing prominence of private coaches in the university. The author does not approve of this development but his discussion of the subject indicates its *de facto* importance at this time. See *The Student's Guide to a Course of Reading Necessary for Obtaining University Honours, by a Graduate of Oxford* (Oxford, 1837), 97. The growth in the importance of private coaching can be gauged by the fact that another student guidebook of 1860, though still hostile to private coaching, is forced to admit that 'as to the Formal Examination, there are but few, if any, colleges where the help supplied is of itself sufficient to insure a man a high place in the Class List. It is pretty nearly a universal rule with class-men to read two terms at least with a Tutor [coach] before the day of trial.' Montagu Burrows, *Pass and Class: An Oxford Guide-Book* (Oxford, 1860), 60.

As usual, the *Edinburgh Review* was the first to attack. In 1831 Sir William Hamilton wrote two articles[13] in which he argued that university education ought to be conducted by professors who taught one subject which they knew well, rather than by college tutors each of whom had to teach all subjects, though generally not qualified to teach any particular one in depth. He argued that the fellows, from among whom the tutors were always selected, were not elected for their intellectual merit, but rather, were usually chosen according to the capricious will of the founder of the college and through fortuitous circumstances. Furthermore, he complained that the institution of the fellowship did not induce tutors to view teaching as a serious occupation.

The fellow who in general undertakes the office [of tutor] and continues the longest to discharge it, is a clerical expectant whose hopes are bounded by a college living and who, until the wheel of promotion has moved round, is content to relieve the tedium of a leisure life by the interest of an occupation, and to improve his income by its emoluments. Thus, it is that tuition is not engaged in as an important, arduous, responsible, and permanent occupation; but lightly viewed and undertaken as a matter of convenience, a business by the by, a state of transition, a stepping-stone to something else.[14]

The old criticism of the venality and corruption of fellowship elections took on a new specificity in the situation of the 1830s. Instead of criticizing these practices as misappropriations of charitable endowments, one reformer argued that 'the manner of the appointment of . . . tutors, and the body out of which they are chosen, do not in general afford the least security for their being fit repositories of the trust committed to them'.[15] One step toward the solution of the problem was that fellowships should be awarded on the basis of intellectual merit. Thus the reformer was forced to sanction

---

[13] 'Universities of England—Oxford', *Edin. Rev.* liii (June 1831), 384–427, and a review of the 'The Legality of the Present Academical System of the University of Oxford, Asserted against the New Calumnies of the *Edinburgh Review* by a Member of Convocation', ibid. liv (Dec. 1831), 478–504.

[14] 'Universities of England—Oxford', 396–7.

[15] *Letters to the English Public on the Condition, Abuses and Capabilities of the National Universities, no. 1, by a Graduate of Cambridge* (London, 1836). See also *Thoughts on Reform at Oxford, by a Graduate* (Oxford, 1833), esp. 15–16.

the altering of founders' wills or even parliamentary intervention in order to achieve his end.[16] Other reformers
believed that the root of the problem was that fellowships
had to be resigned on marriage.

> If a person who has neglected all means of improvement, be once selected
> Fellow anywhere, he is far less likely to give up his advantages by mar-
> riage, than a man of cultivated and powerful mind. The former has looked
> to his fellowship as a maintenance, and thinks that if he lose it, he shall
> never get so good a thing again. Thus the natural inclination to marry,
> thwarted by the Oxford law of restriction, cannot but operate to draw
> off from the Colleges just those men whom the University should wish
> to keep; and if those who remain clinging to her through life are but the
> refuse intellect of the place, it is not to be wondered at. We believe that
> the Colleges which have the cleverest body of Fellows, generally find
> them pass off most quickly, either by marriage or by other appointments.
> This appears more desirable than stagnation; yet a quick succession of
> very young tutors is by no means desirable. On the present plan the two
> evils co-exist to a great degree.[17]

These critics of the 1830s did not all go so far as Hamilton
in implying that the colleges should be reduced to boarding-
houses for those rich enough to afford them and that all
instruction be given over to university professors. Some
proposed both a reform of the fellowship system and a
revival of the professoriate,[18] in order to obtain more effective
teaching. Others timidly asserted that 'professorships should
be made the means of as much good as the altered system of
education will permit'.[19]

In his articles, Hamilton did not emphasize the deficiency

---

[16] Ibid., *Thoughts on Reform at Oxford*..., 10-12.

[17] 'The Oxford University Calender (1837)', *Eclectic Review*, 4th Series, ii
(July 1837), 15.

[18] Ibid., see 21-3. See also 'State of the Universities', *Quart. Rev.* xxxvi, no. 71
(1827), 216-68. This critic was primarily interested in the development of professional education at Oxford as a method of raising the social status of some of
the lower professions (principally surgeons and solicitors). He argued that this goal
could be attained only if each of the teachers in the university were able to
concentrate on one subject and view teaching as a permanent career. Under this
system, the professor would give public lectures while the college tutor would
work with the student in a more personal way. The author conceived his reforms
as modelled on the German professorial system and contrasted this system with
the Scottish universities in which personal contact with the *privat docent* or
college tutor was lacking.

[19] Ibid. 19.

of Oxford from the viewpoint of the advancement of knowledge. Only at one point did he mention this weakness while
alluding to the ideal of the German professorial system.[20]
Another critic, however, concentrated more on this point,
although he also dealt at great length with the deficiencies of
Oxford teaching. Significantly, the ideal of the advancement
of knowledge as a function of the university was again tied
closely to a conception of the professorial system as it existed
on the Continent and particularly in Germany. In Oxford,

philology itself, in which one would expect Oxford to excell, is not
known as the science which it has become in the hands of the inquisitive
Germans . . . That Oxford has exceedingly fallen back in comparison
with her ancient fame, cannot be denied. Once she stood on a par with
the most celebrated foreign universities. Even more recently her Professors were of leading rank in oriental studies. Now we hear of Paris,
Copenhagen and Petersburg as the center of numberless publications in
the languages of the East and North; but of Oxford, nothing of the
kind. She seems to have been living on German classics and on French
and Cambridge mathematics. The Germans have so outstripped her in
Greek, Latin, Arabic, and Hebrew criticism, in Philology at large, in
Biblical antiquities, in Ecclesiastical and other ancient history, that for
a length of time she will have nothing to do but translate from German
authors.[21]

The defenders of Oxford against these criticisms, especially
those of Hamilton, did not really confront the proposal that
teaching ought to be recognized as a life-career. James
Ingram, the President of Trinity, simply enumerated a list of
eminent men who had been Oxford tutors as a defense of the
university against Hamilton's criticisms. Beyond this defence,
his only argument was to assert blandly that the existing
system of education combined satisfactorily the professorial
and tutorial modes of instruction.[22] Vaughan Thomas, an
Oxford city clergyman, merely repeated Copleston's argument
that the personal supervision provided by the collegiate lecture

[20] *Edin. Rev.* liv (Dec. 1831), 486.
[21] 'Reform of the University of Oxford', *Eclectic Rev.* 4th Series, ii (Aug.
1837), 125.
[22] *Apologia Academica or Remarks on a Recent Article in the Edinburgh
Review* (Oxford 1831), esp. vi-x, 12-13. Author identified by Cordeaux and
Merry.

was a far more effective method of education than large professorial lectures.[23] No mention was made of the substantive accusations levelled against the existing collegiate system. The reason for this neglect of specific accusations seems to have been that the defenders basically rested their support of the existing system on its efficiency in preserving the university from the religious heresy rampant in the continental universities. Thomas accused the *Edinburgh* reviewer of being 'just fresh from the classroom of a Dr Birchschneider or a Dr Wagschneider, or some other Teutonic Gamaliel, with a name as unutterable as his blasphemies'.[24]

> Be the imperfections of our seminaries what they may, I am acquainted with no other situations where young men can be so largely stored with principles that may enable them to detect the fallacy, and to escape the contamination of those metaphysical novelties, which are said to have gained a wide and dangerous ascendancy on the continent. After the recent downfall, and amidst the rapid decay of similar institutions in foreign countries, OUR UNIVERSITIES are the main pillars, not only of the learning, and perhaps the science, but of the virtue and piety (whether seen or unseen) which yet remain among us.[25]

B. The Tractarian Movement

It is ironic that this last quotation was cited approvingly by the *British Critic*, the organ of the Tractarian party in Oxford, since it was this movement which, in the 1840s, was to undermine thoroughly the credibility of this defence. As one journal remarked after Newman had been received into the Roman Catholic Church, 'Within a recent period the hereditary instinctive confidence of England in its Universities has been broken by painful revelations. The nation has been compelled to believe, what once it would fain have rejected,

---

[23] *The Legality of the Present Academical System of the University of Oxford asserted against the New Calumnies of the Edinburgh Review, by a Member of Convocation* (Oxford, 1831), esp. 116–19. Author identified by Cordeaux and Merry.

[24] *The Legality of the Present Academical System of the University of Oxford re-asserted against the new Calumnies of the Edinburgh Review, by a Member of Convocation* (Oxford, 1832), 22–3.

[25] Quoted from Vaughan Thomas's second pamphlet (above, n. 24), in 'Attack on the Universities—Oxford', *Brit. Crit.*, no. 23 (1837), 399–400. See also the first part of this article in *Brit. Crit.*, no. 22 (1837), 168–215.

as a monstrous libel. The nation has been compelled to accept as a fact, that for years the Universities have been the seat of a dangerous, and too successful conspiracy against the faith of which they were supposed to be the bulwarks.'[26] High Churchmen might complain that 'Tractarian' was simply being used by the enemies of the universities as an effective taunt to undermine their autonomy,[27] but there can be no doubt that, in fact, after the flight of Newman and other Tractarians to Rome, Thomas's argument was largely discredited. Oxford could no longer be regarded as a reliable defender of the Church of England.

But the effect of Tractarianism was not merely to discredit Oxford as a support for the Established Church. In the late 1830s and 1840s, the Tractarians were one of the few articulate groups within Oxford with a coherent programme for reform, albeit a visionary one seemingly calculated to anger the traditional Tory supporters of the university. They argued that the university must overtly embrace a monastic ideal, rather than compromise with the utilitarian values of the day.

If persons like ourselves might presume to offer its [the university's] members any counsel, it would be never to forget that their present life is but a continuation of the life of past ages, that they are, after all, only in a new form and with new names, the Benedictines and Augustinians of a former day. The monastic element, a most important ingredient in the social character of the Church, lingers among them, when the nation at large has absorbed it in the frivolous or evil tempers and opinions of an advanced period of civilization.... Institutions come to nothing when they abandon the principle which they embody; Oxford has ever failed in self-respect, and has injured its inward health and stability, as often as it has forgotten that it was a creation of the middle ages, and has affected new fashions or yielded to external pressure.[28]

[26] 'University Reform', *Oxford Protestant Magazine* i (Mar. 1847), 5–6. Another critic launched his attack on the system of education pursued at Oxford with the argument that the Tractarian Movement was a symptom of the failures of Oxford education and that these ideas could not have taken hold in a more wholesome intellectual atmosphere. See 'The Present State of the University of Oxford – Its Defects and Remedies', *Tait's Edinburgh Magazine* xvi (Aug. 1849), 525–39, esp. 530.

[27] See the four pamphlets attributed by Cordeaux and Merry to W. Sewell, *The University Commission or Lord John Russell's Post-Bag* (Oxford, 1850), esp. no. 4, p. 9 and no. 3, p. 31.

[28] 'Memorials of Oxford', *Brit. Crit.*, no. 47 (1838), 144.

In a review of G. R. M. Ward's translation of the statutes of Magdalen College, the monastic ideal was made more specific. The college ought to return to its original function as a home for forty 'poor scholars', the fellows of the college, and a president, all united in a common life of frugality, prayer, piety, and theological study. The model was not to be a theological college for the training of parish clergy, like the Dissenters' Homerton or the Roman Catholics' Maymooth[29] nor should it be modelled on 'some Prussian or French academy'.[30] Rather, the ideal was to be St. Maur, the monastery devoted to the collection of theological documents by monk-scholars of the order.[31]

Although these ideals in themselves were enough to alienate many defenders of the university, this effect was intensified by the language of these articles. One Tractarian reviewer casually remarked that 'it is really losing time and toil to deny what is as plain as day, that Oxford has, and ever has. had, what men of the world will call a popish character'.[32] This was clearly waving a red flag before the Anglican bull. In discussing the proper social background for a clergyman, another Tractarian reviewer took the opportunity to criticize the Anglican ideal of merging the character of squire and parson. 'Gentlemen . . . the Church must have,' he asserted, 'but they must be priest-gentlemen, not samples of the squirearchy.'[33]

Although the manner and content of the Tractarians' promulgation of an internal idea of reform helped to divide and weaken the defenders of the university, they were as deeply committed as Copleston or Ingram to collegiate autonomy. They opposed, however, the domination of the tight oligarchy of Heads of Houses, who were mostly hostile to their ideas. It was significant that when Newman had the

---

[29] 'The Statutes of Magdalen College, Oxford', *Brit. Crit.*, no. 54 (1840), 387. This unsigned article was written by James Hope (later Hope-Scott), a young follower of J. H. Newman. Newman suggested to Hope that he write this review. A Dwight Culler has written that this review 'gives the most extensive account we have of the sort of reform that Newman would have espoused'. See *Imperial Intellect: A Study of Cardinal Newman's Educational Ideal* (New Haven, 1955), 92-3 and 92-5 *passim*.

[30] Ibid. 365.   [31] Ibid. 394.

[32] *Brit. Crit.*, no. 47 (1838), 146.   [33] *Brit. Crit.*, no. 54 (1840) 390.

opportunity to frame a constitution for the Catholic University of Ireland in 1851, he gave the Heads only domestic powers.[34] Legislative power was vested, instead, in a Senate, three-quarters of whose members were the resident teachers of the university. This decision was also significant since the Tractarians were prominent among the first generation of college tutors to respond to the increased demand for teaching by taking over from the coaches the method of individual instruction. Thomas Mozley noted that Newman, Hurrell Froude, and Robert Wilberforce 'bestowed on their pupils as much time and trouble as is usually only expected from very good private tutors [coaches] '.[35] Although hostile observers considered that theological indoctrination was their purpose in establishing this new policy, more sympathetic critics argued that their goals in this case were largely educational.[36] The fact that Provost Hawkins was able to remove the three Oriel tutors from their offices because he disapproved of their theological influence also must have added to their disgust with the existing structure of authority.

Internal criticism became much more prevalent in the 1840s and with it the issue of providing academic careers came into prominence. The opinion that university teaching ought to be a serious and lifetime occupation had been mentioned by the critics of the 1830s, but it was not the main thrust of their argument. Similarly, the advancement of learning, which had been assumed by the *Edinburgh* critics as early as 1808-10 to be a major role of the university, was also a function capable of justifying a lifetime career. It was used, however, as merely one more point in the attack on Oxford; the university might be denounced for falling behind the Germans or French in scholarship, but the charge was not pursued. The new critics of the 1840s took this earlier side-issue as their point of departure. The increasing devotion of college tutors to teaching and the rising value of the college

[34] See A Dwight Culler, *Imperial Intellect* (New Haven, 1955), ch. viii, esp. 158-9.
[35] See *Reminiscences, chiefly of Oriel College and the Oxford Movement* (London, 1882), i, 229.
[36] See Mark Pattison, *Memoirs* (London, 1885), 85-8 for a discussion of these alternative interpretations.

tutorships clearly had stimulated thought on how these positions could be made more permanent.

As the internal critics developed their ideas, however, it became apparent that there were important, even irreconcilable, differences among them. Since they took seriously the idea of developing an academic profession, rather than merely using it as one of several methods for attacking the existing institution, the question soon arose of what type of profession it ought to be. Was it to be organized to fulfil the need for teaching or the advancement of learning? Even if both functions were accepted as legitimate, which was to predominate? What institutions were to be used to create these careers? Were the college fellowships to be transformed to meet the requirements of these new roles, or were the professorial chairs to be remodelled for this purpose? Finally, there remained the crucial question of status. Was this new profession to equal the social rank and income of the traditional learned professions?

The issue of Tractarianism was, of course, a *leitmotiv* running through all reform positions during the late 1840s. The very presence of the movement in Oxford was taken as a sympton of intellectual malaise. One reviewer wrote of 'Oxford theology' that 'it never could have been produced in a place where scientific thought or historical criticism had flourished. Had Oxford minds understood the laws of evidence, or had they been imbued with the principles of mathematical proof, Newman and his disciples would have laboured in the fire. Had even logic flourished as a science, Puseyism must have been strangled at birth.'[37] The reviewer could argue that his proposed reforms of the educational system would eliminate Tractarianism and, implicitly, would have prevented it had they been instituted sooner. In this example, the author, who wished to alter the curriculum toward more practical subjects, used the need to combat Tractarianism to advance his argument. However, this issue was flexible enough to lend itself to other uses as well. Another critic, desirous of

---

[37] *Tait's Edin. Mag.*, N.S. xvi (Aug. 1849) 530. The issue of Tractarianism was used similarly in 'Oxford and Cambridge: University Reform', *British Quarterly Review*, iii (May 1846), 358–76, esp. 376.

establishing a system of professorial instruction with emphasis on the function of advancing knowledge, could argue that Tractarianism grew because of the lack of scholarly research in Oxford. 'If we have no original philosophy of our own we must import it from abroad', remarked Bonamy Price.[38] This argument was doubly effective since it could be used not only to explain the malaise of Tractarianism but also to criticize the other great enemy of Anglican orthodoxy, German historical criticism of the Bible.[39] Price concluded, 'Surely it is not necessary to say more in order to make evident the urgent need there is of English learning, and, above all, at the Universities.'[40]

C. Practical Subjects vs. Scholarly Research

Despite their agreement on the evils of Tractarianism, the reformers of the late 1840s differed fundamentally in their positive goals. This period saw the development of the idea that the revival of 'the professorial system' would cure Oxford's deficiencies. Although this theory had been advanced first by the critics of the *Edinburgh Review*, only in the late 1840s did it become specific enough to reveal that the advocates of this reform were divided into two groups. Both wished to see the professoriate expanded, given greater scope in the educational work of the university and provided with the opportunity for a professional career. They disagreed sharply, however, concerning the primary function of the university and the duties of the new academic profession they advocated.

One group was interested essentially in changing the curriculum to provide more career-oriented education. One reviewer wrote that 'we cannot think that universities will be at all more successful in cultivating either truth or taste in the abstract, if everything that can be called practical, we may add, professional, be removed to a distance from them'.[41] These reformers rejected the Coplestonian idea that the only

[38]*Suggestions for the Extension of Professorial Teaching in the University of Oxford* (London, 1850), 20. See also 19–20 for critique of Tractarianism.
   [39] Ibid. 21.   [40] Ibid. 22.
   [41] 'Oxford and Cambridge: University Reform', *Brit. Quart. Rev.* iii (May 1846), 356–66. See also 'Reform of Oxford University', *Tait's Edin. Mag.* xvi (Oct. 1849), esp. 709 for another example of the same argument.

purpose of university study was to provide mental discipline and inculcate religious values. According to this theory of 'liberal education', the student derived from classical languages and literature the habits of thought and intellectual skills which could later be applied to the study of any particular profession. The reviewer complained that the effect of this theory was 'to rear clergymen, schoolmasters, and gentlemen, by imparting to all indifferently the knowledge which is professional to the schoolmaster'.[42] In attacking this concept of education, however, the reformer had to choose his words very carefully to avoid the danger that his argument would be dismissed as a call for mere vocational training.[43] 'Deprecating, as we do, low utilitarian notions, which would undervalue all mental culture that does not yield immediate and palpable fruit,' he contended, 'we yet cannot but think that abstract science and what is vaguely called liberal knowledge will wander into absurd or unprofitable vagaries if they are not at intervals checked by demanding some fruit of them.'[44]

The solution to this problem of avoiding 'low utilitarian notions' was to defend the inclusion of new subjects in the curriculum not on the basis of practical utility but as offering alternative sources for abstract 'mental culture'.[45] For example, when W. F. Donkin, the Savilian Professor of Astronomy, advocated the use of his own subject in undergraduate education, he argued that 'practical astronomy is not merely a means of obtaining astronomical results, but is also capable of being made highly useful as an instrument of intellectual discipline and cultivation ... [it] requires very clear conceptions and exact reasoning, without involving (so far as it needs to be taught for educational purposes) the more abstruse parts of Mathematics'.[46]

---

[42] Ibid. 368.

[43] This dismissal was soon to be given its classic statement in Newman's *On the Scope and Nature of University Education*, delivered in Ireland in 1851 and first published in 1852. See esp. Discourse IV, 'Liberal Knowledge its Own End', in edition by W. Ward (London, 1965), 80–102.

[44] *Brit. Quart. Rev.* iii (May 1846), 365.

[45] For changes in the concept of 'liberal education' in the nineteenth century, see Sheldon Rothblatt, *Tradition and Change in English Liberal Education* (London, 1976).

[46] *Oxford University Commission* (1852), Evidence, 110.

Another critic, while making this same type of argument for modern subjects, added that the teachers must be *'students of truth'* not practitioners for gain'.[47] In this way, the stigma of 'low utilitarian notions' was further removed. By including modern subjects under the rubric of 'liberal education' and by constructing a scholarly ideal for the teacher of these subjects, the taint of vocational education was removed.

For these particular reformers, the establishment of provision for an academic profession grew out of their ideas for changing the curriculum. They argued that so long as instruction was conducted by young graduates who had to seek a life-career outside the university, it was hopeless to expect the successful teaching of the 'progressive sciences'. For these subjects, it was necessary that the teachers be 'men of mature age and whose lives are given to their peculiar branch'.[48]

The emphasis among these reformers was clearly on the role of teaching in the academic profession. The idea that the teacher should also be a 'student of truth' was of distinctly secondary importance. This attitude was revealed in one reviewer's suggestion that the fellowship system be dismantled exclusively in the interests of improved teaching.

The possession of a fellowship implies the right to receive so much money for doing nothing. As, however, the founders did impose duties on the fellows, let the duty of affording public instruction be imposed on them, in place of the duties required by the founders, which are either become illegal or obsolete; and if needful, let two or more fellowships be consolidated to provide an adequate stipend for an efficient public teacher; and above all, let the fellow be allowed to marry. This permission will deprive the efficient instructor of his inducement to leave the university.[49]

The reviewer argued that the 557 fellowships in the colleges could be transformed into about 200 professorships of £450 per annum. In this way an adequate staff of teachers would be provided for instruction in the new 'progressive sciences'.

[47] *Brit. Quart. Rev.* iii (May 1846), 366.
[48] Ibid. 368. See also *Tait's Edin. Mag.* xvi (Aug. 1849), 536 for another example of the same argument.
[49] *Tait's Edin. Mag.* xvi (Oct. 1849), 708. For a similar argument see *Brit. Quart. Rev.* iii (May 1846), 371.

Although some of these reformers wished to preserve the fellowship system, their only purpose was to improve the organization of instruction by introducing an element of hierarchy. As one reviewer wrote, 'The body of fellows employed in tuition, in strict subordination to the professors, would be an invaluable assistance. The number of fellows in each college might be easily so arranged that they should all be employed, and all render tuition gratis; for surely common sense suggests that they should do something for their fellowships . . .'[50] For these reformers the primary concern was expanding the curriculum and improving teaching; they advocated the development of academic careers only as a necessary corollary to their major goal.

There was, however, a second position which also involved advocacy of 'the professorial system' but which viewed the encouragement of learned research rather than the improvement of the curriculum as the prime objective. These reformers also demanded the creation of academic careers but the type of careers they required differed markedly from the needs of the first group of critics. This second ideal of the professorial system reached its full expression in the report of the Oxford University Commission published in 1852. However, in its general outlines, it can be seen also in the years immediately before the calling of the Commission, for example, in the views of Bonamy Price, a master at Rugby who later became Drummond Professor of Political Economy at Oxford.[51] Price's argument differed fundamentally from that of the other advocates of the professorial system since they placed their emphasis on the deficiencies of the university as a place of education while he focused on its shortcomings as a seat of learning: 'One of the primary functions of the University — the pursuit of really profound knowledge for the benefit of the nation and the University — is almost entirely abandoned', he complained. 'Study and self-improvement and original investigation are sacrificed to the educational office.'[52]

---

[50] *Tait's Edin. Mag.* xvi (Aug. 1849), 533. Another of these critics suggested that 'the professors ought to have a chief voice in deciding the course of academic instruction'. *Brit. Quart. Rev.* iii (May 1846), 375.

[51] *Suggestions for the Extension of Professorial Teaching* (Oxford, 1850).

[52] Ibid. 8.

Price argued that the root of the problem was that the university did not offer sufficient opportunities for academic careers. Beyond the college fellowship, which had to be vacated at marriage, the existing system provided only a small number of professorial chairs, most of which were insufficiently endowed, and the college headships, for which scholarly excellence was generally not considered an important qualification.[53] These positions were too few and too unrelated to original research to serve as a stimulus to the scholarly labours of tutors. Price wrote of the college tutors, 'They cannot look upon their office as their home, or their profession. It cannot be anything else than a temporary post . . . [T]he evil here is that the Tutorship is a preparation for no other post; it leads to no further station for which it trains and qualifies the tutor. A tutor must ever be on the lookout for some call which shall terminate his teaching; and this fact alone is sufficient to show that he cannot connect the cultivation of knowledge with his office.[54] This argument was superficially similar to that of the first group of reformers, who also called for the establishment of academic careers, but the priorities were exactly reversed. For the first group, a career had to be provided for teachers because this was the only way subjects of practical or professional value could be introduced into the curriculum. For Price, the curriculum had to be broadened because this was the only way the university could provide a proper scope of activity for scholars.[55]

Price argued that the solution was to create posts awarded on the basis of scholarly merit toward which the tutors might aspire. He suggested that the professorships could serve this purpose if there were more of them, if they were better endowed, and if they were better integrated into the studies of the university. To achieve this goal he proposed that the existing *Literae Humaniores* examination be altered to permit its being taken by the end of the second year of study. Students would be instructed during these two years by the college tutors, who would receive their tuition fees. The final year would be devoted to preparation for a second set of

[53] Ibid. 14–17.   [54] Ibid. 12–13.   [55] Ibid. 6–8.

examinations in history, divinity, and philosophy. During this period, instruction would be largely through professorial lectures. There would be three professors for each of the three subjects and tuition fees would be divided among them. Each professor would give two courses of lectures, one for undergraduates preparing for the examinations and one for fellows, tutors, and coaches. Tuition fees, together with the endowment of the chair, would provide an income for each professor of about £1,500 p.a.[56]

The primary objective of this plan was to supply the need for an orderly professional hierarchy for academics. The tutors would have a stimulus to advance their own learning since they could look forward to one of the well-paid professorial chairs if they were successful in their researches. The fellowship would become a step on the ladder of a genuine profession rather than, at best, a mere prize for past performance. With these reforms, Price argued that it would be possible to provide academic careers analogous to those possible in the other learned professions.[57]

Were the educational system of Oxford placed on this footing, the prospect opened to the young Batchelor, if he decided to become a resident would be altogether different from what it is now. He would have a real profession, and that a noble one. As a Fellow, he would enjoy maintenance from his College; and by continuing his studies under the direction of a professor, he would, in the fullest sense, be carrying out the purpose for which the founders of his College bequeathed to him that maintenance. As a private tutor [i.e. a coach], he would be keeping up his course of improvement. In due time he would become professor; and that with a mass of knowledge which had been constantly accumulating from the day of his entrance into the University. Here too progress would be sustained. The responsibilities of his office, and the immediate value of knowledge in the Academical system, would be effectual guarantees that the efforts to advance would be unbroken; the University would gain a great name in science, recognized and honoured as such throughout England; and beyond all estimation would the influence of Oxford be increased in the country, when her professorships — not from accident, but from the necessary actions of the institutions — were known to contain the highest literary authorities with the nation could boast; and it would not then be easy to tempt men away from the University. For a post which implied a sphere of

[56] For Price's specific suggestions for reform, see ibid. 25–31.
[57] Ibid. 11–12.

action worthy of it — which confered station, wealth, authority, influence and, not least, increasing self-improvement — such a post would indeed be one of the noblest things which this land contained.[58]

This high ideal of a scholarship orientated academic profession which could compete in status and income with the rewards of the other learned professions was far removed from the desires of the first group of reformers to create careers for teachers of practical subjects at salaries of £450 p.a. Both schemes, however, would be equally offensive to those college tutors who accepted their traditional clerical role or feared the loss of their personal and collegiate autonomy.

D. *The Royal Commission of 1850–2*

The Royal Commission of 1850 was the arena in which the rival ideals of the university crystallized and attained the form they were to retain. The task of framing specific reforms or defending existing institutions led to the conscious artic-ulation of explicit conceptions of academic life. The calling of the Commission was the result of long-term, cumulative, and diverse grievances combined with a situation in which the strongest argument for the *status-quo* — the position of the university as the bulwark of Anglican orthodoxy — had been destroyed by the Tractarian Movement and the defections to Rome. The harsh but ineffective responses of the Hebdomadal Board also had highlighted the need for reform in university government. Both these sources of vulnerability to govern-ment intervention were expressed in a satire containing a mock legal opinion of some 'Stable-keepers' [the Hebdomadal Board] protesting against a 'Subcommission' [the Royal Commission]. The barrister for the 'Stable-keepers' concluded his brief,

Having read your case submitted for my opinion, I have no hesitation whatever in declaring that the Subcommision of March 1851 is . . . neither constitutional nor legal . . . The true source of power being his Holiness the Pope and under him the Cardinal Wiseacre, and the only Bull now in force in Oxford being decidedly opposed to its proceedings, it follows that Aniseed [the 'Secretary of the Subcommission'] and his

---

[58] Ibid. 32–3.

associates are acting on no better authority than the recommendation of one John Russell, a discharged servant of the temporal power.[59]

Earlier attempts at government intervention had failed for lack of such vulnerabilities. In 1834 pressure from Dissenters had led to attempts in Parliament to modify or abolish religious tests in the universities and, in 1836, a bill was introduced to establish a commission for the reform of college and university statutes. In neither case, however, did the bills survive their second readings. In the 1840s, James Heywood, a Unitarian MP, took up the cause of university reform and his calls for a royal commission became a 'hardy annual'.[60] It was declining public confidence in the university and its leaders which encouraged Lord John Russell to heed Heywood's speech of 23 April 1850 and issue a commission of inquiry.

Not surprisingly, the Royal Commission met with bitter opposition in Oxford. The prospect of parliamentary intervention awakened nightmares of the seventeenth century, when both the Puritan Commonwealth and James II had attempted to crush the autonomy of the university.[61] This feeling was especially strong on the Hebdomadal Board, however, similar sentiments were also felt by the majority of college residents. Although many harboured their own resentments against the Hebdomadal Board, they knew that most critics who called for a government inquiry were hostile to the collegiate system itself.

The result was that the Heads of Houses, with the single exception of Francis Jeune of Pembroke, and most college officials as well refused to recognize the legitimacy of the Royal Commission. They declined to serve on it, nor would

[59] *Eureka, No. II. A Sequel to a Sequel to Lord John Russell's Post-Bag* (Oxford, 1853), 13. This anonymous pamphlet was a specific parody of the four pamphlets published by William Sewell in 1850 (above, p. 23, n. 27).

[60] See Ward, 152. Also see chs. v–vii for the politics of the agitation against religious tests and for a royal commission.

[61] See the reprints of a seventeenth-century account of the trials of the university published by Vaughan Thomas in 1834 and again in 1850. *A Ballad in Macaronic Latin entitled Rustica Descriptio Visitationis Fanaticae, being a country clergyman's tragi-comical lament upon revisiting Oxford after the root-and-branch reform of 1648 (1649), by John Allibond, with Preface and notes, the verses being done into doggerel 1834 in Usum Parliamenti Indoctorum, Ejusdem Nominis Secundi* (Oxford, 1850).

they supply either factual information or evidence of their
opinions. The Hebdomadal Board decided to present their
views through a commission of their own. They collected
evidence and printed it with a report upholding the traditional
clerical and collegiate ideal. In this report, the rationale for
the existing system of university government, education, and
academic life could be explicitly stated and defended. The
college tutors were placed in a dilemma since they could not
voice their opinions before a Royal Commission hostile to
the collegiate system nor could they acquiesce silently to the
views expressed by the Hebdomadal Board. The experience
of fifty years of increasing importance in the work of the
university had engendered in many tutors a consciousness of
group identity as college teachers. For this reason, they
formed an association and published a series of pamphlets
setting forth their own ideas on university reform.

The Royal Commission fell by default to the advocates
of the scholarly version of 'the professorial system'. The
Commission was the ideal forum for their views since they
had a few articulate spokesmen and could expect no sympathy
from existing collegiate or university institutions. In all the
Commission's recommendations, the raising of the status,
powers, and importance of the professoriate was stressed at
the expense of the colleges. In remodelling the government of
the university, the commissioners would have destroyed the
dominance of the Heads of Houses, giving power instead to
the professors, who would form a majority in the 'remodelled
Congregation' which was to replace the Hebdomadal Board.[62]
The commissioners were also most enthusiastic about the
plan for 'university extension' which would have destroyed
the monopoly of the colleges over admission to the university
by creating a new class of non-collegiate students.

The commissioners' intention was to make the Oxford
professoriate a class of dignified professionals whose primary
task would be the advancement of learning. In relation to the
educational work of the university, the professors were to

---

[62] This new Congregation would consist of all professors (at least fifty under
the commissioners' plan) together with all Heads of Houses and the senior tutors
of each college (totalling forty-one including the halls).

form faculty boards which would have exclusive control over the examination system. 'It is generally acknowledged that both Oxford and the country at large suffer greatly from the absence of a body of learned men, devoting their lives to the cultivation of Science, and to the direction of Academical Education; it is felt that the opening of such a career within the University would serve to call forth the knowledge and ability which is often buried or wasted, for want of proper encouragement.'[63] The commissioners proposed to establish a hierarchically organized profession for academics. At the bottom would be the college tutors who would take over the role previously fulfilled by the coaches.[64] The commissioners argued that the very existence of coaching on a large scale was evidence of the deficiencies of collegiate instruction.[65] 'Private Tutors [coaches] would (it is to be hoped) be resorted to only where individual and solitary supervision was required', the commissioners noted in their report. 'Even in these cases they would be superseded to a great extent by the College Tutors . . . Private Instruction would be rendered unnecessary, during Term at least, by the improved Instruction accessible to everyone from the Professors and Lecturers.'[66]

The purpose of fellowships would be little altered except that restrictions of family or locality would be removed so they could be awarded solely on the basis of intellectual merit. They would continue as prizes to enable young graduates to begin their professional careers. The only difference would be that instead of having to choose between the Church, the Law, and Medicine, the young fellow would have one more choice: a professional career as an academic. 'If the Professoriate could be placed in a proper condition, those Fellows of Colleges whose services the University would wish to retain, would be less tempted and would never be compelled to leave it for positions and duties, for which their academical labours had in no way prepared them, but would look forward to some sphere of usefulness within the University of which they would have been fitted by their previous occupations.'[67]

[63] *Oxford Univ. Comm.* (1852), Report, 94.   [64] Ibid. 90.
[65] Ibid. 88–90.   [66] Ibid. 101.   [67] Ibid. 94.

This new career clearly was not to be merely one of several choices; it was to be the most appropriate path for winners of academic distinctions. The commissioners pointedly attacked the use of the fellowship as a rung in the professional hierarchy of the Church: '. . . it is evident that, for literary men, Academical rather than Ecclesiastical offices are the fittest rewards and the most useful positions'.[68] In regard to the use of advowsons by colleges to provide Church livings for fellows, the commissioners argued that 'it is very doubtful whether either literature or the Church derive any benefit from the ecclesiastical patronage of Colleges. That a College should be deserted by any of its abler men in their full strength, for a country living, in which they are for the most part lost to learning, is a great evil even when they are suc-ceeded by young men of promise.'[69] The commissioners did not suggest, however, that fellowships themselves be made into professional career positions. Therefore, they advocated no change in the requirement that fellows resign when they married.

This new profession to which the fellows might aspire would be organized into a two-tier hierarchy. The basic teaching of the university would be performed by a new class of lecturers of sub-professors, who would be appointed by faculty boards composed of the professors. Although the commissioners were somewhat vague about the exact position of these lecturers, it seems clear that they would rank above the tutors who would view these positions as their entree to the academic profession: '. . . it is evident that such an inter-mediate grade of Lecturers would at once serve the purpose of opening prospects of advancement to the Tutors, Collegiate and Private'.[70] These university lecturers would specialize in particular subjects and would be free from all clerical and celibacy restrictions. The commissioners also suggested tentatively that college tutors appointed to university lecture-ships might be permitted to retain their fellowships though married.

At the summit of the academic profession would be the university professorships to which the lecturers would look

---

[68] Loc. cit. [69] Ibid. 171. [70] Ibid. 100.

for professional advancement. The professors and the faculty boards, composed exclusively of professors, would have full control of the examination system and the appointment of lecturers. Their own tasks would be the cultivation of their subjects and the administration of the examination system, while the actual teaching would be done largely by the lecturers and college tutors. The generous incomes of the professors — at least £800 p.a. from endowment in addition to fees which would bring the total to between £1,000 and £1,500 p.a. — also would serve to make these posts objects of ambition to the lower ranks. The professors also would become *ex officio* fellows of the colleges who would provide their endowment incomes by suppressing and combining fellowships.

This Royal Commission plan for the creation of a hierarchical academic profession was important as a fully explicit expression of the scholarly professorial ideal. In terms of practical results, however, it was virtually a dead letter. When the government came to formulate the Oxford University Bill of 1854, these recommendations were almost completely ignored. Instead, the major provision of the act was to give each college leave to alter its statutes in consultation with a board of executive commissioners. This sealed the fate of the Royal Commission's plan, which was seen as a menace to all collegiate interests. To the Heads of Houses, it threatened the loss of their dominance in the government of the university; to the fellows, it threatened to make them underlings of the professors.

The commissioners might have predicted this reaction if they had been more attentive to the evidence they received. Although many witnesses desired the establishment of some type of academic profession, only a few, most notably H. H. Vaughan, Regius Professor of Modern History, wanted schemes similar to the commissioners' plan for professorial dominance. This was an ominous sign since the strongest opponents of reform refused to submit evidence at all. The positions taken by the Royal Commission's witnesses reveal quite clearly the paucity of support for the commissioners' plan, even among those who favoured some measure of reform.

The fundamental issue was power. Many witnesses advocated

the integration of the professors into the studies of the university, particularly in teaching the 'higher aspects' of their subjects.[71] According to these proposals, the professors would be responsible for teaching undergraduates in their third year. This third year was often conceived as a concession to the demands for 'professional education',[72] since those intended for careers in Law would study modern history, law, and political economy with the professors in those fields while aspiring physicians would study with the professors of the natural sciences. The commissioners rejected this proposal, citing with approval Professor Vaughan's view that such a plan would degrade the professor into merely 'a Tutor of the third year'. Although they did not reject entirely the desirability of catechetical instruction by professors, the commissioners implied that this task would be more suitable for the subordinate university lecturers.[73]

On the issue of private coaching, the witnesses generally did not share the commissioners' repugnance for this mode of instruction. Although only a few doctrinaire advocates of *laissez-faire* totally defended the existing system,[74] most witnesses saw its substantial advantages in relation to existing methods of collegiate tuition despite their dislike for its

[71] See 'Answers from the Rev. Richard Congreve, MA, Fellow and Tutor of Wadham College, Oxford', 151-4, esp. 153; 'Answers from the Rt. Rev. Thomas Vowler Short, DD, Bishop of St. Asaph', 164; and 'Answers from N. S. Maskelyne, Esq., MA, Deputy Reader in Mineralogy in the University of Oxford', 185-91, esp. 188, all in *Oxford Univ. Comm.* (1852), Evidence.

[72] For the use of law professors for pre-professional training for barristers, see 'Answers from Stephen Charles Denison, Esq., MA, late Stowell Fellow of University College, Deputy Judge Advocate General', 197-200. For a similar argument for medicine, see 'Evidence of H. W. Acland, Esq., MD, Lee's Reader in Anatomy, Late Fellow of All Souls', 235-9. Only Charles Lyell advocated the establishment of full professional training in medicine in Oxford; see 119-23. All in ibid.

[73] 'Many of the Lecturers, at least might have classes not larger than those which attend College Tutors, and would naturally adopt the same mode of teaching.' *Oxford Univ. Comm.* (1852), Report, 101. For the commissioner's entire argument, see 99-101.

[74] See 'Answers from the Rev. H. L. Mansel, MA, Fellow, Tutor, and Dean of Arts, of St. John's College', 21, for the only total defense of the existing system of private coaching. See also, 'Answers from Robert Lowe, Esq., MA', 13, for a recommendation that private coaching completely replace college tuition. Even Lowe, however, suggested some changes to insure the moral and religious character of the teacher and to discourage taking too many pupils. All in *Oxford Univ. Comm.* (1852), Evidence.

unregulated and unofficial character. For example, W. C. Lake of Balliol argued that for the student, 'it is an obvious advantage to read alone with a sensible Private Tutor [coach], who can understand and enter into his difficulties better than can be done by his College Tutor in a large lecture'.[75] The colleges' reliance on catechetical lectures attended by large classes of varying abilities and attainments was also condemned directly by several witnesses. 'The plan . . . of teaching in large lectures,' Robert Lowe complained, 'while it gives but little instruction to the less advanced, is inexpressibly tedious and disgusting to the more forward student.'[76]

The system of private coaching was considered valuable as well because it offered the coach an opportunity for subject specialization which was denied to the college tutor. George Rawlinson of Exeter praised the coach's 'greater diligence in mastering the especial field of knowledge on which his instruction are given'.[77] Arthur Hugh Clough, a former fellow of Oriel, characterized the college tutor's role as 'three hours a day of subjects not his choice, very often his unpleasant necessity, . . . belonging to the most various and heterogeneous departments'.[78] Furthermore, Clough bluntly stated that coaching was also valuable since it was 'the only permanent business open to married residents'.[79]

The defects of private coaching were viewed as simply the result of its unofficial position in the university. Many

---

[75] Ibid. 168. Another witness also argued that 'almost every subject may be more easily and thoroughly taught to an individual than to a class'. 'Answers from W. F. Donkin, MA, Savilian Professor of Astronomy, Mathematical Lecturer and late Fellow of University College, Oxford', 108. See also 'Answers from the Rev. George Rawlinson, MA, late Fellow and Tutor of Exeter College, Oxford', 216–17, for a similar argument in favour of honours coaching though not for pass coaching.

[76] Ibid. 12. 'Boys from the Remove and boys of three years' standing in the Sixth Form of public schools are indiscriminately set to work together', another witness complained. 'Answers of A. H. Clough, Esq., MA, late Fellow and Tutor of Oriel College, and Principal of University Hall, Gordon-square, London, and Professor of English Language and Literature at University College, London', 214.

[77] Ibid. 218. See also 'Answer from the Rev. Bartholomew Price, MA, Fellow, Tutor, and Mathematical Lecturer of Pembroke College, Oxford', 63, for a similar argument.   [78] Ibid. 213.

[79] Ibid. 215. Another witness also argued that coaching provided 'scope for men of learning to exercise their vocation'. 'Answers from the Rev. Edward Arthur Litton, MA, late Fellow of Oriel College, now Vice-Principal of St. Edmund Hall', 178.

witnesses argued that the inevitable tendency of a system in which the students chose their own teachers and paid them directly was to encourage 'cramming'. Bartholomew Price of Pembroke complained that 'the teaching has respect rather to the examination, than to the cultivation of the intellectual powers, and the formation of character'.[80] 'Cramming' also was considered detrimental to the coach's own intellectual advancement. 'They go over the old ground again and again,' E. S. Foulkes of Jesus observed, 'and five or ten years after they have taken their first Degree, they know no more of Philosophy or Theology than they did when they commenced.'[81] Arthur Hugh Clough stated, with characteristic bluntness, the central deficiency of private coaching from the viewpoint of the teacher. 'Some stimulus of the competitive kind may be useful,' he noted, 'but some freedom from dependence on the Pupil is surely no less desirable.'[82] While several witnesses hoped that improved university lecturing would help to bring private coaching within reasonable limits,[83] none foreshadowed the commissioners' view of coaching as appropriate only for infrequent, remedial instruction.

Although several witnesses recommended the recognition

[80] Ibid. 63. 'Cramming' was also condemned in 'Answers from the Rev. R. W. Browne, MA, Prebendary of St. Pauls, Professor of Classical Literature at King's College, London, Chaplain to the Forces and late Fellow and Tutor of St. John's College, Oxford', 8; 'Answers from the Rev. W. Hayward Cox, BD, Late Fellow of Queens College and formerly Vice-Principal of St. Mary's Hall', 98; 'Answers from the Rev. Richard Congreve, MA, Fellow and Tutor of Wadham College, Oxford', 154; 'Answers from Travers Twiss, Esq. DCL, FRS, Late Tutor and Dean of University College and Late Professor of Political Economy', 157; 'Answers of Sir Edmund Head, MA, KCB, Governor of New Brunswick and late Fellow and Tutor of Merton College, Oxford', 161; and 'Answers from B. Price, Esq., MA, Late Fellow of Worcester College and formerly assistant Master in Rugby School', 195.

[81] Ibid. 227. For similar criticisms, see also 'Answers from the Rev. W. C. Lake, MA, Fellow and Tutor and Senior Dean of Balliol College', 168; 'Answers from the Rev. George Rawlinson . . .', 216–17, applied to pass coaching only; 'Answers from the Rev. R. W. Browne . . .', 8; 'Answers from the Rev. W. Hayward Cox . . .', 98; 'Answers from the Rev. Richard Congreve . . .', 154; 'Answers from B. Price . . .', 195; and 'Answers from W. F. Donkin . . .', 108.   [82] Ibid. 216.

[83] See, for examples, 'Answers from the Rev. Bartholomew Price . . .', 63; 'Answers from the Rev. W. C. Lake . . .', 168; 'Answers from the Rev. R. W. Browne . . .', 8; 'Answers from the Rev. Richard Congreve . . .', 154; 'Answers from Sir Edmund Head . . .', 160–1; 'Answers from B. Price . . .', 195; and 'Answers from the Rev. Edward Arthur Litton . . .', 179.

of the claims of advanced study in relation to the professor-iate,[84] H. H. Vaughan was one of the few who advocated the commissioners' plan of combining this role with control over the examination system.[85] John Conington of University College, for example, preferred to allow fellowships to be used for this purpose with the prospect of life-tenure without celibacy restrictions after a ten-year probationary period.[86] Other witnesses wished to see fellowships used to provide teaching careers for college tutors, who would be entitled after ten years of service to hold their fellowships for life without clerical or celibacy restrictions.[87] The commissioners, however, explicitly rejected both these views. Their plan for the expansion of the professoriate and the creation of univer-sity lectureships was meant to attract those who could not countenance any tampering with college foundations but who nevertheless wished to see life careers for teachers in Oxford. One witness argued that this reform would make 'provision in the University itself, unclogged with the heavy restriction of celibacy, for men of high academic honours. Justice to the able men, who now, amidst many difficulties, discharge most conscientiously the duties of college tuition, requires that Oxford should not be wanting to herself in holding out to her best sons adequate encouragement to continue in her service.'[88] The problem with the commis-sioners' plan was that it actually reduced the current position of college fellows, subordinating them to the professors, while holding out the possibility of a professorship in the future. But this future possibility was not likely to be con-sidered by the tutors an adequate recompense for their present

[84] See 'Answers from the Rev. H. L. Mansel . . .', 19–21, esp. 20; 'Answers of the Rev. Robert Scott, MA, Rector of South Luffenham and Prebendary of Exeter, Late Fellow and Tutor of Balliol College, Oxford', 110–14, esp. 112. All in *Oxford Univ. Comm.* (1852), Evidence.

[85] See 'Answers of Henry Halford Vaughan, Late Fellow of Oriel College, and Regius Professor of Modern History', 82–92; 'Answers from Sir Edmund Head . . .', 157–61, esp. 160–1 for an argument for professorial control over the examination system, but with less emphasis on the role of the professor in learned research. In ibid.   [86] Ibid. 115–19.

[87] See 'Answers from the Rev. Bartholomew Price . . .', 59–67; 'Answers from the Rev. W. Hayward Cox . . .', 92–9, esp. 97, in ibid.

[88] 'Answers from the Rev. John Wilkinson, MA, of Merton College, and Rector of Broughton Gifford, Wilts', 75, in ibid.

loss, and the commissioners might well have understood this from a study of their own evidence. It revealed a variety of discontents with the existing state of the university, but few for which their plan could be considered an acceptable solution.

E. The Tutors' Association

The publication of the Royal Commission's report in 1852 galvanized into action the college tutors who were the most coherent of these discontented groups. In the royal commissioners' report, there was a basic consistency in the evidence submitted by college tutors. They complained of the temporary nature of their occupation as tutors. As Mark Pattison of Lincoln asserted. 'The transitory nature of the occupation, which in most cases being adopted "in transitu" to a totally different pursuit, has none of the aids which in the regular professions are derived from regard to professional credit, and the sustained interest which a life-pursuit possesses.'[89] This complaint was generally combined with criticism of the lack of possibility for specialization in subjects. Arthur Hugh Clough emphasized the bad effects of unspecialized tutorial work on the tutors' intellectual development: 'I can conceive nothing more deadening to the appetite for learning than this three-hour-a-day tuition, leading as it does in general, and always must be expected to do, to no ultimate learned position − a mere parenthetical occupation uncontemplated in the past and wholly alien to the future.'[90] The plan of the royal commissioners did little to answer these complaints of the tutors. It confirmed their position as temporary and merely preparatory to a professional career, and it degraded their teaching into that of mere drill instructors under the supervision of the professors.

The threat presented by the recommendations of the royal commissioners forced the tutors into unified action and a definite expression of their ideas. Although the tutors were allied with the other clerical and collegiate interests against the Royal Commission, they felt the need for a separate expression of their views despite the danger that this action

[89] Ibid. 48.   [90] Ibid. 213.

would lead to conflict among the opponents of the royal commissioners. About sixty tutors formed the Tutors' Association to articulate their views on various aspects of university reform and on the commissioners' recommendations.[91] The reports of the Tutors' Association contained an ideal of an academic career designed to rival that of the Royal Commission but expressed with sufficient circumspection to minimize the ill-feeling which this action would create among the college tutors' more traditional allies.

In its diagnosis of the defects of the system of instruction in Oxford, the Tutors' Association came strikingly close to the royal commissioners. They identified two main problems: 'The first is the want of a body of instructors who, confining their attention to a single branch of study, shall be capable of prosecuting it to its utmost limits . . . The second deficiency is the want of an adequate means of producing and retaining within the University men of eminence in particular departments of knowledge.'[92] For the royal commissioners, the first of these problems was to be dealt with by the creation of the group of university lecturers who would each specialize in a particular subject. The second problem would be solved by the selection of professors for scholarly merit and providing for them lucrative positions with extensive powers. For the Tutors' Association, the commissioners' plan to create new classes of teachers was completely unnecessary to meet these admitted deficiencies. The college tutors could supply both these needs if they were offered professional careers: 'Hardly any of the present teachers of Oxford can look upon their occupation either as the business of their whole life, or as affording any preparation for a subsequent employment . . . [H] is tutorial position is not, under the existing restrictions of College Fellowships, such as most men will regard with satisfaction as a permanent occupation.'[93] This situation contrasted unfavourably with that of the German universities

---

[91] See Ward 180–4 for the formation of the Tutors' Association; also *No. 1. Recommendations Respecting the Extension of the University of Oxford, Adopted by the Tutors' Association, January 1853* (Oxford, 1853), 4.

[92] *No. 3. Recommendations Respecting the Relation of the Professorial and Tutorial Systems as Adopted by the Tutors' Association, November 1853* (Oxford, 1853), 62.   [93] Loc. cit.

where 'the . . . teacher is a scholar or a philosopher by profession, instead of being compelled, as is too often the case at Oxford, to take up scholarship or philosophy as a mere temporary occupation'.[94] The clear implication was that if college tutors were offered the opportunity for academic careers by removing 'restrictions' on fellowships and permitting more specialization, they could be expected to be as scholarly and productive as their German counterparts.

The Tutors' Association based its case for the superiority of its reform proposals over those of the royal commissioners on the superiority of tutorial instruction to professorial lectures and on the unfairness of granting dominating powers in the university to the professoriate. In criticizing professorial lectures as a mode of education,[95] the Tutors' Association relied heavily on the traditional Coplestonian defence of liberal education. They argued that the professorial system had three major defects in relation to collegiate instruction: in lectures to large classes, there was an inherent tendency to attach 'too much importance to the person teaching and too little to the things taught;' the lecturing situation tended to place a premium on innovation for its own sake rather than for the sake of 'Truth'; and lectures provided an easy and superficial education, memory being the major mental faculty cultivated, while the ability to reason was not developed. In regard to the increased powers of the professoriate envisaged by the commissioners, the Tutors' Association argued that 'it would not be doing justice to many of the Tutors of Oxford, to degrade them to mere mouthpieces or subordinates of superior teachers'.[96] They argued that many tutors were equally qualified to hold a professorial chair, yet under the commissioners' plan, if one were appointed, he would suddenly be raised to a position of dominance over all the others. This situation would certainly induce many able tutors to leave the university. In general, the Tutors' Association concluded that the royal commissioners' plan to give the professors a dominating voice in the university 'would destroy the independence of thought among the equal members of an

[94] Ibid. 63. [95] Ibid. 74. [96] Ibid. 75.

intellectual republic, to make way for the energetic rule of an official despotism'.[97]

The Tutors' Association was especially hostile to the royal commissioners' plan for the reform of university government, although they agreed that the existing Hebdomadal Board was unrepresentative of university opinion and gave too much power to the college heads. They argued that the commissioners plan 'gives an indefinite, but palpably a very undue preponderance to the Professorial element, which would not only predominate in the "remodelled Congregation", but would have the entire control of all its votes and proceedings'.[98] The Tutors' Association proposed instead that the existing Hebdomadal Board ought to be replaced by an initiative board composed of 27 members, 9 elected by the heads, 9 by the professors, and 9 'by the Tutors and other Resident Members of Convocation'.[99] The Tutors' Association contended that 'as it is in no way desirable that the instruction of Professors should ever become the main instruction of the place, so it seems unfit that its dispensers should have the chief influence in University legislation'.[100] By their proposal, the danger of professorial 'despotism' would be averted and dominant power in university legislation would remain in collegiate hands while the influence of the college tutors would be greatly enhanced.

The Tutors' Association was not opposed, however, to the expansion of the professoriate if the professors did not infringe the independence of the college tutors. Several areas were suggested among the traditional classical studies of the university in which more professorial chairs would be useful, although the need for new chairs in the natural sciences and modern history was considered less certain.[101] New professorships in classical studies clearly would have been attractive for providing possibilities for advancement to college tutors,

---

[97] Ibid. 76.

[98] *No. 2. Recommendations Respecting the Constitution of the University of Oxford, as adopted by the Tutors' Association April 1853* (Oxford, 1853), 41. See above, p. 35, n. 62 for the commissioners' plan.

[99] Ibid. 48. This inclusion of 'resident members of Convocation' was undoubtedly a concession to the coaches who were members of the Tutors' Association.

[100] Ibid. 42.   [101] *Tutors' Association, No. 3*, 78-9.

while this was less true for subjects not taught on the college level. The Tutors' Association suggested a somewhat lower salary for professors than the commissioners had recommended — £600 p.a. plus fees rather than £800 p.a. plus fees. None the less, their proposal still would have meant a considerable improvement in the value of most chairs. This salary, with duties of three lectures per week rather than three classes per day, would have made these professorships into definite objects of ambition to college tutors even without broad powers in university government. Under the Tutors' Association plan, professors would not have power in the colleges either, since the funds for endowing the chairs would be derived from a general tax on collegiate revenues rather than from appropriating fellowships.

In regard to the fellowship system, the general principle of the Tutors' Association was that fellows ought to be resident and involved for the most part in tutorial work. The theme of providing more opportunities for teaching was a constant motif in their reform suggestions. In discussing plans for 'university extension', the Tutors' Association suggested that one of the benefits of increased student numbers was that 'it is important to provide work for that large number of Fellows who may be expected at any one time to be resident in Oxford'.[102] They argued that the present situation 'excludes from Oxford many teachers who would add fresh life and energy to her instruction'.[103] The Tutors' Association clearly felt that many fellows wished to make Oxford teaching a career but could not be employed in the limited number of college tutorships under the existing system. Advocating 'university extension', subject specialization by college tutors, and cautious expansion of the professoriate was their plan to overcome this problem.

Although the Tutors' Association rested its case for increasing official posts in Oxford almost wholly on the need for teaching, college tutors were defined as 'learned men' rather than exclusively as teachers. It was argued that the university ought to function as an antidote to the utilitarian spirit which dominated a commercial country. It ought to

[102] *Tutors' Association, No. 1,* 29.   [103] Ibid. 8.

be the 'centre and source for the exercise and encouragement
of that unproductive thinking which to be successfully
prosecuted must be adequately endowed'.[104] Since teaching
often was denigrated as a mere 'trade' and even defenders of
the teaching role, such as Copleston, tended to view it as a
'homely duty',[105] it was necessary for the tutors to insist
on their learned status. This difference in valuation between
teaching and scholarship was, of course, translated into
concrete material terms. One witness before the Royal Commission stated the prevailing view with great bluntness. '[I] f
it be required only to have a body of tolerably competent
teachers,' W. F. Donkin asserted, 'moderate endowments are
sufficient. But if it be desired that the University Professors
should generally be amongst the most distinguished cultivators
of their respective sciences to be found in the country, then
much more liberal endowments are necessary.'[106] Material
and status considerations clearly dictated at least a perfunctory
bow in the direction of scholarship by the Tutors' Association.
In advocating that the fellow might be entitled to a professional career in Oxford either on the basis of teaching or by
residence for the purposes of advanced study, the tutors
avoided the unpleasing status connotations of reducing the
fellowship from an independent income to a mere salary for
a teacher.

The crucial question of celibacy restrictions on fellowships
presented the Tutors' Association with a dilemma. The logic
of the argument for the provision of academic careers pointed
clearly toward allowing tutorial fellows to marry. In defending
the collegiate system and their own position against the
onslaught of the royal commissioners' scheme, however, the
tutors had to rely on the 'sacredness' of founders' statutes
and the 'illegality' of tampering with them. Since married
fellows were explicitly forbidden by the statutes of every
college, the Tutors' Association could not advocate the
marriage of fellows without destroying their own best argument

[104] *Tutors' Association, No. 3,* 64.
[105] See, for example, 'Answers of Herman Merivale, Esq., MA, Late Fellow
of Balliol College and Professor of Political Economy, Oxford', in *Oxford Univ.
Comm.* (1852), Evidence, 200–2.
[106] Ibid. 108. Also see 106–10.

against the royal commissioners. The result was that they had to content themselves with weakly suggesting that perhaps fifteen years of residence in Oxford for the purpose of either teaching or private study might entitle fellows to marry and yet retain their fellowships.

The basic difficulty for the Tutors' Association was reconciling their strong loyalty to the college system with their desire to enhance and expand academic careers. Faced with the threat to the collegiate system posed by the report of the Royal Commission and impending parliamentary legislation, the tutors were forced to defend the *status quo*. In a letter to Gladstone in 1853, for example, Charles Marriott of Oriel, one of the leaders of the Tutors' Association, declared that the founders' will 'is *everything* as a *typical germ*, giving the principles and organization of the Foundation'.[107] Unfortunately, this type of argument could cut both ways. It was meant to attack the plans of the Royal Commission, but it could be used to frustrate all desires for reform, including those of the Tutors' Association itself.

F. The Report of the Hebdomadal Board

While the tutors were formulating their conception of an academic career in opposition to that of the Royal Commission, the Hebdomadal Board was busy collecting evidence and preparing its report. Their original idea was that the college residents should present a united front against the commissioners. However, they were not able to reach agreement with the representatives of the Tutors' Association on the important question of representation on the committee which would prepare the Hebdomadal Board's report. The Heads of Houses were unwilling to admit the propriety of accepting college tutors as a separate class in the university. This attitude was expressed by Provost Hawkins in his discussion of university government. '[I] f any changes should be recommended in the Hebdomadal Board,' he wrote, 'it should not be such as should destroy its *representative* character; as representing, that is to say, all the several Societies

---

[107] BL Add. MSS 44251 pt. I, fols. 74–6 (Gladstone Papers), cited by Ward, 184, n. 26.

of which the University is actually composed . . . Nor do I perceive any good reason for a special representation of the Professors, or the Tutors, or any other Functionaries, with reference to Academical Legislation generally . . .'[108] This attitude was, of course, as unsatisfactory to the Tutors' Association as the attitude of the royal commissioners themselves. This cleavage was regretted. The Vice-Chancellor urged the need for *'singleness* of action' and stigmatized the Tutors' Association as 'a self-constituted' body,[109] but the developing group consciousness among the tutors made it impossible for them to join forces with the Hebdomadal Board.

The report of the Hebdomadal Board defended existing institutions against the plans of both the Royal Commission and the Tutors' Association. The particular plan of the Royal Commission was denounced on the traditional grounds that it would destroy the liberal character of Oxford education and would be inimical as well to the interests of Anglican orthodoxy: '. . . the system of the Commissioners, with its ample staff of well-endowed Professors, its array of Lecturers, and its multitude of Unattached Students, is one which this University has never known and, we may be permitted to hope, will never know. For, remote as are such results from the contemplation of the Commissioners, it would tend, we fear, to substitute Information for Education, and Sciolism for Religion.'[110] The report also recommended no changes to meet the Tutors' Association's complaints. Their calls for increased residence of fellows and greater tutorial specialization both were ignored.[111] In considering university extension, the report concerned itself only with the maintenance of the collegiate system, giving no mention to the desire of the Tutors' Association to expand the possibilities for employment of fellows in Oxford.[112] Similarly, regarding the government of the university, the report attacked both the royal commissioners' plan for professorial dominance,

---

[108] *Report and Evidence Upon the Recommendations of Her Majesty's Commissioners for Inquiring into the State of the University of Oxford, Presented to the Board of Heads of Houses and Proctors, Dec. 1, 1853* (Oxford, 1853), Evidence, 370.   [109] Ibid. 381.
[110] *Report and Evidence . . . Presented to the Board of Heads of Houses and Proctors* (1853), 59–60.   [111] Ibid. 93–8.   [112] Ibid. 42–5.

and the Tutors' Association's plan to represent the tutors and resident MAs as a separate class.[113] Their own recommendation was to leave the government of the university unchanged, compromising only to the extent of suggesting the appointment of 'Delegacies' of members of Convocation to make suggestions on given subjects. The report defended the existing institutions in virtually every detail. They concluded that the only change required was for Parliament to promulgate an enabling act to permit the university and the colleges to alter or abrogate statutes which altered conditions had rendered obsolete. Their view was that such an act was needed not to make reforms, but only to bring the statutes into consonance with the actually existing system.

This report of the Hebdomadal Board, though diametrically opposed to the royal commissioners' report in all substantive areas, was none the less similar to it in one formal respect; in ignoring the evidence submitted to it. The two sets of evidence present many similarities which link them more to the suggestions of the Tutors' Association than to either of the 'official' reports.

The Hebdomadal Board's witnesses were as opposed as the Board's report itself to the royal commissioners' plans for the dominance of the professoriate. But for many of these witnesses, a definite desire for the development of an academic career in Oxford was evident. Even Dr Pusey, the commission's most important witness and most vociferous opponent of German ideas of professorial power, developed in his testimony basic criticisms of the existing fellowship system. He denounced the fact that 'the incomes of colleges have practically been employed in eking out poor curacies'.[114] He argued that fellowships ought to be used for resident teachers and scholars, not as prizes to help young graduates begin their professional careers outside the university. Specialization of subject was also demanded: 'The greatest disadvantage of the Tutorial system, at least in smaller colleges, is that the same Tutor is required to teach upon too varied subjects.'[115]

---

[113] Ibid. 65–86.   [114] *Report and Evidence . . . Presented to the Board of Heads of Houses and Proctors* (1853), 79. Also see 112–13 for his objection to the use of law fellowships in 'eking out the income of Junior, and other, Barristers until they marry'.   [115] Ibid. 78.

Pusey argued that one attractive aspect of university extension would be that it would necessitate 'an addition in the number of Tutors employed, and this increase of Tutors would facilitate the division of subjects'.[116] Pusey concluded that if these reforms were instituted 'more Fellows might readily be induced, or might be glad, to stay, if there were definite occupation for them'.[117] Finally, Pusey went even beyond the Tutors' Association in advocating the removal of the celibacy requirement to facilitate the development of a genuine profession: '. . . since the Heads and Canons are allowed to marry, in order to retain older men for important offices, there is nothing which can be objected to, on any principle, in allowing certain Tutors and Lecturers to marry, and yet retain their fellowships'.[118]

Although Dr Pusey developed these ideas for an academic career based on the college fellowship more fully than any other witness, the call for increased residence and specialization appeared in several witnesses' evidence.[119] William Sewell of Exeter, one of the strongest opponents of the Royal Commission among the college tutors, even suggested that the desire of the fellows for teaching work was so great that no expansion of opportunities in Oxford alone would satisfy it. In a public letter addressed to the Vice-Chancellor, Sewell proposed a plan for affiliating new colleges to be founded in other cities with Oxford colleges. The method of 'affiliation' which he recommended was to use the fellows of the Oxford college as the tutors and lecturers of these new colleges. One important advantage of this plan, for Sewell, was that it 'would immediately open a wide field of occupation for Fellows of Colleges, who, being at present not engaged in tuition, are often obliged to quit the University, to seek a maintenance'.[120]

---

[116] loc. cit.   [117] Ibid. 79.   [118] Ibid. 112.

[119] See 'Evidence of the Rev. Edward Arthur Litton, MA, Vice-Principal of St. Edmund Hall, Late Fellow of Oriel College', 405–13; 'Evidence of Edward A. Freeman, Esq. MA, Late Fellow and Rhetorical Lecturer of Trinity College', 415–40; 'Evidence of the Rev. James T. Round, BD, Formerly Fellow and Tutor of Balliol College', 463–95; all in *Report and Evidence . . . Presented to the Board of Heads of Houses and Proctors* (1853).

[120] *Suggestions for the Extension of the University; submitted to the Rev. the Vice-Chancellor* (n.p. [Oxford], n.d. [1850]), 10. Sewell printed this pamphlet

The implication was clearly that many college fellows left the university, not to seek the richer prizes available outside, but simply because the university did not provide them with sufficient opportunities for teaching.

In regard to the professorships, the witnesses revealed the same ambiguity as those who gave evidence to the Royal Commission and the Tutors' Association. They were unanimous in their dismissal of any plan which would make the professors as a class into the rulers of the university, but the idea of expanding the number and value of professorial chairs to provide advancement for college tutors proved attractive. One witness asserted:

I hold firmly that, among other wants, the University needs a great extension of the Professorial body . . . [T]here is at present hardly any means of keeping in the University men of ability, who wish to marry. There is no sort of promotion in their own calling offered to able and successful College Tutors. We want some means of permanently fixing in Oxford men of eminence in their several pursuits, which can only be done by offering them situations of emolument equal to at least the more moderate 'prizes' in other professions. And surely it would be better for a situation of this sort, rather than a College Living, to be the goal set before the College Tutor. The diligent and able Tutor should have, as in other professions, the prospect of rising to a higher place in his own line, that is, to a University Professorship.[121]

As in the Royal Commission's evidence and the Tutors' Association's reports, the logic of this conception of the professoriate necessitated defining their role primarily in terms of research. One witness recommended that professors not be permitted to give more than two courses of lectures per year 'in order that sufficient time may be secured to every Professor for carrying on his private studies, and for advancing

---

because he considered the Royal Commission to be 'illegal' and, therefore, he had refused to answer the set of questions which the commissioners had submitted to him. He felt, however, that some statement ought to be made in order to guard against a charge of indifference which might be placed on his refusal were he to remain silent. Since Sewell's motivation was identical to that which compelled the Hebdomadal Board to establish a committee of their own and to collect evidence after the Royal Commission's report had been published, this pamphlet may be considered as part of the evidence submitted to the Hebdomadal Board.

[121] 'Evidence of Edward A. Freeman . . .', *Report and Evidence . . . Presented to the Board of Heads of Houses and Proctors* (1853), 433.

the progress of the science which he professes'. In this way, 'provision [could be] made for securing the services of men who have attained the greatest eminence in their several departments of Literature, Science, and Art'.[122] It was necessary to define professors primarily as scholars to justify the high position which they would have to occupy if their position was to serve as an object of ambition for college tutors. A scholarly conception of the professoriate was, of course, also useful in justifying their exclusion from the educational work which was the preserve of the tutors.

A remarkably consistent ideal of an academic profession emerges from the two sets of evidence given to the royal commissioners and the Hebdomadal Board, together with the reports of the Tutors' Association. This ideal was a distinctive Oxford product, produced to suit its conditions and to fit the aspirations of Oxford dons. While the ideals of academic life which had been expressed in the period before the Royal Commission and in the Commission's report itself had grown from basic criticisms of the colleges and the theory of liberal education, this new ideal grew from a basic acceptance of the Oxford system. Its goal was to expand the possibilities for careers in the university while altering the system of collegiate autonomy and the traditional concept of education as little as possible. This ideal was particularly important because, in its broad outlines, it was this conception of an academic career which was to prevail.

[122] 'Evidence of the Rev. James T. Round . . .', ibid. 471.

Chapter II

THE RISE OF THE TUTORS 1854–1876

The period between the first and the second Oxford university commissions saw the steady growth in importance, power, and group-consciousness of the college tutors. This development was made possible by the Oxford Act of 1854 and the work of the executive commissioners appointed under that act. College tutors increasingly came to desire the acceptance of academic work as a life-career and a recognized profession. They came to see teaching as the primary function of the colleges and the most fitting use for college fellowships. These views inevitably made for conflict since they antagonized three other decernible 'parties' in Oxford. First, they angered supporters of the Church who continued to insist on the essentially religious purposes of the colleges. Second, 'prize fellows' resented the implication that all other uses for fellowships were an abuse of 'educational endowments'. Third, the emphasis of the tutors on the primary importance of college teaching was attacked by those who saw the advancement of knowledge as the most important function of the university.

The relations between these groups was to prove very complex since any specific issue tended to polarize opinion and create a series of shifting alliances. The attack on religious tests united the advocates of a teaching profession with the supporters of 'the endowment of research' against the Church party. However, the Church party and the advocates of a teaching profession could combine to foil the plans of the researchers. The situation was complicated further by conflict over methods of teaching and the distribution of collegiate resources. Through these conflicts the college tutors were able to achieve a significant degree of success for their viewpoint concerning both ideals of education and conceptions of academic life.

A. The Effects of the Oxford Act of 1854 and of the Executive Commission

Although the Oxford Act of 1854 by no means represented a victory for those who wished to see an academic profession created for college tutors, it established the pre-conditions on which future victory would rest. This situation was the result of the government's decision to leave the framing of the bill to W. E. Gladstone, the MP for the university. Lord John Russell's government had been replaced since the appointment of the Royal Commission by Lord Aberdeen's weak coalition which had no desire to tackle the controversial issue of university reform. Gladstone was a loyal 'college man' who had questioned the legality of appointing the Royal Commission.[1] He was in close contact with the leaders of the Tutors' Association,[2] however, and eventually came to accept their views as most representative of Oxford opinion. The result was that the most important provision of the Act of 1854 was to give each college the right to remodel its statutes under the benign scrutiny of executive commissioners notably sympathetic to the collegiate system.[3] The only exception to the general victory for collegiate attitudes and interests was that Dissenters in Parliament managed to insert clauses which made it possible to matriculate and take the BA without signing the Thirty-nine Articles.[4] This change had little practical significance, however, since the colleges could continue to insist on any religious observances they wished, and all scholarships and fellowships remained restricted to members of the Church. Few Dissenters were willing to entrust their sons to Oxford colleges under these conditions.[5]

---

[1] See his *Speech on the Commission of Inquiry into the State of the Universities of Oxford and Cambridge, July 18, 1850* (Oxford, 1850).

[2] See Ward, 180–200. See also above Ch. I, p. 49, n. 107 for an example of this contact.

[3] 17 and 18 Vict. cap. 81, arts, 104, reprinted in L. L. Shadwell (ed.), *Enactments in Parliament specially concerning the Universities of Oxford and Cambridge the Colleges and Halls therein, and the Colleges of Winchester, Eton and Westminster* (Oxford, 1912), iii. 153–4. See also Ward, Chapter IX, 180–209.

[4] 17 and 18 Vict. cap. 81, arts. 43–4, in Shadwell iii. 168.

[5] See below, pp. 77–81 for a discussion of the complete abolition of religious tests in 1871.

Although the act did not recognize the college fellowship as the basic institution for an academic profession, it established an essential prerequisite by insisting on the basic principle that 'Headships, Fellowships and other College Emoluments' should be 'conferred according to personal merit and fitness'.[6] Furthermore, in the methods chosen to accomplish this goal, it showed that the intention was unequivocal regarding fellowships while, for other collegiate prizes, the general principle was simply the basis for negotiation. For example, in cases where this principle conflicted with the advantages enjoyed by a particular school, the governing body of the school had the right to reject any statute concerning previously closed scholarships and exhibitions. They had no unilateral right of rejection, however, in regard to previously closed fellowships.[7] None the less, even in the case of fellowships, some compromises would be necessary since all statute revisions had to gain the acceptance of both the colleges and the commissioners before they could be presented to Parliament.[8] Perhaps because the colleges had the right to submit the first proposal, the commissioners felt that the onus would lie with them in cases of failure to reach an agreement. The result was that they were willing to make large concessions in areas where the principles of their commission and the sentiments of the college conflicted.

During the period 1854-8 in which the Executive Commission operated, compromises were reached with virtually every college making 'open competition' the rule in fellowship elections though some restrictions were allowed in a few colleges where before 1854 all awards had been narrowly closed. At New College, since previously all fellows had been chosen from the scholars of Winchester, the compromise permitted half the fellows to be elected from those educated at either New College or Winchester. In the case of scholarships, however, all were to continue to be restricted to Winchester, though the favoured group was broadened to include commoners as well as former scholars.[9] Similarly, at

---

[6] 17 and 18 Vict. cap. 81, art. 28, in Shadwell iii. 160-1.
[7] Ibid., art. 31, in Shadwell iii. 163-4.
[8] Ibid., arts. 28-9, in Shadwell iii. 160-2.
[9] See, Hastings Rashdall and R. S. Rait, *New College* (London, 1901), 224-5.

Jesus, where previously all fellowships and scholarships had been confined to specific localities or particular schools in Wales, the college's historian has noted that 'point after point had been conceded to the strenuous resistance within the College'. After much hard bargaining, the executive commissioners and the college finally agreed that half the fellowships would be 'open' and half would continue to be restricted to Welshmen. In regard to the 'closed' half, the only change was that they would no longer be limited to specific localities or particular schools. All scholarships, however, were to remain restricted to Welshmen although some modifications were made regarding schools and localities.[10]

Only St. John's[11] used to the fullest their rights of obstruction by rejecting all the commissioners' plans as 'prejudicial to the . . . college as a place of learning and education'.[12] Early in the negotiations the chief strategist of the college, W. A. Rew, had written to Philip Wynter, the President, that 'it is very clear, that the Commissioners are squeezable; . . . if we take a bold attitude, leaving to the commissioners to make some further offer, if we do not altogether carry our point, we shall at least get far more favourable terms'.[13] The college took Rew's advice and was able to obtain considerable concessions especially on the sensitive issue of opening St. John's scholarships and fellowships. The majority of these has been confined previously to scholars from Merchant Taylors' School. The remainder were restricted to four other grammar schools and to 'Founder's Kin'. As in the cases of New College and Jesus, the commissioners were so desperate to gain agreement that they finally suggested that half the proposed eighteen fellowships would be 'open' while half would continue to be restricted. Merchant Taylors' School

[10] See, E. G. Hardy, *Jesus College* (London, 1899), 198–9. Citation on p. 198. It is clear from the context that Hardy felt that the commissioners had been most unwise to concede so much to the desires of the college. He argued that the result of these new statutes was that all the most intellectually talented Welsh students took open awards at other colleges while only the weaker candidates in general competed at Jesus.

[11] See, W. C. Costin, *The History of St. John's College, Oxford, 1598–1860* (Oxford, 1958), 256–77, for an excellent, detailed account of the process of negotiation between the commissioners and the governing body of the college.

[12] 17 and 18 Vict. cap. 81, art 29, in Shadwell iii. 161–2.

and the other preferred grammar schools would still receive the scholarships (the number of which was to be increased) while the founder's kin preference was to be abolished. Merchant Taylors' School decided to accept the compromise; the increased number of scholarships presumably serving as recompense for the lost fellowships. Although this solution was almost identical to the one accepted after hard negotiation by New College and Jesus, the college rejected this compromise. They argued that the commissioners' plan would lead to constant dissension and demanded a distribution of ten 'closed' to eight 'open' fellowships. The commissioners refused to make this further concession and an impasse was reached since the time allotted to attain an agreement had been exhausted. St. John's was the only college to carry their rights under the Act of 1854 to this length.

Due to this failure to reach a settlement, the final decision had to be made by a separate bill framed in the Privy Council. At this stage, it was no longer necessary to reach a negotiated agreement with the college. Even Gladstone, a staunch supporter of college interests, was angered by St. John's inflexibility. He wrote to the President of the Council that 'the Commission . . . acted in this case with the utmost moderation and were very obstinately and irrationally opposed'.[14] The result was that the Privy Council conceded less to the college than had the commissioners. All fellowships were opened and only the majority of the scholarships were reserved for the favoured schools. It was in this form that the bill was passed perfunctorily through Parliament without discussion or alteration.

St. John's lost in this way the concessions which had been granted to New College and Jesus through their miscalculation of how far they could push their rights of negotiation. After the work of the Executive Commission, in these two colleges only were a substantial number of restricted fellowships maintained. St. John's entered fully into the new era of 'open competition' and 'prize fellowships' along with the rest

---

[13] W. S. Costin, *The History of St. John's College, Oxford, 1598–1860* (Oxford, 1958), 269.

[14] PRO G/D, Granville Papers, 26 June 1860, cited in ibid. 277.

of the colleges. This change was essential for the creation of an academic profession since it would have been unthinkable to make fellowships the mode of payment for college teachers while they continued to be used for the purposes of charity and to gratify local, school, or family preferences. In regard to scholarships, more traditional restrictions could be tolerated.

The Act of 1854 also directed that a distinction be made between fellows and scholars in those colleges, such as New College, Christ Church, and St. John's, in which all members on the foundation, undergraduates as well as MAs, were undifferentiated by title and held their awards on the same terms. This basic principle was adhered to in all statute revisions made by the colleges and the executive commissioners. The change was also necessary if the fellowship system was to serve the needs of a profession of college teachers. The removal of these restrictions and anomalies could not in itself establish the position of the college tutor as a professional career; yet this later development could not have been accomplished without these prior changes.

The Oxford Act also contributed to the development of the 'tutorial profession' by giving fellows engaged in college work a substantial plurality in the reformed legislature of the university. Under the pre-1854 system, college tutors had little power in university legislation. The Heads of Houses, who comprised 22 of the 24 members of the Hebdomadal Board, promulgated all legislation with only the 2 Proctors, appointed by the colleges on a rotating basis, to represent all other interests. These other interests were supposed to be represented also by Convocation, the body through which all legislation had to pass. This institution, however, was considerably less powerful than the Hebdomadal Board because proposals had to be accepted or rejected without amendment and no genuine debate was possible since only formal Latin speeches were permitted. Furthermore, since Convocation was composed of all MAs who had kept their names on the books of their colleges, college tutors were vastly outnumbered by the non-residents. In theory, the college tutor had no more power in Convocation than any other MA. Since college tutors, however, were resident during term while the vast majority of graduates were not; in practice, the tutors often were able to control Convocation. Only an exceptionally controversial issue would be likely to bring the non-resident MAs to Oxford to vote. Unfortunately for the college tutors, these often were the most important ones.

This situation was altered radically by the reconstruction of university government under the Act of 1854. A new 'Hebdomadal Council' was established consisting of 22 members; the Chancellor, the Vice-Chancellor, the two proctors and 18 elected members of whom 6 must be heads of houses, 6 university professors and 6 members of Convocation of 5 years standing.[15] The18 representatives of the heads, professors and members of Convocation were elected by a revived 'Congregation' which consisted of all professors, certain other university officials and all members of Convocation resident for 20 weeks in the year within one and a half miles of Carfax, an intersection in the centre of the city of Oxford.[16] University legislation would be promulgated in the future by the new Hebdomadal Council, debated in English in the new Congregation, and accepted or rejected by that body without amendment. If accepted by Congregation, legislation also would have to pass through Convocation, whose limitations and powers remained unchanged.[17]

These reforms in university government were closest in spirit to the proposals of the Tutors' Association.[18] The power of the heads of houses was drastically reduced and domination by the professoriate was averted while the influence of the college tutors was correspondingly increased. In one crucial respect, the Act of 1854 was even more favourable to the college tutors than the plans of the Tutors' Association had been. Instead of allowing the heads and professors to elect their own representatives, it gave this power to Congregation. Although this body was required to elect 6 heads and 6 professors to the Hebdomadal Council, the college tutors, who were expected to be the largest single interest-group in Congregation, would be able to select representatives sympathetic to their own interests rather than those

[15] 17 and 18 Vict. cap. 81, art. 6, in Shadwell iii. 155.
[16] Ibid., art. 16, pp. 157–8.   [17] Ibid., arts. 17–20, p. 158.
[18] See above, Ch. I, p. 46, n. 99 for the proposal of the Tutor's Association regarding university government.

committed to the heads or professors as separate classes. The clear intention of this reform was to give dominant power in university legislation to the college tutors. Since most fellows not engaged in academic work were non-resident, they would be ineligible for membership in Congregation. The residence requirement was expected also to provide some representation for the private coaches, although it was assumed that they would decline in numbers with the increasing commitment of college fellows to tutorial work. The inclusion in Congregation of private coaches and also of local clergy who were resident MAs was not expected seriously to diminish the hegemony of the college tutors. Although unforeseen changes in the composition of Oxford society were later to thwart this intention of the Act of 1854,[19] this reform of university government was of crucial importance since it encouraged the development of group-consciousness among college tutors by providing them, for the first time, with an effective political forum.

An analysis of the academic duties fulfilled by the 289 MAs who were qualified to vote in Congregation in 1858 illustrates graphically the revolution which had been effected in the distribution of power.[20] The largest interest group in the new Congregation was the fellows holding official teaching positions in Oxford, who comprised 27 per cent of the total. Although they were equalled by the other resident fellows, these others were unlikely to develop much group-consciousness.[21] They ranged from Oxford curates, Biblical scholars, and antiquaries, to college bursars and failed barristers. The college tutors were much more homogeneous since they were drawn together increasingly by the performance of common duties. Clearly, they had gained greatly in power from the recent past when their status in university government had been no more than that of any other members of Convocation.

The method of voting in Congregation, particularly in

---

[19] See below, Ch. III, pp. 114–22 and Ch. V, pp. 212–14 for further discussion of this problem of university government.

[20] See below, Appendix 4, p. 289.

[21] There were 77 college tutors or lecturers and 78 other resident fellows. This second figure was obtained by combining 'Fellows holding other college offices' and 'Fellows not engaged in college work' on Appendix 4, p. 289.

elections to the Hebdomadal Council, also tended to put a premium on group-consciousness and concerted action. The act called for the election of half the 18 elected members of the Council every 3 years for 6-year terms. Of the 6 seats in each category 3 were to be vacated for each election. Each member of Congregation would have 6 votes in total, 2 for the 3 vacant seats in each of the 3 categories.[22] In such a system of multiple voting, the effect of concerted action would be to increase the power of any bloc beyond its numerical significance. If a group of voters agreed not to use all their votes, the value of those they did cast would be enhanced. This was a powerful stimulus to the development of the party spirit which was the most striking characteristic of academic politics in Oxford.

The method of reforming the collegiate statutes also had the effect in most cases of giving the college officers and especially the tutors dominant influence. The only exceptions were the few colleges in which fellows were partially or wholly excluded from the governing body.[23] The resident fellows would be certain to take a more active role than the non-residents in negotiations with the executive commissioners and about 70 per cent of the residents were college officers.[24] Tutors alone comprised 50 per cent of the residents.[25] Although the proportion of college officers and tutors among the resident fellows varied, only in Magdalen were they in the minority. It was significant that Christ Church, the only college in which tutors and other officers were wholly

[22] 17 and 18 Vict. cap. 81, art.21, in Shadwell iii. 158–9.

[23] In only one college, Christ Church, were the fellows (called 'students') totally excluded from the governing body. That function was in the hands of the Dean and Chapter instead. In three other colleges only part of the fellows constituted the governing body: in New Colleges and St. John's, a portion of the senior fellows, and in Queen's, the fellows on the 'Old Foundation'.

[24] Of the approximately 160 resident fellows in 1858, 115 or 72 per cent were college officers. The figure for 'college officers' was obtained by combining 'Fellows engaged as official tutors or lecturers' and 'Fellows holding other college offices' on Appendix 4, p. 289. To these were added the four BA fellows who were college tutors or lecturers. The figure for 'resident fellows' was obtained by adding 'Fellows not engaged in college work' to the number of college officers. This figure is only approximate since there were probably several other resident BA fellows who held no college office.

[25] See Appendix 3, below p. 288. To the 80 fellows who taught for their colleges in 1858 can be added one more who was a lecturer at a hall.

excluded from the governing body, was also the only college which became so dissatisfied with its statutes that it required a complete rewriting of them before the second University Commission of 1877.[26]

The fellowship system was still in a far from satisfactory state if it was to serve as the basic institution of the academic profession. The acceptance of the principle that intellectual merit ought to be the major qualification for the awarding of fellowships and the rejection of all charitable conceptions of their function clearly had been major victories for the tutorial ideology. However, the act had also allowed 'personal merit and fitness' to be legitimate criteria for the awarding of fellowships. This vague standard left a wide margin for extra-intellectual qualifications. While the obligation to sign the Thirty-nine Articles had been removed for matriculation and for taking the BA, subscription continued to be required for all higher degrees and also for all college and university offices.[27] In effect, 'fitness' for a fellowship or tutorship was interpreted to require a religious qualification. Also, in those colleges where holy orders had been required previously for the continued tenure of fellowships, the act did nothing to abolish this restriction.

More seriously, the confining of fellowships to unmarried men continued to be a crucial obstacle to their use as the basic institution of a profession. The difficulty was that any change would necessitate fundamental alterations in the entire system. So long as fellowships did not entail specific duties, it was necessary to have some method of ensuring an adequate turnover rate. The celibacy restriction had the advantage of accomplishing this goal, albeit indirectly, in the great majority of cases. The alternatives were fraught with danger for the proponents of the 'tutorial profession' since they all tended to diminish the value of the fellowship itself. The fellows' independence and high status were largely the result of the fact that their position was held for life and entailed no necessary duties. Changes could easily destroy these values

---

[26] See E. G. W. Bill and J. F. A. Mason, *Christ Church and Reform 1850–1867* (Oxford, 1970).

[27] 17 and 18 Vict. cap. 81, art. 44, in Shadwell iii. 168.

which made the system worth preserving. As Archbishop Whately noted in his evidence to the Royal Commission, '[A] man who has no thought (as few have) of sitting down on a Fellowship for life, yet derives a great *consolation* from the reflection that *if* all his plans of life fail, . . . he at any rate has his Fellowship to secure him a decent maintenance and a respectable position'.[28]

A critical aspect of the fellowship's status value was that it was legally a type of property and not a salary. The importance of this legal status may be judged by the reaction of Charles Neate of Oriel to Lord John Russell's ill-advised reference in Parliament to a fellowship as a 'salary'. 'Does Lord John Russell know that I can mortgage my Fellowship, that I can made over to a creditor or an assignee the right to receive during my life my share of the revenues of my College? Salary indeed! I have no more a salary than Lord John Russell himself and I work less for it.'[29] Neate argued that it was precisely this characteristic which made Oxford and Cambridge pre-eminent as 'places of education'. Because a fellow's income was derived largely from property and could not be viewed as a mere salary, 'the teachers . . . are more independent of their occupation for a maintenance than anywhere else . . .'[30] It was this independence which '. . . leads the Undergraduate to respect in his own Tutor the spontaneous exercise of an honourable calling . . . teaching is less with him a necessity, less a trade, . . . he might live if he liked as an idle gentleman, taking his ease in his College, and borrowing from the shadow of its ancient walls, which are his property, something of dignity in his ease'.[31]

---

[28] *Oxford Univ. Comm.* (1852), Evidence, 27. Mark Pattison wrote in a similar vein to his sister when he won his fellowship at Lincoln in 1839, '. . . anxiety for my temporal provision is removed . . . I feel so easy & comfortable to what I did before — not that I for a moment think of giving myself up to a state of stagnant vegetation. I have had training enough to know that an idle life is an unhappy one and whether called yet farther to any active duties, or left to books & study . . . I feel sure that I shall work no less industriously than before — perhaps more so — just as a gentleman who digs for pleasure or exercise exerts himself more than the labourer who has his bread to earn by it.' Lincoln MS Pattison letters 1836–52, MP to EP, 10 Nov. 1839.

[29] *Objections to the Government Scheme for the Present Subjugation and Future Management of the University of Oxford* (Oxford, 1854) 20.

[30] Ibid. 32.   [31] Ibid. 33.

The problem was that all feasible plans for allowing fellowships to be held by married men necessarily would infringe, to some degree, on the independence and status of the position. It would not have been practicable simply to allow fellows to marry while leaving all other regulations the same. This would have meant that the only means of vacating a fellowship would have been the attainment of an income over a certain amount, generally £500 p.a. Except for clergymen, it had always proved difficult for this method to be effective. Increases in income often could be concealed while legal problems made this method even more uncertain.[32] In practice, marriage had been the major means of vacating fellowships and the abolition of this necessity would have virtually eliminated turnover except through death. Even Charles Neate probably would have admitted the undesirability of encouraging these 400 fellows who were 'independent of their occupation for a maintenance' to actually become 'idle gentlemen'. The only solution would have been to make a distinction between fellowships held by college officers and those not used for this purpose. College officers could have been allowed to retain their fellowships as married men while maintaining the old regulations for other fellows. Alternatively, all fellows could have been permitted to marry while limiting the tenure of those who were not college officers. One objection to both of these solutions was that they would have had the effect of making a fellowship held by a college official into a type of salary, since his special privileges would be dependent on the fulfilment of work-obligations. Another objection was that any attempt to differentiate between college officers and other fellows certainly would be viewed by the latter as an invidious distinction.

The existing system for awarding and retaining fellowships was clearly at the centre of the difficulty of organizing a

[32] This problem continued as long as the celibacy restriction was in effect. The value of Church livings was a matter of public record while other types of income were more difficult to determine. For two examples of the complicated legal battles which occurred on this issue, see Oriel MS ETC F.16 and B.4 (in which C. L. Shadwell was able to retain his fellowship despite a private income of £837 p.a.) and University College MS Legal Opinions and Papers on Various Matters *c*. 1820–1906 (in which Lazarus Fletcher kept his fellowship despite his appointment to a lucrative keepership at the British Museum).

tutorial profession in the colleges. The allocation of college resources also would be a problem, however, since the creation of a tutorial profession would necessitate devoting a larger percentage of endowment income to educational uses than previously had been the case. Funds would be needed for both increased numbers of college tutors and for retiring pensions. Tuition fees could not satisfy these demands. An enlarged educational fund would be needed especially if holy orders were no longer required of most fellows and college livings could no longer serve as retirement sinecures.[33] The need to provide retiring pensions for college officers who were not in holy orders would also create pressure for the sale of advowsons. An expansion in the number of fellows engaged in college work would probably also mean a decline in the number of fellowships available for non-academic uses. Thus the financial needs of a tutorial profession, as well as the necessity of altering celibacy restrictions on fellowships, would be certain to arouse opposition in the colleges since they inevitably would disturb the career prospects and other vital interests of the non-academic fellows.

The new legislative and executive institutions created by the Act of 1854, Congregation and the Hebdomadal Council, also were not ideally suited to the needs of the tutorial

---

[33] This use of advowsons also was coming under attack at this time as deleterious to the interests of the Church. As Anthony Trollope wrote, 'Does any man believe that that very pleasant fellow whom he has known at college, and who has sparkled so brightly in common room, who has been so energetic in the management of the college finances, and in the reform of college abuses, — who has gradually succeeded in putting off all those outward clerical symbols which as a novice he found himself constrained to adopt, and who during his annual visit to London has become a well-instructed man of the world, — can any one, we say, belief that such a one at the age of forty can be fit to go into a parish and undertake the cure of the parochial souls? There are, we fancy, some who do so believe; but they are those who think that nothing is necessary to make a parson but orders and a living, — that the profession of a clergyman is unlike any other trade or calling known, requiring for due performance of its duties no special fitness, no training, no skill, no practice, no thought, and no preparation.' See *Clergymen of the Church of England* (London, 1866), 86. Scepticism about the easy connection of holy orders and college offices was also spreading in Oxford during this period. Although one reason C. L. Dodgson of Christ Church never took full orders was his unclerical fondness for the theatre, he also questioned whether a college tutorship was genuinely a 'cure of souls'. See, R. L. Green (ed.), *The Diaries of Lewis Carroll*, 2 vols, (New York, 1954). On the growth of professional ideals among the parish clergy, see Brian Heeney, *A Different Kind of Gentleman* (Hamden, 1976).

profession. Although they were a vast improvement over the pre-1854 situation, they still did not place all power in the hands of those engaged in academic duties. In 1858 over a third of the voters in Congregation were not officially engaged in academic work.[34] To understand the importance of this group, one only has to imagine the distribution of power in Congregation if the fulfilment of official academic duties had been the voting criterion.[35] The result would have been to give the college officers a substantial majority in Congregation. They would have controlled 59 per cent of the votes while the tutors alone would have had 41 per cent. In the actual Congregation, assembled on the basis of non-academic criteria, neither college tutors nor college officers as a whole had such overwhelming power. They were a plurality in Congregation but needed allies to achieve a majority.

The final problem left unresolved by the Act of 1854 was the desire of the tutors for increased opportunities for specialization. Although the Tutors' Association had urged this need in 1853,[36] neither the provisions of the act nor the activities of the Executive Commission had ameliorated this complaint. The royal commissioners had suggested that the creation of a new category of university lecturers would meet this desire, but their plan contained elements which were highly repugnant to the supporters of the tutorial profession. The first priority of the tutors clearly had been to secure its defeat and they succeeded so well that it was not even proposed in Parliament.[37] The result, however, was that the

[34] This figure was obtained by combining 'Fellows not engaged in college work,' 'Resident MAs holding other college offices' and 'Resident MAs not engaged in any official academic work' in Appendix 4, p. 289. The 'Resident MAs holding other college offices' were all college chaplains while the 'Resident MAs not engaged in official academic work' were virtually all Oxford city clergy. The total was 103 of the 289 members of Congregation.

[35] See Appendix 5, below p. 291. I have departed from the strict rigour of my hypothetical criteria to include the Chancellor, the non-professorial canons of Christ Church and a few other high university officials in this imaginary Congregation. It would have been unrealistic to assume that any definition would have excluded these dignitaries.

[36] *No. 2. Recommendations Respecting the Constitution of the University of Oxford, as Adopted by the Tutors' Association April 1853* (Oxford, 1853). One recommendation was for 'an increased liberty of teaching in the University' (p. 22).

[37] For an account of the attack by the Tutors' Association on the report of the Royal Commission, see above, Ch. I, pp. 43–6.

tutors' own desire for expanded opportunities for specialization remained unsatisifed. A plan addressed to this grievance was proposed in 1859 by D. P. Chase, the Principal of St. Mary's Hall.[38] Chase was an energetic university politician whose main concerns were the preservation of the Church connection, the recognition of the charitable purposes of collegiate endowments and the reduction in the cost of Oxford education through the establishment of halls for 'frugal men'.[39] Chase's proposal was significant since his major concerns often placed him in opposition to the proponents of a tutorial profession. His motive clearly was to gain support for his primary objectives by linking them to a cause which was growing in popularity among the academic residents.

Chase argued that college tutors ought to confine their duties to the regulation of undergraduates' moral and religious lives and to the supervision of their reading. Specialized instruction ought to be entrusted to the coaches and the professors outside of the colleges. They would receive payment directly from the undergraduate, a portion of whose collegiate tuition would be refunded for this purpose. Students would be free to select the teachers they thought would help them most, while the teachers would be free of all the statutory restrictions placed on college fellows. They would be able to specialize in any subject or portion of a subject they wished, constrained only by the need to find students willing to pay for instruction in a given area. The sacred metaphor of political economy, Adam Smith's 'pin factory', was invoked to show that this 'voluntary system' would lead to more effective teaching. 'Hitherto each man has made the whole pin himself, why not try what may be done by employing men on separate processes in the manufacture?'[40] Chase argued that since his proposal 'would enable those men who had a real vocation for the work to make it ['academical instruction'] a profession, they would take the line for which

[38] *The Voluntary System Applied to Academical Instruction* (Oxford, 1859).

[39] See his *The Rights of 'Indigentes' in Respect to College Foundations* . . . (Oxford, 1856). Also see *Education for Frugal Men at the University of Oxford. An Account of the Experiments at St. Mary's and St. Alban's Halls* . . . (Oxford, 1864).

[40] *The Voluntary System Applied to Academical Instruction* (Oxford, 1859), 9-10.

they were best fitted, and in that line they would be *facile principes*'.[41]

Although it offered the possibility of a professional teaching career in Oxford, Chase's plan contained features unacceptable to most tutors. It was merely a restatement of Robert Lowe's utilitarian advocacy of coaching as the best system for organizing the teaching work of the university.[42] For Chase, the real advantage of this 'voluntary system' was that, by organizing education outside the colleges, it would preserve collegiate endowments for religious and charitable uses. This advantage from Chase's perspective was precisely the crucial drawback of this plan from the viewpoint of the tutorial profession. For both material reasons and reasons of status it was essential to base the profession on the institution of the college fellowship. To purchase professional specialization at the price of reducing the tutor to total dependence on fees received directly from the student would have been a worse bargain even than attaining this goal at the cost of subservience to a staff of university lecturers and professors.

So long as the colleges remained separate and autonomous institutions for the purposes of education, however, the tutors' desire for opportunities for specialized teaching was certain to be frustrated. All colleges except perhaps the very largest were too small to allow much division of labour. Chase's plan, like the royal commissioners', would have surmounted this problem simply by organizing most teaching outside the colleges. For the tutors this was not an acceptable solution since the colleges were the basis of the tutors' importance in the university. The result was a seeming impasse: increased opportunities for specialized teaching could not be provided within the existing college system, while the tutors were committed to the colleges by all their most essential interests.

B. *College Tutors versus the Prize Fellows and the Heads*

The period between the two university commissions saw the development of conflict in the colleges between fellows and heads and between tutorial fellows and prize fellows. These

---

[41] Ibid. 15.   [42] *Oxford Univ. Comm.* (1852), Evidence, 12–13.

divisions had existed before the Royal Commission, but they had been muted in the interest of forming a united front against the threat to the college system itself represented by the plans of the royal commissioners. After the defeat of these plans, however, these intra-collegiate rivalries became increasingly important. The central issues were how power was to be apportioned among these different groups and the related question of how the endowment income of each college was to be divided among conflicting uses.

An instance of this type of dissension occurred at University College in 1872 when G. G. Bradley was elected Master. The resident fellows took this opportunity of having an inexperienced head to promulgate a number of far-reaching changes in the college statutes. According to Bradley's account, the fellows gained his approval before he had a chance to understand fully the revolutionary significance of the proposed changes. When Bradley realized with horror the importance of the reforms to which he had given his assent, he wrote to the Visitor of the college, the Lord Chancellor, asking that the new statutes be abrogated.[43] This desperate action, however, was only partially successful. The new statutes were, in the main, approved by the Queen in Council on 28 May 1872, although he was successful in having a few of the provisions disallowed. None the less, whether they were ratified or not, all the statutes approved by the college were significant as indications of the aspirations of the fellows, particularly of those who were resident and engaged in educational work.[44]

In regard to the distribution of power in the college, the new statutes decreased the importance of the master in

---

[43] See, *Private and Confidential. Two Letters to the Right Honourable the Lord High Chancellor of Great Britain, Visitor in Behalf of the Crown of University College, Oxford* (n.p. [Oxford], n.d. [1873]).

[44] See Bradley's letter to the Cleveland Commission, printed in PP 1873, xxvii, part ii, 202. He clearly did not conceal in Oxford his discontent with the final settlement. An undergraduate magazine in 1874 expressed in doggerel their understanding of Bradley's attitude, 'I come from Rugby, and my name is Br*dl*y, I am a master; and regret it sadly:' See, 'The New Inquisition', in *The Shotover Papers*, I, no. 4 (1874), 60. It was not until 1881 that Bradley was able to leave his uncongenial position at University College for the deanery of Westminster.

relation to the fellows.[45] The master was no longer to be elected for life, but instead for a term of twenty years with only limited possibilities for extension. At the age of seventy retirement would be compulsory. The powers of the mastership were also curtailed in one other important respect. Previously, he alone had appointed two of the three college tutors. By the new statutes, all three would be elected by the entire governing body.

In regard to fellowships, the new statutes also made some important changes. A division was made between those who held college offices and those who fulfilled no duties in Oxford. The plan was to have three categories. The first would be prize fellows who, either by their own choice or by the decision of the majority of the governing body, would never hold college office. They might be resident or not as it suited their convenience and their tenure would not be limited by marriage or income. Their fellowships would last, however, only for a non-renewable term of seven years.[46] The second category would be fellows who served as college officers for between ten and twenty years. They too would be freed from all restrictions on marriage or income but would only be allowed to retain their fellowships after they had ceased to be college officers for the same number of years as they had served the college. Finally, the third category would be composed of those fellows who held college offices for twenty or more years. They alone would be allowed to retain their fellowships for life, freed from restrictions on marriage or income.

By the new statutes, the number of tutors also was to be increased and extra funds were to be set aside for retiring pensions for tutors who were not clergymen. It was argued that pensions were needed since the fellowship was only a portion of the college tutor's income and would be insufficient for retirement, especially if the tutor was married. Although

---

[45] 'By certain clauses in these statutes, great changes, partly immediate, partly prospective, are made in the tenure and therefore in the pecuniary value of the Mastership', complained Bradley to the Cleveland Commission (PP 1873, xxxvii, part ii, 202).

[46] 'Non-resident Fellowships . . . under the New Statutes are already tenable for a limited period only', wrote the bursar to the 1871 commissioners. Ibid. 195.

the scheme for a generous pension plan was disallowed by the Visitor,[47] it is still worth examining more closely for the indications it gives of collegiate priorities.

The most striking fact was the largeness of the proposed pensions. In the case of tutors who had served twenty years, the pensions were to be £200 p.a. for life. This was about half what they had received from tuition fees above their fellowships and would give them from about age forty-three at least 50 per cent and perhaps 70 per cent of their full tutorial income.[48] The tactical value of a research ideology for the proponents of a tutorial profession is well illustrated by this proposal. The best argument which the fellows could bring forward for their pensions was that they would be granted only 'with a view to important and productive study in the future'.[49] As P. G. Medd, the senior fellow, noted in a marginal comment to a letter in which the Master rejected the notion that a tutor needed to retire so early because he was 'worn out': 'He may not be worn out, but may have earned a studious leisure which may be far from unproductive when based on the experience of 20 years as a teacher.'[50] The fellows also argued that pensions beyond the retained fellowship for the retired tutor of twenty years service were to be granted only by a two-thirds vote of the governing body, but this was well-known to be a weak argument since the inevitable tendency was for such permissions to become entitlements.

Perhaps the most explosive aspect of the proposed pension plan was that much of the capital for the fund was to be obtained by selling three of the college's best livings.[51] Money

---

[47] The elaborate provisions of this plan which did not become part of the new statutes approved by the Visitor, were printed in full in ibid. 202–3.

[48] The higher calculation was made by estimating the fellowship at £250 p.a. Tutors with fifteen years service would receive £150 p.a. and those with less than fifteen but more than ten years would receive £100 p.a. See ibid. 202, items (C), (D) and (E). The lower calculation was based on the clause (9) in some versions of the pension scheme which would have limited the pensions to a maximum of £350 p. a.

[49] University College MS letter, Fellows to the Lord Chancellor, 10 Nov. 1873 (fair copy), p. 11.

[50] University College MS letter, G. G. Bradley to Lord Chancellor, 28 June 1873, p. 5. In box marked 'College Statutes and Pension Scheme (1872–1884)'. The marginal comment is signed 'P.G.M.'.

[51] PP 1873, xxxvii, part ii, 203, clause 13, note (d) (4).

also would be raised by discontinuing the practices of augmenting benefices[52] and paying an allowance to non-resident
fellows for the use of their rooms in college.[53] In his remarks
to the 1871 financial commission, C. J. Faulkner, the bursar,
continued the battle for the pension plan and against the
prize fellows. He stated that 'it is the opinion of the College'
that the increased income which they expected to receive in
the near future 'should not as at present fall into the sum
which is annually divided among the master and fellows,
whether resident and engaged in college work or not. The
prevailing opinion is that non-resident Fellowships . . . should
. . . be limited in value to about £200 per annum.' First among
the uses to which this surplus ought to be put was 'the
adequate remuneration of College officers, educational and
other'.[54]

Taken as a whole, these new statutes revealed clearly
the aspirations of the tutors and other college officers. As
the fellows asserted in their letter to the Lord Chancellor
defending themselves against the Master's accusations, 'The
aim of the College in drawing up its new Statutes was, while
limiting the tenure of sinecure Fellowships, to offer on its
educational staff a professional career to Laymen as well as
Clergymen.'[55] In attempting to secure these goals, the college
officers were led inevitably into sharp conflict with clerical
interests, the prize fellows and the head for the limited
amounts of power and funds available for their purposes.

An analogous conflict occurred at Christ Church, where
the statutes written under the auspices of the Executive
Commission proved so unsatisfactory, particularly to the
college tutors, that revisions were made in 1867.[56] The
main issue was the struggle for power and income between
the senior students (who corresponded roughly to the fellows
of other colleges), especially the college tutors, and the dean
and chapter (who were the governing body of both the
cathedral and the college and, therefore, held all power and

---

[52] Ibid. 203, note (a) (III) and note (b) and note (d).
[53] Ibid. 203, note (a) (IV).   [54] Ibid. 'General Observations', 195.
[55] University College MS letter, 10 Nov. 1873, p. 16 (fair copy).
[56] See, E. W. G. Bill and J. F. A. Mason, *Christ Church and Reform 1850–1867*
(Oxford, 1970).

controlled all revenues). Given the differences in constitution between the two colleges, this struggle was markedly similar to that which rocked University College a few years later.

The battle in Christ Church began when 'Oxoniensis' suggested in a letter to *The Times* of 29 November 1865 that the incomes of the canons ought to be curtailed to £1,000 p.a. so that those regius professors who were not canons might have their incomes brought to this level.[57] The origin of this letter was the long-standing grievance that Benjamin Jowett, though Regius Professor of Greek, had not been given the Christ Church canonry traditionally connected to his chair because the governing body disapproved of his theological views. This letter elicited an angry reply on 1 December from a 'Student of Christ Church' who did not defend the canons but rather asserted that the surplus income 'could be devoted to the work for which Christ Church was endowed — teaching Christ Church men'.[58] This letter was followed on 7 December by a call for revolutionary changes by Osborne Gordon, a former senior student and censor. He called for '1. such an improvement of the condition of Students as shall raise them in all respects to the level of Fellows of Colleges;' i.e. the students ought to be members of the governing body, and '2. either fixed stipends to the Dean and Chapter or a due allotment of estates;' i.e. either total control of revenues ought to be given to the students since they would dominate the reformed governing body which Gordon proposed, or the property ought to be divided between the college and the cathedral.[59]

Although the battle which developed from this beginning principally involved the senior students against the dean and chapter, there was conflict as well between the senior students, who were generally resident and engaged in college work, and the 'Students on the Old Foundation', who had been appointed under the pre-1858 system and who were generally non-resident. The resident senior students, especially those engaged in college work, took the lead in presenting demands to the dean and chapter. This situation was partly the inevitable result of the fact that they were able to meet together

[57] Ibid. 102–3.   [58] Ibid. 104.   [59] Ibid. 105.

easily while the non-resident students could only come to Oxford for meetings infrequently. It was significant, however, that the non-residents were not even asked to attend those meetings. When J. M. Collyns, the first of them to attend a strategy session in Oxford, asked angrily why they had not been summoned, the leaders could only placate him by announcing that ultimately the non-resident students would be consulted.[60]

The statutes which the senior students succeeded in having accepted by the dean and chapter and, eventually, by Parliament represented total victory for the senior students, especially for the tutors, and total defeat for the canons. They also showed little evidence of the proposed consultations with the non-resident students on the old foundation.[61] By these new statures, the non-resident students on the old foundation remained outside the governing body, while the senior students, especially those engaged in college work, became the dominant voice in collegiate affairs.[62] They became the majority of the governing body and all revenues, except fixed sums for the canons and the cathedral, were placed in their hands for educational purposes.[63] Several unsuccessful attempts also were made to include a clause allowing senior students engaged in college work to retain their studentships though married.[64] This struggle at Christ Church foreshadowed the later battle at University College. The issue at University College was clearly the division of power and income between the college officers and the rest

[60] Ibid. 123.

[61] Dr Mason implied that these consultations were not to play any important role in the promulgation of the statute revisions since he referred to Collyns's inquiry as having been 'smoothed over' by the leaders. Ibid. 123. See also Christ Church MS Estates 117, nos. 101–7 for examples of the skill of T. J. Prout in foiling the attempts of non-residents to influence policy decisions.

[62] The new statutes were printed in full in ibid. 241–61. See especially Statute II, 242.   [63] See Statute VIII, ibid. 245.

[64] Ibid. 169. The students approved a resolution asking the referees, who had been appointed to decide the issues between students and canons, to allow R. G. Faussett, a student on the old foundation and the steward, to be allowed to marry and still retain his studentship. The students' recommendation was not accepted. Faussett also attempted to have an amendment added to the bill 'to allow himself and certain other officers to marry' but Ward Hunt, the Christ Church-educated MP whom he approached, declined to act. Ibid. 180, n. 1.

of the governing body. Making allowances for institutional differences, the battle in Christ Church was precisely the same.[65]

It should be emphasized, however, that these struggles for power in the colleges did not imply any alienation from the college system itself. Although many tutors questioned collegiate values when they interfered with their own career aspirations, the importance of collegiate autonomy was still a matter of virtually universal agreement. The interests of the tutors were often in opposition to those of the heads or the non-resident fellows, but in most colleges the tutors were able to use their substantial tactical advantages to make progress toward their goals. The effect of this situation was to strengthen the commitment of the tutors to a policy which one historian has characterized as 'radical conservative reform'.[66] These partial victories were of critical importance since they tended to fix the tutors' collegiate allegiances during a period when old alliances and old loyalties were being subjected to searching re-evaluation.

C. College Tutors versus the Church Party:
The Abolition of the Tests

The period between the two university commissions also saw the development of irreconcilable conflict between the interests of the college tutors and those of the Church on the issue of maintaining religious tests for fellowships and advanced degrees. The total abolition of these tests by Parliament in 1871 represented a substantial victory for the proponents of the tutorial profession. The differences between the tutors and the Church supporters reflected opposing fundamental conceptions of the proper qualifications for a collegiate or university teacher. If religious tests were no longer to be required for the holding of fellowships,

---

[65] Dr Mason concludes, 'In the main, the struggle was a special version, in a unique context, of the well-known struggle of Tutors against Professors.' Ibid. 187. It was not, however, that the canons were professors that angered the tutors and caused them to take action at this time, but that they were the governing body of the college and, therefore, stood in the way of the movement of Christ Church tutors toward professional status.

[66] E. G. W. Bill, *University Reform in Nineteenth-Century Oxford, A Study of Henry Halford Vaughan 1811–1885* (Oxford, 1973), 1.

then, as D. P. Chase angrily observed, 'what security is left that even the bare profession of Christianity will be considered an essential qualification of the teachers and (what is far more) the trainers of the next generation of Oxford men?'[67] Chase himself stated the opposing viewpoint in terms which might well have been accepted by the tutors themselves: '. . . it is proposed that our Colleges should hereafter be liable to be composed of men selected simply for intellectual gifts, no two of whom may agree upon questions vital to Christianity itself'.[68] Another unsympathetic critic paraphrased the position of the opponents of religious tests in similar terms. 'Fellows had obtained their endowments by dint of hard study; was it not intolerable that inquiries into their belief should step in between them and their rewards.'[69]

The tone of the tutors and their supporters toward the Church became increasingly truculent during this period. At its most diplomatic, this attitude could be seen in the attack on the 'ecclesiastical monopoly' made by George Brodrick of Merton.[70] Brodrick called for the abolition of religious tests for all university degrees but was careful to preserve the traditional collegiate distinction between the rights of government over the university and its rights in relation to the colleges.[71] He argued that ·the university was a 'national institution' and, therefore, its degrees ought to be available to all, Dissenters as well as Churchmen. The colleges, on the contrary, were private corporation and, therefore, ought only to be freed from the necessity of imposing religious tests. He smoothly suggested that such a reform would not destroy the religious tone of the colleges; rather, it would merely allow them to remove the obstacle of sectarianism to their greater

---

[67] *The Voluntary System Applied to Academical Instruction* (Oxford, 1859), 9-10.

[68] *The De-Christianizing of the Colleges of Oxford* (reprinted from *The Standard* of 27 Oct. 1868) (London, 1869), 5.

[69] 'University Tests', *Blackwood's Edinburgh Magazine*, cvii, no. 652 (1870), 148.

[70] 'University Tests', *Journal of Social Science* (Mar. 1866), 117-36 *passim.*

[71] Ibid. See also 'The University and the Nation', *Contemporary Review*, xxvi (June 1875), 63-86 for a further example of Brodrick's defence of, and loyalty to, the college system. In this article, he defended the colleges and their fellows against the bad impressions which had been drawn from the publication in 1874 of the report of the Duke of Cleveland's financial commission of 1871.

usefulness. Brodrick also recommended this reform on the basis that it would lead to increased collegiate enrolments. This was a shrewd argument since the 1850s had generally been a period of stagnant or declining matriculations.[72] A much less diplomatic version of the same argument was made by Lyulph Stanley, a former Balliol tutor. He argued that 'the country has well made up its mind that it is not going to set up and sanction with the prestige of a university, a number of sectarian institutions doling severally out as much truth as they think consistent with their own opinions'.[73] Although there was a great difference in the tones employed by Brodrick and Stanley, their substantive positions were identical. They would have been equally repellent to such critics as D. P. Chase.

The 1860s saw a constant succession of meetings of Oxford dons to support the abolition of tests, petitions to Parliament, and periodic but unsuccessful attempts to abolish the tests by act of Parliament.[74] This agitation was important not only for the specific issue involved but also as a stimulus to the development of a consciousness of group identity. One hostile observer to these meetings suggested that such a recognition of common interests was developing in Oxford. 'Fellows and their wrongs filled the minds of the speakers . . . The possessors of endowments constituted for these speakers the University itself: no one could have gathered from the speeches delivered that undergraduates were at Oxford and Cambridge, or that they were worthy of a moment's consideration.'[75]

In 1871 religious tests for advanced degrees were abolished by Parliament.[76] The effect of this bill was to make Dissenters eligible for the first time for fellowships and for voting priviliges in Convocation and Congregation. The circumstances under which the bill actually was passed also served to embitter relations between the Church supporters and the tutors.[77] The government attempted to compromise between these two interest groups. As a concession to the tutors, the college headships were included under the operation of the

[72] See Stone, Table IA, 91.
[73] *Oxford University Reform* (London, 1869), 11.
[74] See Ward, 235–62.
[75] 'University Tests', *Blackwood's Edin. Mag.* xxvi, no. 652 (1870), 148.
[76] 34 Vict. cap. 26, in Shadwell iv. 14–18.   [77] See Ward, 252–61.

bill[78] while, as a concession to the Church, the number of clerical fellowships in each college was maintained.[79] The attempt was made to convince Church supporters that they ought to accept their losses as a prudent compromise to forestall more radical measures. As Gladstone wrote to H. P. Liddon of Christ Church, one of the leaders of the Oxford Church party, 'The present state of things was unmaintainable: if left as it was there might be a few years resistance followed by a measure sweeping away everything.'[80]

Gladstone clearly wished to present the bill as the product of unanimous university sentiment, but he was disappointed in this hope. The Church party used its influence with Lord Salisbury in the House of Lords to insert a number of amendments designed to weaken the bill. Headships were to be explicitly excluded from its operation. No college statutes concerning clerical fellowships were to be altered except by act of Parliament. An oath was to be required of all tutors or lecturers that they would 'not teach anything contrary to the teaching or divine authority of the Holy Scriptures of the Old and New Testament'.[81] Although all these amendments were struck out by the Commons and Salisbury was not able to carry the attempt in Lords to reinsert them, the struggle in Oxford while the bill was being debated had polarized further the Church party and the proponents of the tutorial profession.

The abolition of religious tests indicated the existence of a growing belief that academic life ought to be a profession separate from that of the clergyman. It established the principle that religious qualifications ought not to be

---

[78] An Oxford committee under the chairmanship of Benjamin Jowett, the newly-elected Master of Balliol, had enthusiastically supported this inclusion when it had first been proposed in Parliament. They did this despite the fact that they had earlier acquiesced to the view of the Church party that the headships ought to be excluded from the operation of the bill. See ibid. 259.

[79] 'Bill 6: A Bill to alter the law respecting Religious Tests in the Universities of Oxford, Cambridge, and Durham, and in the Halls and Colleges of those Universities, 10 February 1871', (PP 1871, vi).

[80] Liddon House MS Liddon Diary, 4 Sept. 1866, cited in Ward, 253. Liddon's correspondence with Dr Pusey, preserved in the pamphlet room of Pusey House, Oxford, constitutes the best single source for the activities of the Church party.

[81] 'Bill 145: A Bill (as amended by the House of Lords) to alter the law respecting Religious Tests in the Universities of Oxford, Cambridge, and Durham, and in the Halls and Colleges of those Universities, 16 May 1871' (PP 1871, vi).

expected of a college or university teacher. In 1871 the question of what ought to be the proper qualifications for an academic was still undecided. The traditional conception of university teaching as a quasi-pastoral office remained. Since the Oxford ideal of education stressed 'training' rather than 'information', the teacher still needed more than intellectual qualifications alone. The result was that a vague standard of good moral character came to replace the more explicitly sectarian standard of the past.

D. The Development of the 'Combination System'

The discontent of the tutors with the settlement of the 1850s with respect to the unsolved problem of academic specialization was alleviated to some degree through the development of the 'combination system'. This new mode of instruction ended the collegiate isolation which had been imposed on both teachers and students under the traditional catechetical system. In contrast, all students of the 'combined' colleges were allowed to attend the lectures of any college participating in the system. The college teachers in a particular examination school would meet at the end of each term to decide what classes should be given during the next term. They would divide among themselves the necessary lecturing duties. If a certain topic was to be covered by one lecturer, others were freed to devote their classes to different subjects. One effect of this system was to offer each college lecturer more opportunity for specialized teaching than had been possible previously. The effectiveness of this division of labour, however, varied a good deal among the different schools since the entire system was informal and unofficial. No one could compel any lecturer to teach a particular area or not to teach another which was covered already. The formal arrangements also varied a good deal in different examination schools and in different colleges. In some combinations, it was the colleges which decided to pool their teaching resources in a particular subject while in others it was a group of college lecturers who decided among themselves to work together. In some combinations, fees were charged to students from outside the lecturer's college while in others only students from outside the combination were charged fees.[82]

None the less, it was possible to see in the combination system the embryo of a movement toward the effective organization of university teaching. '[T]he most remarkable phenomenon in Oxford teaching during the last few years has been the growth and increase of these commercial treaties ... between different colleges, which have formed a network embracing nearly every college at the University', wrote one sympathetic critic in 1872.

> These confederations may be more or less complete, and may extend to all, or only to a part, of the subjects professed to be taught; in their completed form they involve the entire intercommunion for teaching purposes, a common staff of lecturers, and the settlement in common of a comprehensive program of lectures open to all members of the confederated societies. In fact for teaching, as distinguished from disciplinary purposes, the college has disappeared, and the confederation, under the management of a common board of tutors and lecturers, has taken its place.[83]

Although this account certainly exaggerated the effectiveness of the existing combinations, it was significant as an indication of the tendencies of the system and the ideals of its most enthusiastic supporters.

The combination system began in the mid-1860s among the collegiate lecturers for the recently established School of Law and Modern History.[84] The initial motivation was the desire of four lecturers to rationalize their work. They were already 'combined' lecturers in the sense that each taught for several colleges. No single college had enough students

---

[82] There is much information about financial arrangements for teaching among the colleges buried in the college returns prepared for the Cleveland Commission (PP 1873, xxvii, part ii). See below, pp. 93-9 for an account of the work of this commission. For example, in reply to some questions about the tuition fund, the bursar of Wadham stated that 'occasionally, the tutors send undergraduates to attend lectures out of College, and pay their fees' (p. 823). Similarly, at University College, £16.5*s*. was paid in 1871-2 to 'occasional lecturers at other colleges' (p. 191).

[83] 'Can Colleges Reform Themselves?' *Macmillan's Magazine*, xxv, no. 150 (1872), 469.

[84] A. H. Johnson of All Souls, who was a modern history lecturer in Oxford for forty years, published an account of the association of history tutors in the *Oxford Magazine*, 12 June 1919. See, also C. H. Firth, *Modern History in Oxford, 1841-1918* (Oxford, 1920), 14-15.

reading for the new school to justify a full-time lecturer. The combination system 'originated in my rooms', said Robert Laing of Corpus Christi to the 1877 commissioners, 'Mr Talbot, now warden of Keble and Mr Shadwell of Oriel and Mr Creighton, who was at Merton, and myself, I think set it going as an experiment.'[85] It began purely as a private arrangement among the four lecturers; however, by 1868, it had become somewhat more formal, since in February of that year, Mandell Creighton obtained official permission to participate in the system. He did this to avoid the obloquy which had fallen on William Esson, the mathematical lecturer at Merton, who had attempted to establish such a combined system for mathematical teaching without the authorization of the college.[86]

From this time, the history combination grew rapidly in size, power, and importance. In 1869 a formal association of tutors of modern history was organized and in 1874 the tradition of dining together, which still continues, was begun. By 1877 there were ten collegiate teachers of modern history, mostly fellows of colleges and they were all members of the combination. The system also included the professors, although it had not included them at the beginning. 'We set it going independently of the professors,' Robert Laing remarked proudly, 'but in time the professors asked whether their lectures might be advertised with our scheme.'[87] C. W. Boase of Exeter identified himself to the 1877 commissioners as 'a member of the combined scheme of history lectures, the members of which arrange every term all of the lectures that are to be given in the university'.[88] When asked whether the combination included many colleges, Boase replied, 'The whole of the university except Worcester, Hertford and the Unattached, but any member of these three bodies may join any course of lectures by paying a sovereign.'[89] Clearly, at least in the field of modern history, the combination system had become so successful as to attain a quasi-official status.

---

[85] *Oxford and Cambridge Act, 1877: Evidence before the University Commissioners* (PP 1881, lvi), 79.
[86] [Louise (van Glehn) Creighton,] *Life and Letters of Mandell Creighton, DD Oxon. and Cam., Sometime Bishop of London, By his Wife* (London, 1904), i. 60.   [87] PP 1881, lvi. 79.   [88] Ibid. 76.   [89] Loc. cit.

The 'combined lecturers' also had a significant impact on the style of Oxford teaching. The traditional catechetical lecture on a set text was replaced by more formal lecturing on periods or subjects. When Robert Laing was asked by Lord Selborne, the chairman of the 1877 commission, 'In the actual system of instruction by the college tutors, or upon the combined system, are books read to the students?' he replied, 'Not very much now.'[90] In the modern history lecture list for 1877, which Montague Bernard read to his fellow commissioners, virtually all of the lectures were organized by period and subject, only one seemed based on a text.[91] One history lecturer argued that this departure from catechetical teaching was an inevitable result of the combination system itself. 'One can have a catechetical lecture with one's own pupils, men who all know one another more or less, and who all know the lecturer,' said H. B. George of New College, 'but if, as is sometimes the case, you have to lecture to 20 men with 12 or 13 colleges represented in it, they will not answer.' 'It is useless to attempt it,' he noted complacently, 'and all the lectures, therefore, became practically professorial.'[92]

Others, however, complained of this growing tendency toward a professorial style among college lecturers. They asserted that lecturers were adopting this method of teaching simply because it was more gratifying to their self-esteem to lecture to large audiences than to undertake the difficult and often dreary work of catechetical teaching, especially for passmen. 'I think there are a great many, too many, lectures of college tutors and that it would be better both for the men and for the tutors if the men were less lectured', asserted Charles Neate.[93] He complained that the tendency, particularly in philosophy, was toward the teaching of 'speculative philosophy' and away from the more wholesome catechetical teaching of classical set texts of 'an authoritative character'.[94]

---

[90] Ibid. 83.

[91] Loc. cit., Q. 1394. Some examples were 'Mr. Owen on Anglo-Scotch history from the accession of Elizabeth, . . . Mr. Kitchen on the Papacy in the 16th century, . . . Mr. Bright on European history 1713–1763, . . . Mr. George on the age of the Hohenstaufen, . . . Mr. Jaune on English constitutional history from 1688.' Only 'Mr Willertsen on . . . Commines and Machiavelli' seemed to indicate concentration on a particular set text.   [92] Ibid. 287.

[93] Ibid. 282.   [94] Ibid. 285.

'My idea is that the higher education of the university should be in the hands of the professors, and that the college tutors should accept the position of being assistants or critics to the professors.'[95] Neate maintained this view despite the perceptive remarks of two of the commissioners questioning whether college tutors would accept these 'modest functions'.[96]

An unsympathetic critic like Charles Neate might well have felt his suspicions of tutorial egotism justified if he had been permitted to read a letter written by Mandell Creighton in 1871. 'Today I began my lectures, and was at first frightened, though afterwards gratified, to find my class for Italian history numbered the huge amount of sixty-three. I began originally by lecturing to four or five, they have gradually increased to twenty, thirty and forty, but sixty-three surpassed my wildest expectations.'[97] The unsympathetic critic might have grumbled that, although these large numbers were undoubtedly gratifying to the tutor's self-esteem, they also surpassed the proper number for effective teaching.

There were also those who saw the combination system as a threat to 'liberal education' itself. When Provost Hawkins was presented in 1868 with a plan to obtain more specialized and effective teaching by sharing lectures with other colleges, he reacted strongly against what he considered a threat to both education and religion. He argued in a closely reasoned twenty-eight page memorandum that '. . . any over-teaching, and excess of instruction, which may spare the Students' independent work, whilst it may place him in a higher class, may rather hurt his mind than strengthen it. What we should aim at is Education not mere Instruction; but this scheme appears calculated to promote the latter at the expense of the former.'[98] Hawkins was particularly incensed that the plan opened the possibility for the separation of religious teaching from higher instruction for the honour schools, since the new

[95] Ibid. 282.
[96] Dr Bellamy asked pointedly, 'Do you think that a tutor would continue to take much interest in looking over abstracts of lectures given by other people.' Mr Bernard questioned whether the tutor 'would be contented with the modest functions that you assign to him'. Ibid. 283.
[97] *Life and Letters of Mandell Creighton*, i. 64.
[98] Oriel MS ETC Al, p. 20. This plan had been approved by a college meeting on 30 Jan. 1868. It was largely implemented despite the Provost's objections.

combined lecturers need not be college tutors as well. If this occurred, the effect would be 'to lessen the value of . . . Divinity lectures in the eyes of the students, since the Tutors are supposed incapable of lecturing in the higher departments of Classics & Mathematics, History, Logic & Philosophy.' 'The mischief may be much worse than this,' he added in a note; '. . . the young men may be exposed to positive evil from the teaching of Lecturers who may be clever teachers, but unsound, and who may be Unbelievers'.[99] It clearly was possible to question the value of the combination system and of the more specialized and formal mode of lecturing; it was also possible to disagree on whether this new method was inevitable under the combination system or whether it was the result of the tutors' professorial aspirations. All commentators, however, were agreed that a more formal and subject-orientated style of lecturing by college tutors was developing in Oxford before the second university commission and that this change had occurred in conjunction with the introduction of combined lectures.

The combined lecturing system also had the effect of contributing to the declining popularity of private coaching.[100] Of the two advantages of this mode of instruction over college tuition which the tutors had emphasized in their evidence before the Royal Commission,[101] individual attention for the student and subject specialization for the teacher, the former was attained in the period between the two commissions largely through the incorporation of the methods of private instruction into official tutorial work. In fact, it was this system of 'private hours' which came to be regarded as the most distinctive and valuable feature of Oxford's 'tutorial

[99] Ibid. 7–8. Hawkins was also angered because the plan would greatly diminish his own control over teaching appointments. The separation of pass and class instruction was also intended to encourage more specialized teaching.

[100] In law, T. E. Holland, Chichele Professor of International Law, and, in modern history, Robert Laing of Corpus Christi, agreed to their evidence before the 1877 commissioners that coaching had declined in their subject. See PP 1881, lvi, 60–9, especially Q. 991 and 79–85, especially Q. 1340. Cited in F. H. Lawson, *The Oxford Law School 1850–1965* (Oxford, 1968), 48. Lawson has noted that law became a special exception to the Oxford rule in that coaching revived after the second university commission.

[101] See above, Ch. I, 39–40 nn. 74–9.

system'. This change was accomplished through the expansion in the number of college tutors and lecturers[102] during a period in which the bad publicity engendered by Tractarianism and the Royal Commission had caused a stagnation in the growth of student numbers. Between 1845 and 1858, there was a 40 per cent increase in the number of collegiate teachers and the teacher-to-student ratio declined from 1:19 to 1:15. Although rising student numbers outpaced by 1874 another 40 per cent growth in the number of teachers, raising the ratio to 1:17, this figure was still well below the high ratios which had characterized the pre-1850 period.[103]

The combined lecturing system contributed to the decline of coaching by increasing the effectiveness of the official teachers in Oxford. Through this new method of organizing lectures, an approach was made toward incorporating in the collegiate system the second advantage which private coaching had been considered to enjoy before 1850, the opportunity for subject specialization. There was a 78 per cent increase in the number of official teaching positions in Oxford between 1858, before the combination system had begun to operate, and 1874, after it had come into use.[104] Between 1845 and 1858, the increment had been only 40 per cent. While this

---

[102] All the figures cited below underestimate the number of collegiate teachers to some degree. Throughout the nineteenth century, those teachers who were employed either on a temporary or part-time basis by the colleges, or by private agreement with an official college tutor were often not listed in the university calenders from which these figures were derived. For example, E. G. W. Bill mentioned that the number of college tutors at Christ Church in the early nineteenth century 'was often increased by resident BAs' but he provided no specific numbers. See *University Reform in Nineteenth Century Oxford: A Study of Henry Halford Vaughan 1811-1885* (Oxford, 1973), 13. Similarly, R. R. Marett noted in his autobiography that he was employed by Balliol, his undergraduate college, in 1890 'as a sort of half-don' to relieve the college tutors of some of their work, but the university calender does not list him among Balliol's teaching staff. See *A Jerseyman at Oxford* (London, 1941), 104. Unfortunately, these extra teachers cannot be counted since the colleges rarely kept records of these informal arrangements. However, this problem does not invalidate the official figures. First, since there is no evidence that these omissions were more common at any particular time, the official figures can be used for comparative purposes. Second, the absolute ratios cited below can still be considered roughly accurate since it is unlikely that these part-time teachers added greatly to the aggregate teaching strength of the colleges.

[103] For all figures for teacher and student numbers, see below, Appendix 3, p. 288.

[104] See Appendix 7, below, p. 292

earlier rise had been exclusively the result of an expansion in the total number of teachers in Oxford, the increased rate of increment in the period 1858–74 was largely the result of the introduction of the combination system.[105] The effect of this rise in the number of teaching positions was to organize collegiate teaching more efficiently. By allowing college tutors to master thoroughly the subjects on which they lectured, the combination system reduced the desirability of coaching and served to bring Oxford teaching more exclusively under the control of collegiate institutions.

As the advantages of private coaching, especially for honour-men, were adopted within the collegiate system, the hostility of the college tutors increased toward the pass coaching which remained. One of their goals came to be to foil, through alterations in the examination statutes, the efforts of the 'Cramming Fraternity'.[106] Only rarely was their animosity directed toward the coach as an individual; however, they increasingly came to view the system as a whole with distaste. By the 1870s, even the few defenders of private coaching betrayed a mood of defeat. James Rumsey, a former fellow and tutor of Pembroke, portrayed the coaches of Oxford as selfless martyrs, 'who, now unendowed, unprotected, without recognition or place, without guarantee, give their life (heart and soul) to teaching; men to whom their work is their art, their passion; men who do this for moderate fees, and who do it contentedly, in the conviction of the worth, the usefulness of this toil'.[107] The invidious comparison was clearly implied with the college tutors who were endowed, protected, and re-cognized, but still discontented. Rumsey viewed these privi-leged competitors with evident hostility. One has only to compare his defensive tone with the confidence and pride of the combined lecturers in modern history to perceive which system of teaching was gaining in importance and which was on the decline.

From its beginnings in the school of modern history, the

---

[105] Compare the rates of growth on Appendix 3 and Appendix 7, below pp. 288 and 292.

[106] For an example, see *Reasons for Certain Amendments to the New Examination Statute* (Oxford, 1871).

[107] *A Few Words on Teaching in Oxford* (Oxford, 1871), 7.

combination system quickly spread to all other examination schools. Lyulph Stanley, a critic who was favourable to this development, was able to declare optimistically as early as 1869 that 'division of labour' was replacing the 'old college system, by which a tutor was supposed to be responsible for the whole instruction of his pupil'.[108] By 1877, combined lecturing schemes existed in the teaching of law, mathematics, natural science, and classical studies. However, in none of these schools did it flourish to the extent that it had in modern history. In natural science, collegiate teaching had never flourished since only Christ Church and Magdalen had the laboratories and equipment required. Not even combined collegiate instruction could compete with the professors and their well-equipped new Museum. In law, there was little attempt to avoid duplication of lectures.[109] The historian of the Oxford law school has noted that 'a number of tutors would combine to make a co-ordinated list of lectures which all their pupils in their several colleges could attend. Otherwise, there was little co-ordination.'[110] Perhaps H. B. George was correct when he ascribed the relative lack of success of the law combination to 'personal reasons'.[111] He certainly would have known of any personal animosities among the law tutors and professors, since he had continued to teach both law and modern history when the schools were divided in 1875. In mathematics, George only reported that 'there is one combination of lectures, but it does not embrace anything like the whole number [of colleges]'.[112] Probably the reason was that the colleges had experience providing the very limited amount of mathematical teaching they required without resorting to combinations.

The reasons for the relative lack of success of the combined system in *Literae Humaniores* were of greater significance, both because this school contained many more students and teachers than all of the other examination schools together and because these reasons reveal the limitations of the system

---

[108] *Oxford University Reform* (London, 1869), 16.
[109] See, 'The Rev. H. B. George, Esq., MA (Fellow of New College), examined', 288 (PP 1881, lvi).
[110] F. H. Lawson, *The Oxford Law School 1850–1965* (Oxford, 1968), 47.
[111] PP 1881, lvi. 288.   [112] Loc. cit.

for alleviating the grievances of the tutors. D. B. Monro of Oriel gave the 1877 Commission an account of the founding and contemporary arrangements of the combined system for classical studies.

At the present moment there are two large systems of combinations for the purposes of the classical schools . . . I think it first originated in the combination between Balliol and New College; and then soon afterwards about five or six tutors of other colleges made an arrangement between themselves which at first was purely private . . . The list of lectures used to be marked 'private,' and that grew so as to include a number of other colleges. The two systems are quite different in one respect; in the one case it is an arrangement between the colleges, as between Balliol and New College, and in the other it is an arrangement between the individual lecturers of which the college has no official cognizance.[113]

Although the secretary of one of the combinations for *Literae Humaniores*, H. P. Richards of Wadham, told the 1877 commissioners that '[t]here is a considerable amount of labour in lecturing spared to the tutors, so that they are able to devote themselves better to particular subjects',[114] most witnesses were less enthusiastic about the efficiency of this combination. C. W. Boase thought that the complete explanation for the lack of success of the classical combination was that, as opposed to the history scheme, it charged fees among the participating colleges. 'In the classical scheme you will very often find that there are several Ethic or Republic lectures going on at the same time . . . [I]f there is payment from the colleges,' he concluded, 'the colleges from which that payment comes employ their own men, and therefore, there is a great multiplication of lectures.[115] Even a very junior fellow who had returned only recently from study in Germany could see that this was the problem with the classical combination. J. Cook Wilson of Oriel suggested modestly to the 1877 commissioners that Oxford needed 'some sort of control over the times when the subjects come on by the different lecturers'.[116]

---

[113] Ibid. 13.   [114] Ibid. 331. Q. 5056.   [115] Ibid. 76.
[116] Ibid. 56–7. See below, Ch. IV, p. 169, nn. 42–3 for the acceptance of these criticisms by the commissioners.

Any combined system could be considered successful only if it reduced the duplication of lectures to a large extent. It had achieved this goal in modern history while it clearly had been less successful in *Literae Humaniores*. 'Even the meeting of the lecturers which takes place does not control the lectures which are given by its members', Monro complained. 'The colleges are quite independent of each other. Each has its own staff and its lecturers in each of the three or four principal subjects; and the combination is really a mere gathering into one of the different lectures which would be given. There is a great want of system and arrangement.'[117]

One reason for this relative lack of order in the classical combination was that too many lecturers were involved to use effectively an informal method of decision-making. It was easier to exert social pressure among ten modern history lecturers than among the approximately sixty classical teachers. H. B. George's account of how the division of lecturing work was accomplished in the history combination is revealing on this point. 'There is no sort of attempt at formal division of the subject, and no pressure whatever is put upon anybody to lecture in a particular way', he explained.

They do as a matter of fact find out what subjects are vacant; the younger men coming in find out to what subjects their seniors have devoted themselves, and choose something else; and also if it is found in a given term that a particular subject is not going to be lectured upon, and has not been lectured upon in the last term or so, somebody who has not made up his mind to the exact subject of his lectures for the next term will probably select it if he can; but that is the total amount of pressure that is exercised in any way.[118]

Although well-intentioned classical tutors also attempted to practice 'division of labour' on an informal basis;[119] in general, the lack of central authority could only lead to the 'great

[117] Ibid. 13–14.   [118] Ibid. 287.
[119] For example, Francis Paget, a young senior student and classical tutor of Christ Church, wrote to his brother in 1879, 'I found at the beginning of the Term a demand for a Juvenal lecture: so I have been grinding at that'. See Stephen Paget and J. M. C. Crum, *Francis Paget, Bishop of Oxford* (London, 1912), 60.

want of system and arrangement' which led D. B. Munro to more basic criticisms, not only of the combined lecturer system, but of the college system itself. 'Fellows 'take college work' as it is called, mainly according to seniority; and their place in any inter-collegiate teaching depends upon their place in their own college. Such a system can hardly secure the appointment of the best men as lecturers, or even enable lecturers to choose the subjects which they have studied most themselves.'[120] Seniority clearly played an important role in both the modern history and the classical combinations while social influence was expected to accomplish the rest. In a group of ten this method could be lauded for its lack of formality and 'pressure', but, among sixty collegiate teachers, it could only be condemned for its lack of order and 'control'.

The basic problem was that the existing unofficial system could not solve this difficulty while an officially-recognized combination system with clear lines of authority would inevitably infringe on collegiate and tutorial autonomy. There was the danger also that such an official system might be used as a vehicle for professorial power. The Tutors' Association had fought the Royal Commission on this issue of freedom from 'official despotism'[121] and there was no reason to suspect that the college tutors valued less highly their independence twenty-five years later. D. B. Monro saw as insurmountable the problem of attaining order under the existing system. He argued that the only solution was to dismantle the combinations and build a full system of university teaching outside the college.[122] A few history lecturers suggested to the 1877 commissioners that it would be beneficial for their combination to be made official. Even one of these few, however, admitted candidly that he saw little likelihood that the proposal would be welcomed by his colleagues. 'I do not think that a certain number of us would like to be disciplined', admitted J. F. Bright of University College. They 'would rather carry on their lectures upon their

---

[120] PP 1881, lvi, 14.   [121] See above, Ch. I, pp. 45–6, nn. 96 and 97.
[122] PP 1881, lvi, 12–13.

own ground than be brought into discipline by any professor whatever'.[123]

Despite these difficulties, many tutors found it possible through the combination system to achieve some opportunities for specialization. The informality which allowed the combination system to grow without endangering collegiate and tutorial autonomy, however, placed a definite limitation on the degree to which this new system of instruction could aid the cause of the tutorial profession. It was found to be more effective for enabling scarce teaching resources to cover broad examination fields than for eliminating the duplication of standard lectures by tutors in several colleges. The development of the combination system during the period between the two university commissions indicated both the degree of flexibility of the collegiate system in accommodating tutorial aspirations and the inherent rigidities of that system which would thwart those aspirations.

E. The Financial Commission of 1871

The advocates of the tutorial profession were also able to strengthen and advance their cause indirectly through the publicity given to the findings of the financial commission of 1871. This commission, under the chairmanship of the Duke of Cleveland, had been appointed to collect 'the fullest information respecting all matters of fact connected with the property and income either of the Universities [of Oxford and Cambridge] themselves, or of the Colleges and Halls therein [,] . . . the prospects of increase or decrease in such property and income, and a statement of the uses to which it is applied'.[124] The desirability of this inquiry had been suggested by the government during the debates in Parliament surrounding the abolition of religious tests in 1871. Virtually

[123] Ibid. 79. the plan which both Bright and C. W. Boase (see p. 76) endorsed was for an official council under the *ex officio* chairmanship of the Regius Professor of Modern History. Perhaps they had forgotten, in their fondness for Professor Stubbs, how they might feel about such an arrangement were the government to present them with an antipathetic professor, such as H. H. Vaughan. Of course, they might have decided that elections within the combination would be more conducive to breeding animosity than an occasional hostile chairman.

[124] See Gladstone's letter of 24 Oct. 1871 to the Vice-Chancellors of both universities, p. 7 (PP 1873, xxxvii, part i).

all the Oxford colleges had refused to supply the 1850 Royal Commission with financial information and, even if they had, it would have been of little value twenty years later since the administration of collegiate property had been completely revolutionized by the Universities and Colleges Estates Act of 1858 and its extension of 1860. After some negotiations, minor concessions on the part of the commissioners, and much grumbling, the heads and bursars of the Oxford colleges agreed to supply the necessary information.[125] Perhaps the colleges were reassured by Gladstone's pledge that 'it would be no part of the duty of the Commission to pass judgement on the present appropriation of their resources, and to recommend alterations in it'.[126]

When the report of the commissioners was published in 1873, it was clear that they had abided by the terms of their commission quite scrupulously. Only fourteen of the close to 2,000 pages which comprised their three part blue book were occupied by their report. Even these fourteen pages did not bristle with judgements. The numbers themselves, however, were enough to cause a public stir. The aggregate figures revealed the immensity of the wealth of Oxford and its colleges. The university and colleges owned 192,447 acres of land, mostly in agricultural use.[127] Their total income from property amounted to £413,842 in 1871.[128] The advowsons for 444 livings worth £188,675 in 1871 were also held by the university and its colleges.[129] The greatest beneficiaries of this large income were the heads and fellows of colleges. The commissioner's report revealed that in 1871, the nineteen

[125] Ibid. 19-20. See Oxford heads' and bursars' resolution of 19 Mar. 1872 and the commissioners' reply. The major objection in Oxford was not conceded by the commissioners. The colleges were not permitted to withhold their accounts of income derived from student fees, room rents, and battels from their returns. The heads and bursars had argued that such income ought not to be considered since it was too much subject to fluctuation with the popularity of the college.

[126] Ibid. 7.

[127] Ibid. 26. The university owned only 7,683 acres, while the colleges owned 184,764 acres.

[128] Ibid. 29. The university had only £47,589 including income from fees, while the colleges received £366,253. In these figures and in all subsequent financial data, shillings and pence have been eliminated.

[129] Ibid. 28. The university held five livings worth £1,036 and the colleges presented to 439 worth £187,639.

heads of houses received £30,543 while £101,171 was expended on the 345 fellows.[130] All scholarships consumed only £26,225 while more was spent to augment the incomes of the benefices held by the colleges — and thus to raise the stipends of ex-fellows — than was paid to the university professors.[131]

The report demonstrated that comparatively little of this vast endowment income was spent for educational purposes. All scholarships and professorships together accounted for little more income than the nineteen headships alone. The tuition funds in virtually all colleges were practically self-supporting. The commissioners noted that 'the tutors and lecturers are almost wholly paid by means of fees charged directly on the students for this purpose'.[132] It was true that the value of the fellowships held by tutors and lecturers was not charged against the tuition fund. Also, some colleges did augment their tuition funds to a small extent. New College, for example, contributed a subsidy of £350 in 1867–8, which had risen to £500 in 1870–1.[133] However, even if one added to this subsidy the value of the four fellowships held by college tutors, approximately £1,000, the total still would be small compared to New College's endowment income of £23,856 in 1871.[134]

It was even possible that the colleges as a whole profited from their function as educational institutions. The commissioners remarked that in several poorly-endowed colleges, the revenues directly from students 'forms a very important part of the whole income of the College, and amply compensates for the insufficiency of the endowment'.[135] For example, over 60 per cent of the income of Exeter in 1871 was derived from this source.[136] For the university as a whole, however,

---

[130] Ibid. 34.

[131] Loc. cit. £8,772 was spent in 1871 to augment benefices while only £6,994 was paid to university professors. The commissioners did not count the incomes of the professor-canons of Christ Church under this head since the college did not count their income as collegiate expenditure but, instead, included it as a cathedral expense. The figures for professorial endowments would have appeared much more creditable if the £7,500 paid to the five professor-canons had been included.

[132] Ibid. 31.   [133] Ibid., part ii, 380–1.

[134] Ibid., part ii, return A. 18, p. 374.   [135] Ibid. 30–1.

[136] Net income from property amounted to £5,455 (see ibid., part ii, return A. 18, p. 267) while £8,653 was derived from students (see return A. 20, p. 271).

the commissioners were not able to determine whether the net income of the colleges was increased by their activity as educational institutions. They remarked with a trace of annoyance that 'because there is no uniformity in the number of charges included in the expenditure before the striking of the balance . . . We cannot say with any certainty in all cases whether profit, properly so called, accrues to a college from its reception of students or not.'[137] On this point, the commissioners permitted themselves one of their few notes of overt criticism. 'There is one point brought prominently out in the results of this inquiry, the great disparity between the property and income of the Colleges and the numbers of the members. When that number is small, the expense of the staff and establishment is unnecessarily large in proportion.' Aware of their commission to avoid judgement, they hastened to add, 'We do not, however, consider that it lies within the scope of the commission entrusted to us to enter further upon this subject.'[138] Further criticism was not necessary; it was sufficiently clear from the numbers alone that the colleges did not use their large endowment incomes to any great extent for educational purposes.

The commissioners also assumed that these large incomes which the university and the colleges derived from landed property would increase greatly in the next twenty years. This increase was to be the result of the improvements which the colleges had been making in the terms of their leases and the condition of their agricultural estates. The Universities and Colleges Estates Acts of 1858 and 1860 had made it feasible for the colleges to become 'progressive landlords'. The old system of 'beneficial' leases had made the bulk of a college's income dependent on renewal fines rather than yearly rent. This system had the advantage for absentee, institutional landlords that the cost of maintenance and repair was the responsibility of the lessee. This type of lease did not require the landlord to become involved in questions of agricultural improvement. The disadvantages were that this system did not encourage the lessee to make improvements either. It was also inefficient in that the total returns to the landlord were

---

[137] Ibid., part i, 30.   [138] Ibid. 37.

considered to be less than under a system of 'rack-rent', or yearly economic rent. Fines had the further disadvantage of providing the college with an irregular and unpredictable income.

It was not possible, however, for the colleges to convert to rack-rent without extended powers for mortgaging, buying, and selling of land. These powers were needed both to raise money for necessary improvements and to indemnify the existing fellows against the loss of immediate income which they would suffer if beneficial leases were allowed to run out without taking renewal fines. The Estates Acts of 1858 and 1860 granted the colleges the ability to alter this system. About 300 years after the 'agricultural revolution' had begun in England, the colleges took up the fashion of agricultural improvement. They embarked in the 1860s on a large-scale process of conversion to rack-rent and capital expenditure since, as the commissioners were informed, 'on the falling in of beneficial leases a large outlay on building and improvements is ordinarily required'.[139] The commissioners estimated that by 1895, as a result of the introduction of progressive methods, the incomes of the colleges and university ought to rise by £98,835, about 25 per cent. They conceived that even larger increases could be expected in the more distant future until the middle of the twentieth century when the last house properties on long leases would finally come into hand. They did not feel justified, however, in putting this distant growth in income into exact figures.[140]

These expectations of increased income through progressive agriculture turned out to be completely mistaken. In 1871 England was on the verge of an agricultural depression which would destroy much of the prosperity of rural England and which would continue until it was broken, for a short time, during World War I. Between 1873 and 1896, aggregate farm income declined from £154 million to £107 million.[141] Although some modern economic historians have cast doubt

---

[139] Ibid. 35.

[140] Ibid. 32–3, see especially the chart of projected increment until 1895 on p. 32.

[141] See J. R. Bellerby, 'National and Agricultural Income 1851', *Economic Journal*, lxix, no. 273 (1959), 95–104.

on the older 'catastrophic' theory of uniformly bleak agricultural prospects during this period; from the standpoint of the Oxford colleges, the older theory needs little revision.[142] Although several studies have suggested that livestock husbandry was increasing in profitability from 1870 to 1900,[143] the colleges' land was overwhelmingly in grain production where decline is indisputable. The large estates of absentee landlords were unsuitable for successful livestock husbandry because of the intensive labour required. The large capital expenditures on agricultural improvements made by the colleges during this period only served to make the effects of the depression more sharply felt in Oxford.[144] The value of

[142] One attempt has been made to argue that the traditional accounts exaggerate the effects of the agricultural depression on Oxford and Cambridge, but even this study cannot deny that the income derived by the colleges from their estates declined. See J. P. D. Dunbabin, 'Oxford and Cambridge College Finances, 1871-1913', *Econ. Hist. Rev.*, 2nd Series, xxviii (1975), 631-47. Mr Dunbabin does argue, however, that the decline was not great enough to have a major effect on the ability of the colleges to carry out the plans of the 1877 Commission. I have denied this view for Oxford in 'Oxford College Finances, 1871-1913: A Comment', *Econ. Hist. Rev.*, 2nd Series, xxxi (1978), 437-45. Also see below, Ch. V, for a more extensive account of the effect of the agricultural depression on the fate of the 1877 Commission's plans. Mr Dunbabin has replied in 'Oxford College Finances, 1871-1913: A Reply', *Econ. Hist. Rev.*, 2nd Series, xxxi (1978), 446-9.

[143] The traditional view of a pervasive agricultural depression caused by unprogressive methods and overly political, rather than economic, concerns of landlords, has been stated by O. R. McGregor, 'Introduction Part Two: English Farming After 1815' in Lord Ernle, *English Farming, Past and Present*, edited by G. E. Fussell and O. R. McGregor (6th edition, 1961), lxix-cxlv. McGregor was attacked by E. L. Jones, 'English Farming Before and During the Nineteenth Century', *Econ. Hist. Rev.*, 2nd Series, xv (1962), 145-52. The importance of livestock breeding in balancing the admitted decline in grain prices was stressed by T. W. Fletcher, 'The Great Depression of English Agriculture 1873-1896', *Econ. Hist. Rev.*, 2nd Series, xiii (1961), 417-32, also T. W. Fletcher, 'Lancaster Livestock Farming During the Great Depression', *Agricultural History Review*, ix, part i, 1961, 17-42, also E. L. Jones, 'The Changing Basis of English Agricultural Prosperity 1853-1873', *Agricultural History Review*, x, part ii, 1962, 102-19. Bellerby's statistics, however (see above, n. 141), which lump together grain and livestock farming, indicate that rising livestock prices did not counterbalance declining grain prices. During the same period, 1873-96, in which farm income fell by one-third, non-farm income, according to Bellerby, rose from £867 m. to £1,288 m.

[144] The figures which St. John's submitted to the 1871 commissioners seemed to indicate that the college had exceeded its income in every year from 1867 to 1871. (Compare return A. 18, p. 769 and A.20, p. 773 to return C.2, p. 776.) Large sums were being spent during this period on improvements to the college estates. In 1871 nearly 30 per cent of total net income had been expended for this purpose. (See C.2, p. 776, items 18 and 19.) When the bursar was faced with

college livings also declined generally since they were mostly country livings and, therefore, shared the fate of rural society in general. Both the landed property which provided much of the income of the Oxford colleges and the Church livings toward which many of the fellows still looked for their ultimate careers, had declined in value sharply by 1900.

In 1873 when the Cleveland Commission's massive report was published, this future prospect was unknown. Instead Oxford and its colleges were portrayed as extremely rich institutions who were certain to become even richer. From the viewpoint of those who wished to see a tutorial profession established, the commission represented an unmitigated victory, since it made available publicly for the first time financial and statistical information which could be used to support their case.

There had been conflict between the prize fellows and the tutors concerning the allocation of the endowment income of the colleges before the publication of this report. As early as 1866 Goldwin Smith had predicted that 'the nation will not always acquiesce . . . in the expenditure of so large a portion of our funds in sinecure Fellowships'.[145] The conflicts

---

the unenviable task of explaining this situation to the commissioners, he remarked lamely that because of changes in the system of accounting at St. John's, 'the accounts of income and expenditure are not as correct as I could wish them to be. In each of the five years it would appear that the expenditure has largely exceeded the income, but I know, although I was not bursar during any one of those years, that the sum borrowed on current account was nothing like the apparent deficit.' (The letter is printed in full on p. 781.) This excuse could only mean that either the college accounts were being mismanaged or the college was entering into a plan for agricultural improvements beyond its resources. It is most likely, given the rotation of the bursarship, that both of these possibilities were true to some degree. (Returns and correspondence were printed in full in PP 1873, xxxvii, part ii, 741–85.) To give another example, the bursar of University College reported to the 1871 commissioners, 'The total outlay in Wales on the works of building and drainage commenced in 1871, and still in progress, will not fall short of £6,000, the payment of which, seeing that the resources of the college are limited, will prevent any considerable increase in the income derived from these estates for some years to come. After this, a fair return may be expected for the outlay' (ibid. 195).

[145] Goldwin Smith, *The Elections to the Hebdomadal Council. A Letter to the Rev. C. W. Sandford*, MA (Oxford, 1866), 18. Smith added cuttingly that if 'the course of undergraduate study . . . were properly devoted to the objects of life, [it] would be its own reward, and can only stand in need of this costly stimulus because it is intrinsically defective'.

between college tutors and prize fellows at Christ Church and University College[146] were probably not exceptional cases. One anonymous 'Sinecure Fellow' concluded his general defence of prize fellowships with a contemptuous dismissal of the college tutors. The prize fellowship system 'has spread and is spreading through England a free-masonry of critics of all ideas, of connoisseurs of all knowledge', he argued. 'It would be a great pity if this were to disappear and leave nothing but a thriving group of busy, sociable, finishing schoolmasters in its place.'[147]

Prize fellowships also had been the subject of some unfavourable comment in the popular press before the publication of the Cleveland Commission's report. One general attack on 'modern Oxford', for example, had noted the prize fellows with especial dissatisfaction:

> . . . if you want to find the ordinary Oxford fellow of the present day, the last place to look for him is within the immediate precincts of the University. He is anywhere rather than there: toiling away in murky chambers in the Temple, lounging at the Oxford and Cambridge Club, airing himself in the Park, scaling the Matterhorn, or rambling through the art-galleries of Florence or Dresden. The income of his fellowship he thoroughly enjoys, as the necessary responsibilities which that source of income entails upon him are none.[148]

Before 1873 there had been ample criticism of the prize fellowship system both in Oxford and in the press, but there had been available no systematic information on its scale. The individual tutor had, of course, an accurate idea of the extent to which collegiate revenues were used for 'non-academical' purposes, at least within his own college; yet there were no concrete figures which could be placed before the public.

After the publication by the financial commission of almost 900 pages of Oxford collegiate returns, concrete information was no longer lacking. The large amount of endowment income expended on fellowships while the colleges' tuition funds were almost wholly dependent on student fees became

---

[146] See above, pp. 71–7.

[147] 'Strike, But Hear', *Macmillan's Mag.* xxv, no. 148 (1872), 306.

[148] 'Young Oxford in 1870', *Belgravia: A London Magazine,* 2nd Series, ii, no. 8 (1870), 440.

matters of public record. Although the colleges managed to avoid stating exactly how many of their fellows were engaged in educational work in Oxford, it was quite clear from their returns that only a small number of them fulfilled this function.[149] It may have been a clumsy caricature to portray the prize fellows as idle gentlemen, lounging in London clubs or in the Park, climbing mountains or visiting continental art galleries. Yet the bald statement alone of the amount spent on the system proved a powerful argument for the tutors' contention that too much money was being expended on mere prizes and sinecures. Defenders of prize fellowships might still argue that helping young graduates of demonstrated intellectual ability during the struggling early years of their professional careers was a worthy use for collegiate income. Few, however, were able to make this argument with the same confidence when it was discovered that most of the £100,000 per year spent in Oxford alone on fellowships was being used for this purpose only.[150] The college returns also revealed that, in some cases, dividends were so large as to be wholly inconsistent with their supposed character as aids to young professional men. Although most prize fellowships were worth about £250 per year, the returns revealed some colleges, like Magdalen, in which the senior fellows were receiving over £600 per year.[151] Armed with these facts, the case for reform was strengthened greatly.

The tutors, however, were not the only group whose plans for reform were aided by the findings of the Cleveland Commission. There were others who wished to see college endowments put to 'academical' uses; but not to support college teachers. To those who viewed the advancement of learning as the primary function of the university, the existing allocation of collegiate income was as much a misuse of 'academical endowments' as it was to the advocates of the tutorial profession. They saw the £130,000 per year expended

---

[149] In fact, of the 345 fellows in 1873, less than one-third taught in Oxford. See figure for 1874 in Appendix 8, below p. 292.

[150] C. S. Parker, an MP who had been a fellow and tutor of University College, defended prize fellowships strongly on the traditional grounds but had to admit that they were 'too lavish'. See *Academical Endowments* (London, 1875), 12.

[151] PP 1873, xxxvii, part ii, 554, return C (2).

on headships and fellowships as money which ought to be used to establish career positions for scholars devoting their full time to the advancement of learning. The evidence provided by the financial commission was also valuable to those who wished to use Oxford endowments to finance university colleges in other cities. They argued that since the Oxford colleges could operate as educational institutions on only a small percentage of their endowment income, a good deal could be spared to endow 'affiliated' colleges.

The advocates of the tutorial profession had to be very careful to avoid co-option by either of these rivals. Delicate strategy was required since alliances on specific issues would be desirable, although permanent bonds would be impossible owing to differences in ultimate goals. All could combine effectively to attack the existing distribution of collegiate revenues. The supporters of the tutorial professions could ally themselves with the supporters of 'affiliated' colleges to oppose the plans for the endowment of research, since both saw educational work as the primary function of the university. One advocate of 'affiliated' colleges even attempted to cement this alliance by suggesting that lecturers in the new colleges be permitted to marry while retaining the fellowships they held on the foundations of the parent Oxford colleges.[152] Similarly, the supporters of the tutorial profession might combine with the advocates of the endowment of research to insist on the need to keep Oxford endowments in Oxford.[153]

Despite these specific and limited alliances, it was of great

---

[152] See, Joseph Bickersteth Mayor, MA, *Affiliation of Local Colleges to the Universities of Oxford and Cambridge* (London, 1874). Mayor argued that if an Oxford college were to 'move' to a provincial city by selling its buildings in Oxford to adjoining colleges and building new ones in its new home, 'Fellowships would be changed into lectureships and superannuation pensions . . .' (p. 7). One advantage of this plan of 'university extension' would be, therefore, that it would free college fellowships from their restriction to unmarried men; 'lecturers' would clearly not be restricted in this way and the 'pensions' pointed clearly to Mayor's intention that these lecturers view college teaching as a life-career.

[153] See Robert Laing, *Some Dreams of a Constitution-Monger: A Paper on University and College Reform* (Oxford, 1876). 'If I would have the colleges confine themselves in the redistribution of their revenues to Oxford, still more am I obliged, as by the very force and meaning of language, to locate the University, body and soul of it, at Oxford.' (p. 16.)

importance that the college tutors develop articulate counter-arguments to the claims of their rivals for collegiate endowments, especially against the 'endowment of research'. The plans for 'affiliated' colleges were less threatening since it was unlikely that any college's governing body would be tempted seriously by the paltry enticements offered by these schemes. The claims of the 'endowment of research' party, however, required more serious consideration. The obligation of a university to advance knowledge was a traditional ideal which the tutors did not wish wholly to dismiss since the reputation for learning was an important element in their 'gentlemanly' social status.[154] It was argued, therefore, that this obligation would be fulfilled more effectively through the establishment of a small fund from which sums could be paid to individual scholars for limited periods to accomplish specific pieces of research, writing, or experimentation.[155]

In some cases, this position indicated a genuine wish to encourage research and reform the fellowship system. James Bryce, Regius Professor of Civil Law, hoped for 'many most beneficial changes in the application of funds now wasted in needless fellowships'.[156] His scepticism about the 'endowment of research' stemmed not from indifference to the importance of advancing knowledge but from a genuine fear that 'to create places of emolument subject to no obligation but that of research is at best a hazardous experiment, which the wisest men among our men of science disapprove'.[157] The danger was that a researcher paid 'in the hope that he would work' might simply allow his position to become a sinecure.

There were others, however, who recommended the establishment of a small research fund for specific projects not primarily because of the genuine fears which motivated Bryce but simply because such a plan would be less costly than the creation of career posts in pure research. George

---

[154] See above, Ch. I, pp. 47–8, for the support for this traditional ideal displayed by the Tutors' Association in 1853. See also above, p. 73 for the enthusiasm of the fellows of University College in 1873 for 'productive study'.

[155] See George C. Brodrick, 'The Universities and the Nation', *Contemp. Rev.* xxvi (June 1875), esp. pp. 83–4. Also see James Bryce, 'A Few Words on the Oxford University Bill', *Fortnightly Review*, New Series, xix, no. 113 (1876), esp. p. 776.

[156] Ibid. 771.   [157] Ibid. 776, n. 1.

Brodrick of Merton, for example, supported such a fund even though his strongest commitment was to the use of collegiate endowments for educational purposes. 'Most certainly the first and strongest claim is that for the development of the highest academical education within the Universities themselves', he argued. 'This claim must equally take precedence of that for the encouragement of original research, and of that for the encouragement of University lectures to populous towns. It is by concentrating, and not by dispersing the vital energies of the Universities, by exalting their educational function rather than by reviving the monastic idea of self-culture, that we shall best utilize them for the good of the whole Nation.'[158] Brodrick's assigning to the supporters of the endowment of research a 'monastic idea of self-culture' was a pointed criticism. 'Monastic' conjured up threatening visions of Tractarianism and the Roman Catholic Church, which were still in the 1870s potent sources of anxiety. The reference to 'self-culture' implied, at the least, that research was a selfish activity; at worst, it is perhaps not wholly fanciful to note the similarity between 'self-culture' and the contemporary euphemism for masturbation, 'self-abuse' (another disperser of 'vital energies'). The implication was that research was unhealthy as well as selfish and un-English.

Brodrick's support for a research fund was the result of his own indifference to research ideals combined with his recognition of the need to placate its supporters. It was desirable to give the appearance, at least, of making a moderate compromise with their position. At the time of the Royal Commission a loyal college fellow like Brodrick would have recommended an expansion of the professoriate only to the extent that it was needed for teaching; by the 1870s, he was willing to allow that 'the Professoriate ought to be considerably but gradually increased, not according to an abstract standard of perfection, nor out of all proportion to the practical demand for professorial teaching, but somewhat in advance of that demand'.[159]

The findings of the Cleveland Commission were of critical

---

[158] Brodrick, op. cit. 83.   [159] Brodrick, op. cit. 83–4.

importance to the advocates of both the tutorial profession and the endowment of research since its statistics had documented effectively their grievances with the settlement of the 1850s. The confronting of these grievances was to be the major work of the university commission which began its work in 1877. The basic shape of the modern academic profession in Oxford would emerge from this confrontation.

Chapter III

TUTORIAL GRIEVANCES AND 'THE ENDOWMENT OF RESEARCH'

Although the college tutors had improved their position greatly since the Royal Commission, several grievances still remained. The reluctance of most colleges to permit their tutors to marry while retaining fellowships inhibited the development of collegiate teaching into a professional career. The distribution of power in both Congregation and Convocation continued to be unsatisfactory. Furthermore, the college tutors' success in both taking over the function of the coaches and continuing to exclude the professors from educational work was in danger of backfiring by degrading the college tutor to the level of a mere 'teaching drudge', especially as student numbers rose sharply in the 1860s and 1870s.

The call for the 'endowment of research', which began to dominate the polemical writings on Oxford reform during the late 1860s, came to be seen by some of the tutors as a possible solution to this last aspect of their remaining grievances. This was true despite the fact that the demand for the 'endowment of research' originated not among the tutors but among their most bitter enemies. As the goal of an articulate and self-conscious party, led by Mark Pattison, Rector of Lincoln, and C. E. Appleton of St. John's, the editor of *The Academy,* the call for the 'endowment of research' developed as a movement explicitly intended to attack the ascendency which the college tutors had attained since the Royal Commission.

A. Celibacy

One crucial obstacle to the development of collegiate teaching into a professional career was the restriction of fellowships to unmarried men. Although some colleges had obtained, before the second university commission, statute revisions permitting some college officers under certain circumstances to marry, there had been no general solution to this problem.[1] In 1869 New College had been the first Oxford college to obtain an alteration in its statutes which allowed fellows engaged in tutorial work to marry while retaining their fellowships.[2] The Privy Council had approved in 1871 a new set of statutes for Merton permitting four fellows engaged in tutorial work to marry.[3] In 1872 University College had obtained a similar dispensation in their new statutes.[4] Unfortunately, this type of piecemeal solution was inadequate to resolve this issue finally.

One difficulty was well illustrated by the case of University College. Although their new statutes had allowed fellows engaged as college tutors to marry, the Privy Council had rejected the pension plan which had formed an integral part of the statute-revisions as they had been proposed by the governing body.[5] The result was that the retired tutor would receive only the value of his fellowship. Although £250 to £300 p.a. was considered a comfortable income for a bachelor, it was unsatisfactory for a married man, given the tutors' conception of their social position. A partial and mutilated victory of this sort was one of the risks of this piecemeal method of confronting the problem.

Another difficulty was illustrated by the case of Merton. As soon as their new statutes had been approved by the Privy Council, four fellows immediately petitioned the governing body for leave to marry. There followed several months of acrimonious politicking, recriminations, and constant anxiety.[6] In the end the painful situation was resolved by the

---

[1] Lincoln's statutes of 1856 had allowed the two chaplains who held the college's Oxford city livings of All Saint's and St. Michael's to retain their fellowships though married. See V. H. H. Green, *Oxford Common Room* (London, 1957), 187. Beginning in 1858, Exeter had begun to use regularly the practice of allowing college tutors to retain their tutorships when they married and resigned their fellowships. Since the Exeter fellowships were of small value, the financial sacrifice was not great, but the married tutor was placed in an insecure position because the special permission to continue this arrangement had to be renewed by the governing body every three to five years. See Exeter MS Minutes of Educational Council 1856-1937, pp. 7 and 14.

[2] Hastings Rashdall and Robert S. Rait, *New College* (London, 1901), 228.
[3] *Life and Letters of Mandell Creighton*, i. 79, and 86-9.
[4] See above, Ch. II, pp. 72-4.   [5] See above pp. 72-3.
[6] *Life and Letters of Mandell Creighton*, i. 86-9.

governing body voting to allow all four to marry. In this way, Merton put itself in the unsatisfactory position of probably not being able to offer to any college officer for some time the prospect of a permanent position in Oxford. Furthermore, the new statutes opened large prospects for future conflict since the special permission to retain a fellowship had to be renewed by each married official every ten years. This situation obviously was unsatisfactory as well from the viewpoint of the married fellow. In order to obtain the consent of the Warden and the prize fellows to the new statutes, the task of obtaining permission to marry had been made extremely onerous and the position of the married fellow had been diminished.

There was clearly much collegiate sentiment against married tutors. Many, especially among the more old-fashioned fellows, felt that 'a tutor is at his best . . . when he is young, vigorous, and enthusiastic, and not yet sufficiently removed from the standing of his pupils to be unable to comprehend their difficulties'.[7] The celibacy restriction was an effective method of insuring that most college tutors would be young. One 'Sinecure Fellow' in 1872 also argued strongly against the effects of marriage on both the teaching and scholarship of dons.[8] 'Celibacy is not necessarily a school of purity; it is certainly not in itself a school of self-denial, but it is always a school of detachment and of idealism', he asserted. He contrasted the teaching in Oxford with Germany where 'domestic interests are generally admitted to have given an official tone to the teaching of the professoriate upon more subjects than one.' About the advancement of knowledge by

[7] 'Can Colleges Reform Themselves?' *Macmillan's Mag.* xxv, no. 150 (1872), 468. The author did not fully accept this viewpoint himself but recognized its importance in the colleges. R. W. Browne, a former fellow and tutor of St. John's, had expressed this view to the 1850 commissioners. He had written that 'a man is better fitted for dealing with young men when he is himself young, and this advantage appears to me to counterbalance even the evil of frequently changing the Tutor of the College.' Browne had used this argument explicitly against allowing fellows to marry since 'married men have necessarily another sphere for their social sympathies, and cannot live with and mix amongst Undergraduates so much as ought to be the practice of College Tutors'. See *Oxford Univ. Comm.* (1852), Evidence, 7.

[8] 'Strike, But Hear', *Macmillan's Mag.* xxv, no. 148 (1872), all remaining citations in this paragraph on p. 306.

married tutors this critic was pessimistic as well. 'It is equally vain to promise that if we once make the profession of an Oxford tutor half as good for a family man as that of a Rugby master, the tutor will proceed to choose a line of study and to make discoveries . . . It may be taken for granted that when they are married, most of them will have to do like other married men in an expensive country, and take all the remunerative work that they can fairly do.' College sentiments of these types were implicit in the actions of the Merton governing body regarding married fellows. They also were probably behind the successful opposition to the attempt at Christ Church to insert a clause in the new statutes of 1867 allowing college officers to retain their studentships though married.[9] If the question of permitting married fellows were left to each college's revisions of its own statutes, it was clear that, in many cases, permission would be wholly denied. In other cases, only a truncated or otherwise unsatisfactory provision for marriage would be achieved.

The existing obstacles to marriage and, therefore, to the prospect of a professional career in Oxford were felt bitterly by many dons. Both the desire for an academic career and frustration with the existing restriction on marriage could be seen in the attitudes expressed by A. L. Smith during the time he held a prize fellowship at Trinity. Smith had decided to give up Oxford to read for the Bar since he wished to marry and an engagement was opposed on the ground that he lacked a solid income and a definite career. He wrote to his mother in 1876, 'I am sorry to leave Oxford, where the work is so congenial, and *if* I had two hundred a year of my own would spend a year in study abroad and then come back to teach here, instead of involving myself in the "nice sharp quillets of the law" in London. But a Fellowship that is stopped, and with it one's definite career, by the comparatively innocent process of marrying, is not a fair thing to depend upon.'[10]

In the end, however, Smith was not forced to abandon the career he desired in order to marry. In 1879 he was able to

[9] See above, Ch. II, p. 76, n. 64.
[10] [Mary (Baird) Smith,] *Arthur Lionel Smith, Master of Balliol (1916-1924), A Biography and Some Reminiscences by his Wife* (London, 1928), 79.

give up his uncongenial studies, as well as his other efforts to find a career position,[11] when he was offered a lectureship in modern history at Balliol. The lectureship paid enough to enable him to marry and resign his fellowship at Trinity. There was also a tacit understanding that, as soon as the college statutes permitted, he would be elected to a fellowship. Smith wrote happily to his mother about his new position,

> You know that I am settling down into an Oxford tutor, and am now lecturing on 'Modern History' in the pay of Balliol College, which pay is not magnificent at present, as I am new to the work and not able to do it all unaided; but it will improve as I get more competent, and will, at no distant date, I hope, give me a permanent place on the Governing Body of Balliol, and among the Staff of Fellows there, for I vacate my Fellowship at Trinity and lose my connexion with it by marrying, a penalty which leaves it doubtful whether matrimony was, in the eyes of the ancient Oxford legislature, a sin or a luxury.[12]

Smith envisaged that his entire career would be spent in Oxford since he jocularly remarked later in the same letter, after mentioning the 'great opening in the University for the teaching of Modern History', '. . . do not be surprised if some twenty years hence I may be intriguing for the Professorial chair in the subject'.[13]

Smith's predictions of 1879 proved not far wrong. In 1882 he was elected to an 'official fellowship' which could be held by a married college tutor under the new statutes written after the second university commission. 'A. L.' eventually became one of the most famous Oxford teachers of his era. Modern history was considered a subject especially suited to students of high social rank but only moderate intellectual abilities and 'A. L.' proved to be outstandingly successful with undergraduates of this type. Those who had difficulty with the Balliol matriculation examination or with their final modern history school were boarded at 'King's Mound', the large house which the college built for Smith and his family

---

[11] In 1877 Jowett wrote a glowing testimonial for Smith when he was thinking of an inspectorship at the Board of Education. See H. W. Carless Davis *et. al.*, *A History of Balliol College* (Oxford, 1963), 237.

[12] *A. L. Smith, Master of Balliol*, 87.   [13] Loc. cit.

specifically for this purpose. Although 'A. L.' never attained the professorship which he had predicted in 1879 he would be 'intriguing for' in twenty years, his devotion to Balliol was rewarded with the mastership, which he held from 1916 until his death in 1924.

Even in those colleges which had been able to alter before the second university commission their statutes regarding marriage for fellows, the path to the attainment of a position as a married tutorial fellow was rarely smooth. The decision at Merton in 1871 to propose to the Privy Council new statutes allowing college officers to marry had been prompted by the engagement of Mandell Creighton, one of the college's most energetic and successful tutors. The Merton governing body had considered such a change once before, but had deferred action because of the strong objections raised by the Warden and many of the older fellows. In a letter which Creighton wrote to his future wife before the college had decided to revise its statutes in his favour, he discussed his career options at this time of crisis.

I am distracted by advice from every side what to do; several of the Fellows beseech me not to leave the College; they are good enough to say that my continuance here is important to the Society; they beseech me at all events to do nothing hastily, to wait till June, when we have our next College meeting, when they will reopen the question of allowing marriage to tutors. Others of my friends advise me at all events to keep my Tutorship, even if I vacate my Fellowship by marriage, and stay at Oxford taking pupils. I listen patiently and meditate; if Butler [the headmaster of Harrow] makes me a good offer, I still think I should go to Harrow, it opens out a career which residence here does not . . . I should very much like to be a married Fellow here, but I see difficulties in the way of a society doing to meet the needs of one of its members what it deliberately refused to do in the abstract . . .[14]

Creighton did not look forward to becoming a school-master,[15] but he saw this position as his best possibility if he were not allowed to become a married tutorial fellow. He evidently never considered seriously resigning his fellowship

[14] *Life and Letters of Mandell Creighton*, i. 78.
[15] His wife wrote that after he had met a successful schoolmaster, he had written, 'I infer that it requires more energy than thought or profundity to make a schoolmaster.' Ibid. 78.

and remaining in Oxford as a college lecturer and private coach. Although Creighton was in holy orders, waiting for a college living was not an acceptable option either since Merton had few desirable ones. He wrote after the new statutes permitting four married college officers had been approved but before the governing body had decided on his application, 'I shall take the vote as final for myself, and if it goes against me I must look elsewhere.'[16]

As the date approached of the crucial meeting of the governing body at which his fate was to be decided, Creighton became increasingly anxious and irritable. He warned his fiancée not to be too certain that the governing body would approve his application. 'It is perfectly possible I may not reap the fruits of it [the new statutes]', he wrote. 'I speak in all seriousness . . . The voting on such a point is secret, and you cannot over-estimate the amount of private feeling in such things.'[17] He began to feel resentment toward the three other fellows who also had petitioned for permission to marry, even though these college officers had been previously his allies against the more conservative fellows and the Warden. 'I feel quite angry with Esson and Wallace, and am inclined to ask them why in the world they could not have restrained themselves for a while', Creighton complained.[18] He feared that the governing body might decide only to allow marriage to the two older applicants: '. . . all the older Fellows, who are very little interested in the educational aspect of the place, and know very little about its real working, will cut the knot by voting for Edwards and Esson on the ground that they are much older and have served the College much longer than Wallace and myself'.[19] He concluded bitterly, 'that is the sort of argument that always weighs most with an old man. I don't feel particularly merry about the matter. I must candidly own that it appears before me in the light of a sell; so much so, that it seems to me the sooner I look about me for a schoolmastership the better.'[20] The best construction which Creighton was able to put on the possibility of having to leave Oxford was that 'after all, it is only a bore at first going to be a schoolmaster'. It probably was only regard for his

---

[16] Ibid. 85.   [17] Loc. cit.
[18] Ibid. 87.   [19] Ibid. 86.   [20] Loc. cit.

future wife's feelings which induced him to add weakly, 'If Providence decides that I leave Oxford, I have no doubt it is better for us.'[21] In the end, however, 'Providence' was kind: the governing body decided to allow Creighton to become a married tutorial fellow.[22]

These accounts of the problems of A. L. Smith and Mandell Creighton, though not their successful endings, were certainly typical of the difficulties felt by many college tutors in the 1870s. The increasing seriousness with which they came to view their position as collegiate teachers had led many to conceive the possibility of academic work as a professional career. The fact that the college tutorships and lectureships were generally worth £500 to £800 p.a. (including fellowship dividends) at this time was also no small inducement to the development of professional consciousness.[23] These sums were considerably more than a young practitioner still under the age of thirty could hope to obtain in any of the traditional learned professions without exceptionally powerful connections. For the lay tutorial fellow, the traditional ladder, which had led from the fellowship to practice at the Bar, to a school inspectorship, or to a mastership at a public school, seemed no longer appropriate or desirable. It was also possible that a 'crisis of middle-class employment' was a factor in making career prospects outside Oxford less inviting to the college tutor.[24] Even among clerical college tutors, who were still the

---

[21] Ibid. 87.

[22] See below, pp. 124–7 for a discussion of the remainder of Creighton's career.

[23] In 1870, for example, the three University College tutors received £845, £719 and £604 while a lecturer received £567. All these figures include the fellowship dividend for that year of £313. There were also three more lecturers who were only resident for one or two terms and drew smaller sums from the tuition fund. See University College MS Bursar's Ledger 1869–70. At Lincoln in the same year the two tutors received £785 and £652, of which £323 was the fellowship dividend. There were also five other part-time lecturers who received smaller sums. See Lincoln MS Day Book 1869–70.

[24] The existence of such a crisis was argued by F. Musgrove, 'Middle-Class Education and Employment in the Nineteenth Century', *Econ. Hist. Rev.* 2nd Series, xii (1959), 99–111. The statistical basis of this argument has been severely attacked by H. J. Perkin, 'Middle-Class Education and Employment in the Nineteenth Century: A Critical Note', *Econ. Hist. Rev.* 2nd Series, xiv (1961), 122–30. Musgrove's viewpoint is supported by a large mass of literary evidence. Perkins dismisses this evidence of 'over-crowded professions' as merely a chorus which might be heard among discontented practitioners at any point in modern history.

majority, many were beginning to question the desirability of following the traditional route from a fellowship to a college living, although this factor was to become much more important in the 1880s when the serious, long-term decline in Church income, caused by the agricultural depression, had become obvious.[25] The result of this situation was that many college tutors came to resent bitterly the general restriction of fellowships to unmarried men which prevented them from looking forward to professional careers in Oxford.

From the examples of those colleges even where successful attempts had been made to alter their statutes on marriage for tutors and other college officers, it was apparent that special circumstances were required to achieve any solution to this problem on the level of the individual college. In these circumstances, a growing body of college tutors and other officers came to welcome the possibility of another government commission and Parliamentary action as the only effective means of solving their problem.

B. *The Structure of Power in University Government*

Another tutorial grievance on the eve of the second university commission was the inclusion of a large number of 'non-academical' persons in both Convocation and Congregation. Although the influence of the tutors in these bodies was greater than it had been before 1854, the situation had remained far from ideal from their viewpoint. Furthermore, in the 1860s and 1870s there was a marked change for the worse since the power of those residents involved in academic work actually declined in both Congregation and Convocation.

The complaints which began to appear in the mid-1860s from collegiate and university teachers against the existing distribution of power in the university legislatures were based on an accurate understanding of the changes which had occurred in the structure of power since the late 1850s. Comparing the register of members of Congregation in 1858

It does not seem, however, that the statistical data which Perkin uses is so reliable as to justify this easy dismissal.

   [25] See Appendix I, below p. 286. Although 69 per cent of the sample of college officers appointed between 1881 and 1900 were in holy orders, only 9 per cent took Church livings.

with the same list in 1874,[26] the most significant growth in representation was experienced by the 'resident MAs not engaged in official academic work'. Their number grew from 15 per cent to 25 per cent of Congregation. Their expansion was the primary cause of the growth in the total number of registered voters.[27] One hostile critic in 1866 attributed this change to 'among other things, the tendency of the city clergy to increase in numbers, not only from the growth of the city, but from causes connected with the present religious movement'.[28] Since one residual effect of the Tractarian movement had been to make Oxford a centre for innovations in Church ritual, many clergymen desired to remain there even as curates or college chaplains. This was especially true for High Churchmen for whom Oxford exercised a strong attraction as the city in which it was most historically fitting for their theories to be put into practice. It is also possible that in 1858 a significant number of eligible city clergy did not enter their names on the official register of Congregation. The increasing organization of the Church party in the 1860s and 1870s may have induced these men to assert their rights. In any case, 'resident MAs not engaged in official academic work' grew after the 1850s to become the single most important power-bloc in Congregation.

The other change in the structure of power in Congregation between 1858 and 1874 was the decline in resident fellows. They fell from 54 per cent to 38 per cent of Congregation. Clearly, there was at least some truth in the taunt that 'if you want to find the ordinary Oxford fellow of the present day, the last place to look for him is within the immediate precincts of the University'.[29] Tutorial fellows had remained

[26] See Appendix 4, below, pp. 289–90.

[27] In most other categories, the changes were of only minor significance. Although the growth of the combined lecturing schemes had more than doubled the number of 'resident MAs engaged as official tutors of lecturers', they still amounted to only 10 per cent of the total legislature. The moderate expansion of the professoriate which had followed the Act of 1854 had also increased their representation slightly.

[28] Goldwin Smith, *The Elections to the Hebdomadal Council. A Letter to the Rev. C. W. Sandford, MA, Senior Censor of Christ Church* (Oxford and London, Nov. 1, 1866), 7.

[29] See above, Ch. II, p. 100, n. 148. An undergraduate magazine made this criticism in verse.

virtually constant in numbers from 1858 to 1874, the decline had been in other resident fellows, whose number fell from 27 per cent to 15 per cent. The new breed of prize fellows were not likely to remain in Oxford unless they were provided with college work.

Although there actually was a rise in the number of tutorial fellows from 81 to 98 between 1858 and 1874,[30] it was not reflected in increased representation in Congregation since only MAs were qualified to vote. Only four college tutors were still BAs in 1858; by 1874 seventeen had not yet taken their MA.[31] Changes in the practical working of the examination system had tended to place an increasing premium on very young tutors. An undergraduate magazine criticized this tendency in 1874:

> And surely to the world it needs must seem,
> A little strange in this our Academe,
> How easy to the heights of College sway
> The Don all youthful wends his gladsome way . . .
> Securely great, examinations o'er,
> At twenty-three they tread the path to power.[32]

There was a general trend in *Literae Humaniores* to emphasize philosophy rather than the linguistic skills which had dominated this school in the past. The tendency was increasingly to use the rarely altered list of classical texts which were the ostensible subject-matter for the examination papers as points of departure for the discussion of philosophical problems in terms of currently fashionable thought. As Mark Pattison observed with distaste in 1868, 'I do not believe that

---

> See! o'er the seas, as if she [England] ne'er had been,
> Frantic they [the dons] rush upon the Alpine scene,
> And since the fashion Tyndal once began
> Ascend those summits never meant for man . . .
> Self-exiled ever from their land and home,
> They deem a stay in England martyrdom . . .

The Shotover Papers, i, no. 4 (1874), 53. The editorship of this magazine is attributed by Cordeaux and Merry to W. E. W. Morrison, exhibitioner of Queen's 1870-5.   [30] See Appendix 8, below, p. 292.

[31] See notes 6-7 to Appendix 4, below, p. 290.

[32] *The Shotover Papers*, i, no. 4 (1874), 53. For the changing age distribution of college tutors, see Appendix 11, below, p. 294.

there exists at this moment in Europe any public institution for education, where what are called "the results of modern thought" . . . are so entirely at home, as they are in our honour examinations in the school of "Literae Humaniores"'.[33] A thorough knowledge of J. S. Mill's modification of Utilitariansim was crucial for success until the late 1860s when German idealism began to take its place.[34]

In this situation, the most effective tutor would be a recent graduate who had distinguished himself in the examinations. If an older fellow were called back to take up a tutorship, it would be quite possible that the knowledge which had insured his own success would no longer serve to win good degrees for his students.[35] Mandell Creighton's rapid attainment of a Merton tutorship was typical of this period. He took his final classical schools in the spring of 1866 and his second final school of modern history the next fall. He was elected fellow of Merton in late November and took up a college tutorship in modern history with classical work for the pass school

[33] *Suggestions on Academical Organization* (Edinburgh, 1868), 292.

[34] See Diderick Roll-Hanson, *The Academy 1869–1879* (Copenhagen, 1957), 45–57, esp. 52. One critic in 1870 complained, 'At one time a first class is only attainable by those who have been coached along the high *a priori* road of speculation; at another time the honour can only be gained beneath the auspices and leadership of Mr Mill and his friends.' See 'College Tutors: The Old School and the New', *London Society*, xvii, no. 100 (1870), 340. The trend toward philosophical idealism in the 1870s was parodied in an undergraduate magazine of the period. An article on 'What is Philosophy?' began, 'Philosophy, the handmaid of Truth, is like a mirror dashed to pieces, whose each severed part reflects new phases of the great To Be. The time has come for a system which shall restore the fragments to a harmonious unity and point out the errors and shortcomings of previous workers in the illimitable sphere of the Unconditioned . . . What then is Philosophy? . . . Let us scorn the delusions of sects and boldly declare that Philosophy is Humbug.' See *The Shotover Papers*, i, no. 4 (1874), 56–7. The 'unconditioned' was Sir William Hamilton's translation of Kant's *ding an sich*. The concept was popularized in Oxford by H. L. Mansel's influential Bampton Lectures for 1858, *The Limits of Religious Thought* (Oxford, 1858).

[35] When R. W. Macan, later Master of University College, was an undergraduate, his tutor in his last year was Ingram Bywater of Exeter. Bywater disapproved strongly of the current trend toward emphasizing philosophical theories rather than exact scholarship. Noting that T. H. Green, a well-known exponent of philosophical idealism, was to be an examiner that year, Macan asked that he be permitted to write an essay on mysticism. Bywater only agreed with evident distaste. 'Mysticism' was the topic of one of the set papers that year. A less knowing undergraduate clearly would have been in serious trouble if his tutor was unsympathetic to the type of thought then fashionable. See W. W. Jackson, *Ingram Bywater: A Memior* (Oxford, 1917), 64.

immediately after Christmas.[36] The requirements of the examination system tended increasingly in the 1860s and 1870s to place young BAs, like Creighton, in the college tutorships before they were able to vote in either Convocation or Congregation.

The desire to alter this situation in which the academic residents were doomed to being defeated in the legislatures of the university by Oxford city clergy clearly was an issue on which the advocates of a 'tutorial profession' and the supporters of the 'endowment of research' might act together against the Church party. C. S. Roundell of Merton argued privately that the only chance was to outmanoeuvre the non-residents and the Oxford clergy by trying to form an alliance within Congregation 'on the neutral ground of interest in education'.[37] Yet this could not be a satisfactory solution since those who had an interest in education; professors, tutorial fellows, lecturers and coaches were outnumbered by 'non-academical' voters.

In Convocation, the dominance of non-residents was bitterly resented. 'The history of recent academic legislation shows what the spirit of the mass of the non-resident graduates is', Lyulph Stanley asserted.

Men who having many years ago satisfied the examiners in that minimum of knowledge which secures a degree have since then lived on their intellectual capital or hoarded it in a napkin. These gentlemen we have seen again and again brought up (in one case many of them, it was said, by a special train from Somersetshire) to vote in perfect ignorance against some statute on the details of education recommended by the great mass of those practically acquainted with the teaching of the university.[38]

Goldwin Smith, the Regius Professor of Modern History, complained that the balance of power in Convocation was held, for practical purposes by 'some thirty or forty staunch partisans, who having leisure enough to come up whenever

---

[36] *Life and Letters of Mandell Creighton,* i. 42.

[37] C. S. Roundell to J. Bryce, 24 July 1865, Bodleian Bryce MSS Box E 30, cited in Ward, 248. For an attempt to form such an alliance in 1868, see Bodl. MS Top. Oxon. e. 100.

[38] *Oxford University Reform* (London, 1869), 5.

they are called, have put themselves into the pockets of two or three wire-pullers, and thus enabled the wire-pullers to coerce Congregation whenever it presumes to come to a decision of which they do not approve'.[39] Smith suggested that the solution was to abolish the power of Convocation over university legislation. 'The non-resident members of Convocation generally bear no part of the responsibility, which falls on the actual administrators and teachers of the University', he argued. 'Why should those who do not share the responsibility expect to share, and more than share, the power.'[40]

The mood of dissatisfaction among the academic residents with the structure of power in Convocation was so obvious that it became a theme for undergraduate satire. In a mock play, 'Tom Tower' addressed a meeting of thinly disguised academic residents, such as M*gr*th of Q***n's (J. R. Magrath of Queen's) and Mr W*ince (William Ince of Exeter), with the following lament,

> My little friends you all must know that I
> Decided yesterday that I would try
> And work some new reforms in Convocation.
> I tried, I tried — met nothing but vexation,
> For first I thought as it was wood I'd polish it,
> On second thought I said 'I will abolish it.'[41]

In this parody, the organization of academic residents even surpassed Goldwin Smith's suggestion by abolishing Convocation altogether. In reality, the problem was not to be solved so easily. The situation became so hopeless that after 1864, some collegiate and university teachers took to abstaining ostentatiously from voting when they were certain to be defeated.[42]

---

[39] *The Elections to the Hebdomadal Council*, 12-13. Perhaps the most prominent of these 'wire-pullers' was C. P. Golightly, an MA of Oriel and an unbeneficed clergyman of independent means, who devoted his life to academic politics in the interests of the Church but especially against its High Church contingent. Smith probably also had in mind such High Church polemicists as J. W. Burgon of Oriel and H. P. Liddon of Christ Church, both of whom were generally resident in Oxford.

[40] Ibid. 13. Smith's views were enthusiastically endorsed in [H. H. Lancaster,] 'Oxford University Extension', *North British Review*, xlvi, no. 91 (1867), 119-29, esp. 127.　　　　　[41] *The Shotover Papers*, i, no. 4 (1874), 59.

[42] Bodleian Monk Bretton MSS Goldwin Smith to J. G. Dodson, 9 Mar.

There was much dissatisfaction with the composition of Congregation as well. The inclusion of all resident MAs was felt to be a grievance by the tutors and others 'practically acquainted with the teaching of the university'. Some suggested that this problem be solved by balancing these 'non-academical' persons with other senior non-residents involved in educational work outside Oxford.[43] Goldwin Smith urged that the only solution was to remove the non-academic element altogether. He argued that 'Congregation was unquestionably intended to be, what the miscellaneous Convocation was not, a strictly academical assembly . . . [T]he House cannot have contemplated such a result as the ascendency in Congregation of persons who have no connection with academical affairs, the parish clergy and professional men of the city, and chaplains who are without any academical occupation.'[44] He concluded that the university ought to 'ask Parliament to fulfil its original intention, by . . . excluding from that specifically academical body all persons holding benefices or curacies, or engaged in any profession or calling other than Learning or Education'.[45]

Goldwin Smith's angry pamphlet is best remembered today as the butt of a witty, rhyming parody by C. L. Dodgson of Christ Church.[46] Dodgson was an active controversialist in the cause of the Church party, several of whose leaders, such as H. P. Liddon and Dr Pusey, were among the senior members of his college. Dodgson's characterization of Smith's basic suggestion to remove non-academical persons from Congregation revealed clearly which interest group Smith's plan was intended to benefit.

My scheme is this: remove the votes of all
The residents that are not Liberal —

1864. Cf. *The Times*, 7 May 1868, p. 5, cited in Ward. 253.
[43] Bodl. MS Bryce 9, fol. 19, cited in Ward, 247.
[44] *The Elections to the Hebdomadal Council*, 6-7.
[45] Loc. cit. Smith's position was seconded in 'Oxford University Extension' (see above, n. 40).
[46] *The Elections to the Hebdomadal Council. A Letter to the Rev. C. W. Sandford, has been addressed (on this subject) by GOLDWIN SMITH, and may possibly reach a SECOND EDITION* (Oxford, 5 Nov. 1866). Reprinted in *The Complete Works of Lewis Carroll* (London, 1939), 815-22.

Leave the young Tutors uncontrolled and free,
And Oxford then shall see — what it shall see.[47]

Even the enemies of reform were willing to admit that the
tutors had suffered from the changes which had occurred
in the structure of power in Congregation since the 1850s.
They also recognized that the college tutors would be the
principal beneficiaries of the removal of non-academic
residents from Congregation, especially if tutors who were
still BAs were permitted to vote.

The supporters of reform were equally clear as to who
their enemy was. Goldwin Smith characterized the beneficiaries of the existing structure of power in the university
legislatures as 'a great political and theological party (more
political, if we may judge by its ultimate preferences, than
theological), acting for non-academical objects, recruited to
a great extent from non-academical sources, and labouring
under perfect discipline and with fell unity of purpose, to
hold the University in subjugation'.[48] To make the description
more pointed, Smith could not resist making an invidious
comparison between those who sympathized with his position
and his opponents on the basis that 'we cannot promise
Paradise to our supporters'.[49] The enemy was the Church
party and Smith no longer thought it necessary to conceal
the personal venom with which he viewed their continued
influence in Oxford.

One striking aspect of this controversy was the small
amount of public debate it engendered. Perhaps one reason
was the clear danger of such public arguments descending to
the level of personal invective. It was significant that Goldwin
Smith resigned his professorship and left Oxford immediately
after writing his outspoken pamphlet on this issue. If he had
to continue to live and work with his opponents, he might
not have been so blunt in his attack. W. R. Ward has suggested
that public discussion was also tactically inexpedient. All
who made suggestions for reform 'were exposed to the damag-
ing charge of wishing to rig the constitution of the university

[47] Ibid. 818.   [48] *The Elections to the Hebdomadal Council*, 2.
[49] Ibid. 6.

in the party interest'.[50] Even Goldwin Smith felt it necessary to defend himself energetically against the charge that he was attempting to form a 'combination' against the Church.[51] Certainly the total failure of Smith's pamphlet to lead to any of the changes he had proposed would not have recommended this method to other malcontents.

Any attempt to curtail the power of 'non-academical' persons in Congregation and Convocation would necessitate a revival of the battle of the tutors and other academic residents against the Church party. Given the existing structure of power in the university legislatures, however, any such attempt would be doomed to failure. In Congregation, the 'non-academical' persons, although not a majority, were none the less the single largest bloc. Undoubtedly, they would come to the poll in large numbers on an issue so vitally affecting their interests. In Convocation, any legislation of this type certainly would be important enough to bring to Oxford sufficient non-residents to insure its defeat. Therefore, as in the case of the struggle to allow married fellows, the tutors and other academic residents came to welcome the possibility of a second university commission as their only hope for regaining the power they had recently lost in the university legislatures.

C. The College Tutor as a 'Teaching Drudge'

Both grievances which have already been discussed were the result of the incomplete victories which the tutors and other academic residents had won since the Oxford Act of 1854. Their final grievance, however, grew from their success itself. In their struggles against the heads, the prize fellows, and the Church party, the tutors had been forced to emphasize the importance of their role as collegiate teachers to such an extent that they were in danger of losing their status as scholars. The rise in the number of students and the teaching obligations of college tutors during the 1860s and 1870s also contributed to this problem. The teacher/student ratio rose from 1:15 in 1858 to 1:17 in 1874 despite a 40 per cent rise in the absolute number of collegiate teachers.[52] The growing

---

[50] Ward, 247.   [51] *The Elections to the Hebdomadal Council,* 6.
[52] See Appendix 3, below, p. 288.

practice of college tutors seeing their students individually for 'private hours' also intensified this problem by increasing the amount of tutorial work required by each pupil.[53]

This grievance was not as crucial as the other two, nor did it have as wide an appeal among the tutorial fellows. The life of a busy college tutor, reading in the evening the books on which he would lecture in the morning, was a fulfilling and satisfactory career for some, once the permission to marry had been granted. A. L. Smith, for example, probably little regretted his lack of time for advanced study and writing. It seems clear that he was satisfied with the energetic life of a successful collegiate teacher, personally involved with the success of his pupils and the standing of his college in the class lists. Once he had obtained permission to marry while retaining the fellowship which gave his position dignity and permanence, Smith was content to spend the rest of his active life in tutorial work. When A. L. was a young fellow of Trinity, he found coaching 'so congenial' that he regretted only the absence of sufficient private means to allow him to resign the fellowship which prevented his marrying.[54] Similarly, as a young lecturer at Balliol, he looked forward to the time when he could raise his income by doing all of the college's tutorial work in modern history.[55] In contrast, T. H. Green, who had been in an analogous situation as a young fellow of Balliol with no private means, wrote of his work as a coach, 'At first it seemed to do me some good, but now I find that, while it takes up all my time and brings little money, it does nothing to improve the mind. After next term I think I shall give it up, for a time at least, and devote myself for a period to real study away from Oxford.'[56] Skill in teaching was a highly-prized and well-rewarded attribute in Oxford at this time and Smith had no reason ever to regret his devotion to it. As one of his friends wrote, with a perfunctory nod toward the importance of research, 'As for regretting that A. L. didn't write books himself, of course one regrets that his knowledge

---

[53] See above, Ch. II, pp. 86–7 for a discussion of the adoption of this mode of instruction, which previously had been used by the private coaches only, by the college tutors.

[54] See above, p. 109, n. 10.   [55] See above, p. 110, n. 12.

[56] Cited in R. L. Nettleship, *Memoir of Thomas Hill Green* (London, 1906) 41.

and rich appreciation of the Middle Ages was not given to the world, but others may come who have equal knowledge, whereas *his* business was with men'.[57] Smith might have wished that he had become Master of Balliol sooner, but the lack of leisure to pursue learned research did not seem to have been a major discontent for him.

For Mandell Creighton, on the other hand, the situation was quite different. He attained his desire to become a married fellow in 1871 but only three years later he resigned to take the Merton living of Embleton in Northumberland. Neither the desire for pastoral work nor a significant financial advantage were important considerations to Creighton in this decision. His income as fellow and senior tutor was approximately £720 p.a. exclusive of the sums he often received as an examiner for the modern history school and as a lecturer on history and Italian literature during vacations.[58] Since Embleton was worth £840 p.a.,[59] the financial benefits of taking the living were clearly marginal at best. From the viewpoint of the amenities of life, Oxford was clearly superior. Although the vicarage at Embleton was a large and beautiful house, it was situated in a cold, wind-swept region near the sea. To many it would have seemed a kind of exile. It was the prospect of having time for scholarly work that constituted for Creighton the chief advantage of Embleton over Oxford. He composed the following balance-sheet both for his wife and to clarify his own thinking while making the difficult choice.[60]

Advantages of Oxford	*Advantages of Embleton*
1. Stimulus of intellectual society.	1. Quiet and energy undisturbed by struggles concerning your work.
2. Facilities of consulting libraries.	2. Opportunity of uninterrupted work all the year round, and concentration of intellectual energy on one subject.

[57] *A. L. Smith: Master of Balliol*, 160.

[58] See PP 1873, xxxvii, part ii. In 1871 all fellows of Merton received a fixed payment of £300 p.a. (p. 252, return C.1, item 2), the senior tutor received in addition £332 1s. (p. 255, 'Tuition Account'). Creighton also held two other college offices: as 'Principal of the Postmasters' he received an additional £50 p.a. (p. 252, return C.1, item 5), and as the senior dean he received an additional £37 p.a. (p. 252, return C.1, item 5). The total was £719 1s and there is no reason to suppose that three years later it had changed significantly.

[59] Ibid. 260. [60] *Life and Letters of Mandell Creighton*, i. 141.

Creighton had found, to his chagrin, that the busy schedule of an active college tutor was not as conducive to study as he had imagined when he was an undergraduate. It had been the attraction of a life devoted largely to study that had constituted for Creighton the chief value of a tutorial fellowship in Oxford. Fresh from his First in *Literae Humaniores* in 1866, he had written to a friend, 'I am determined, in case I get a fellowship, to give myself up to study and literary labour in general, and seek to do nought else.'[61] Presumably his friend had voiced the conventional objection that such a life was inherently selfish, since he replied in a tone of youthful idealism, 'I could do much more positive good at present as a don at Oxford than in any other capacity I am aware of and could besides have plenty of time for study . . . [I] f I have this I may possibly . . . add something to the knowledge of mankind — add one little stone to the temple which is raising; or if I can only supply a little more mortar for the good of others, I will not have lived in vain . . . Such a life is far from being one of idleness or necessary selfishness.'[62] Seven years as a tutorial fellow, however, had led Creighton to question seriously the desirability of his Oxford life. Part of the problem was undoubtedly the restrictions which had been placed on the security of his position as a married fellow. Every ten years he would have to be re-elected by a two-thirds vote of the governing body. 'I am, though nominally a Fellow of the College, really a subordinate official in the employment of the unmarried Fellows', he complained after three years. 'An Oxford life is delightful if one has it properly; but in seven years I have to sue for re-election.'[63] It was clear from the balance-sheet, however, that lack of time for concentrated research as a college tutor was a crucial grievance as well.[64]

When it became known that Creighton was seriously considering Embleton, some intimations evidently were made

---

[61] Ibid. 40.   [62] Ibid. 40–1.
[63] *Life and Letters of Mandell Creighton,* i. 140.
[64] In 1892 looking back on this important decision, Creighton concluded, 'I had felt that the manifold activities required of me — I was the Senior Tutor, and taught both ancient and modern history for honour men, besides taking a share of the pass work — were obstacles to gaining any thorough knowledge . . . So a desire for less mental dissipation led me into the country.' Ibid. 143.

that he would be elected Warden when Dr Marsham died. Creighton decided that this was unlikely, however, since Merton was one of the few colleges permitted to have a lay head. He felt that the fellows would be reluctant to forgo their privilege by electing a clergyman.[65] None the less, Creighton would have been willing to remain if he had seen a real prospect in the near future for a professorship with its greater freedom from teaching work. Unfortunately, he could not view this possibility as any more substantial than his chance for the headship.[66]

Creighton decided in the end that his undergraduate conception of the life he would lead as a tutorial fellow had been totally incorrect. His blunt conclusion was that 'literary application and tutoring don't run side by side . . . The tendency of Oxford is to make me a teaching drudge, and prevent me from being a literary student.'[67] Creighton chose to take Embleton, therefore, despite the protests of his Oxford friends. This decision was amply justified by subsequent accomplishments. During the ten years which he spent at Embleton, Creighton was able to write the first two volumes of his *History of the Papacy from the Great Schism to the Sack of Rome 1378-1527.*[68] This work was both well received in its time and has continued to command the respect of ecclesiastical historians for its impartiality and accurate use of primary sources.[69] Although Creighton was disappointed in his desire to become Regius Professor of Modern History at Oxford,[70] his life certainly did not lack worldly rewards for his distinction as a scholar. In 1884 he was elected the first Dixie Professor of Ecclesiastical History at Cambridge and, a year later, he was given a canonry at Worcester Cathedral to

---

[65] Ibid. 142. He was probably correct in his judgement since George Brodrick, another layman, was elected when Dr Marsham died in 1881.

[66] 'I have no chance of any University office at present, or I would not dream of going', Creighton wrote in 1874. Ibid. 140.　　　　[67] Ibid. 141.

[68] The first two volumes were published by Longman's in 1882, volumes III and IV followed in 1887, and volume V, the last he was able to complete, was published in 1894.

[69] See Owen Chadwick's inaugural lecture as Dixie Professor of Ecclesiastical History at Cambridge, *Creighton on Luther* (Cambridge, 1959).

[70] When William Stubbs became Bishop of Oxford in 1884, Creighton was a candidate for the chair. See *Life and Letters of Mandell Creighton*, i. 243-4.

hold with the chair. In 1890 Creighton was elevated to the see of Peterborough and, in 1897, he was translated to the richer bishopric of London. His sudden death in 1901 at the age of fifty-eight cut short what undoubtedly would have been an influential as well as a brilliant career.

Other tutorial fellows who did not leave Oxford also resented the deterioration of the 'learned leisure' which had traditionally been the prerogative of the Oxford don, but which rising student numbers and increasing teaching demands were destroying. For example, the scholarly career of W. W. Fowler, who became fellow of Lincoln in 1872, did not begin in earnest until he decided to give up college work in his mid-fifties after twenty-five years as tutor and sub-rector. He complained that he had been 'under the everlasting necessity of making an income by routine college work'.[71] His biographer wrote of the 'long years of tutoring (of which Fowler more than once complained)'.[72] Fortunately, Fowler had a long and productive 'retirement' during which he was able to write extensively on the history of ancient Rome and the social context of classical literature.

Other Oxford dons of this period were not as fortunate as Fowler in this respect. R. L. Nettleship became fellow and tutor of Balliol in 1869 and served the college for the next twenty-three years until his death at the age of forty-six. His posthumously published lectures on Plato and some literary fragments were all that could be salvaged of his knowledge of classical philosophy. Nettleship's literary executor noted sadly that 'he gradually came to recognize that it was beyond his powers to combine both philosophical and historical writing with his College work'.[73] This sentiment mirrors almost exactly Creighton's that 'literary application and tutoring don't run side by side'. Since he was not in holy orders, Nettleship could not, like Creighton, gain the time he needed for writing by leaving Oxford for the quiet of a country living. Nor did he live long enough, like Fowler, to produce his learned work after having served his college as an

---

[71] See the private letter cited in R. H. Coon, *William Warde Fowler: An Oxford Humanist* (Oxford, 1934), 81.   [72] Ibid. 74.
[73] 'Biographical Sketch', in A. C. Bradley and G. R. Benson (eds.), *Philosophical Lectures and Remains of Richard Lewis Nettleship* (London, 1897), xix–xx.

active tutor for twenty-five years. In the end, Nettleship's biographer could only conclude, '[T]he main reason why he did not write more was that he regarded his College Work as his first business, and gave himself to it so ungrudgingly that . . . the bulk of his energy was exhausted in it'.[74] These complaints were too numerous to be dismissed as excuses. Their persistence clearly indicated the existence of grave deficiencies in the ideal of the 'tutorial profession' as a desirable career for those with learned aspirations.

This grievance, like the problems of the celibacy restriction and the unsatisfactory distribution of power in university government, was not amenable to solution on the level of the individual college. An expanded number of college tutors would be one step toward the alleviation of the undue pressure of tutorial work. Such an expansion, however, would only be practical if a more efficient division of labour were created than was possible while each college was autonomous as an educational institution. A beginning had been made in the combined lecturing system but it was clear that some type of formal university organization was needed if this system was to expand successfully. A genuine solution to this problem would require also the 'endowment of research', either through the expansion of the professoriate or through the redefinition of the role of the college tutor to include literary, as well as educational work. Neither of these changes were likely with the existing distribution of power in the colleges and in the university legislatures. Therefore, as in the cases of their other grievances, those college tutors who resented their conversion into 'teaching drudges' came to look toward a second university commission as their only hope of reversing the trend toward the steady erosion of their learned status.

This attitude of the tutors and other academic residents toward university reform was in marked contrast to their attitude before the Royal Commission. At that time, their very existence as a separate group would have been denied by most members of the university. Within the colleges, they

[74] Ibid. xxvi.

were greatly outnumbered by those fellows who did no academic work. Most clerical fellows saw themselves primarily as clergymen, while the few lay fellows generally identified with the secular professions in which they aimed ultimately to make their careers. Even among the tutors, there were few who viewed themselves as collegiate teachers or scholars by profession. The fact that less than thirty years later the tutors and other academic residents could welcome the second university commission with confidence that their voices would be heard and their wishes respected, was a measure of the degree of success which they had attained since 1850.

The period since the Royal Commission also had seen a doubling in the number of official collegiate teachers.[75] Although the greatest expansion had been among lecturers not on the college foundations, the number of fellows engaged in official teaching in Oxford also had risen by almost 80 per cent.[76] This growth indicated a trend toward the greater concentration of collegiate resources on educational work, since the two-thirds rise in the number of students during the same period[77] could not account for the entire growth in college teaching staffs. This expansion in the number of collegiate teachers, especially the rise in the number of tutorial fellows, meant that the power of the tutors had grown significantly. Although serious problems still remained, their existence should not obscure the fact that the college tutors had become a recognized interest group since 1850. They were articulate and their importance clearly was increasing. They looked to a new university commission, therefore, not as a hostile external inquisition, but as the only means of eliminating their remaining grievances.

D. The Emergence of the 'Endowment of Research' Party

In their desire for government intervention, the college tutors were able to make common cause with the advocates of the

---

[75] The total number of collegiate teachers grew from 71 in 1845 to 140 in 1874. See Appendix 3, below, p. 288.

[76] The total number of tutorial fellows grew from 55 in 1845 to 98 in 1874. See Appendix 3, below, p. 288.

[77] The average number of matriculents grew from 410 in 1840–9 to 684 in 1870–9. See Stone, Table IA, p. 91.

'endowment of research'. This alliance was extremely precarious, however, since they disagreed fundamentally on the goals which a new commission ought to achieve. They could agree on the elimination of the celibacy restriction, yet this agreement only concealed their more important differences on what uses fellowships ought to serve. Although both agreed that 'non-academical' persons had obtained too much influence in university government, they differed sharply on the more important question of what measures the academic residents as a whole ought to support.

The party explicitly devoted to the 'endowment of research' evolved in the late 1860s and 1870s from the earlier supporters of a scholarly ideal of the 'professorial system'.[78] The experience of 'reformed' Oxford had convinced many who wished to see the advancement of knowledge recognized as the primary function of the university that the natural harmony of teaching and research duties was illusory. Although many of the earlier advocates of the 'professorial system' had tended to view teaching as the lower aspect of the functions of academics, they had not gone so far as to suggest that it ought to be removed entirely. In the years since 1854, however, the advocates of research had seen the college tutors growing in power on the basis of their devotion to educational work. They had also seen the university becoming increasingly dominated by its teaching and examining functions. The researchers became convinced, therefore, that the only way to promote the advancement of knowledge was to endow career positions completely divorced from educational duties. They also came to believe that the importance of the examination system ought to be reduced, both to create a more wholesome intellectual atmosphere and to diminish the powers of the tutors. The colleges could continue to educate undergraduates but this activity ought not to be subsidized either by devoting fellowships to the support of college tutors or by augmenting tuition funds or pension funds from endowment income.

Those who wanted the advancement of knowledge recog-

---

[78] For a discussion of this ideal, as it was articulated before the Royal Commission, see above, Ch. I, pp. 30–3.

nized as an important, though not the only, function of the university had victory snatched from them between the issuing of the Royal Commission's report and the passing of the Oxford Act. A major value of the 'professorial system' and the university lecturer scheme advocated by the royal commissioners was that they would have supported this function by providing academic careers unencumbered by the many restrictions which made college fellowships inappropriate for this purpose.[79] The total rejection of these plans had been the first step toward the development of the 'endowment of research' party twenty-five years later. The experience of 'reformed' Oxford had increased the alienation of the advocates of research. One member of the 'endowment of research' party in 1876 dismissed 'the actual course of academical reform throughout the present century', with the bitter comment that its only effect 'has been to augment the efficiency of the Universities as examining machines, and to add to the comforts of the Colleges as endowed boarding-schools for adults'.[80] This critic even went so far as to imply that the fellowship system had been better suited for the encouragement of learning prior to the 'reforms' of the 1850s: '. . . endowed sinecures did not turn out a failure until it was announced, with quasi-parliamentary sanction, that the traditional duty of study was no longer to be expected from the fellows'.[81]

This spirit of hostility to the work of the Royal Commission indicated clearly the gulf between the advocates of a scholarly ideal of the 'professorial system' in the 1850s, such as H. H. Vaughan and Bonamy Price, and the supporters of the 'endowment of research' in the late 1860s and 1870s. This hostility can be seen in the defensive attitude of Goldwin Smith, the former secretary of the Royal Commission. He had been an opponent of the 'collegiate monopoly' and a supporter of the 'professorial system', however, by the late 1860s, the attitude of the 'researchers' had become so hostile

---

[79] For a discussion of the royal commissioners' plans for reform, see above, Ch. I, pp. 35–8.

[80] James Sutherland Cotton, 'The Intentions of the Founders of Fellowships', in *Essays on the Endowment of Research* (London, 1876), 30.

[81] Ibid. 70.

that he felt it necessary to protest strongly against their viewpoint. Although Smith attempted to present his views as a statesmanlike compromise by admitting grudgingly that 'the promotion of learning and science may be the highest function of the University', he concluded that, 'its direct function, in the present day, is Education; and . . . educational duties ought to be attached to our emoluments'.[82] Smith also became impatient with the researchers' insistence that the endowments of the colleges and university were essential to the advancement of knowledge. 'We are not living in the Middle Ages, when it might be necessary to draw men at any cost, out of the half-barbarous population, engrossed by war, unscientific husbandry or petty trade, to the only place where intellectual pursuits could be carried on', he asserted.

Modern society has a multitude of callings and positions more or less intellectual, more or less favourable to the pursuit of literature and science. The high education of all those who are to enter such callings and hold such positions is likely to promote learning and science much more than the books occasionally written by the holders of sinecure preferment. It is easy to exaggerate the service done by writing a single book as compared with that done by increasing the general intelligence through the effective discharge of educational duties.[83]

Goldwin Smith's hostility to the 'endowment of research' was certainly stimulated by the publication in 1868 of Mark Pattison's *Suggestions on Academical Organization*. This work criticized severely the unscholarly teaching of philosophy in Oxford. 'Its highest outcome', Pattison complained, 'is the "able editor," who, under protection of the anonymous press, instructs the public upon all that concerns their highest interests, with a dogmatism and assurance proportioned to his utter ignorance of the subject he is assuming to teach. In the schools of Oxford is now taught in perfection the art of writing "leading articles." '[84] This was almost certainly the

---

[82] *The Reorganization of the University of Oxford* (Oxford, 1868), 1.
[83] Ibid. 2–3.
[84] *Suggestions on Academical Organization* (Edinburgh, 1868), 294–5. Cited in Diderick Roll-Hanson, *The Academy 1869–1879, Victorian Intellectuals in Revolt* (Copenhagen, 1957), 46. Pattison repeats this argument later in his article, 'Philosophy at Oxford', *Mind*, i (Jan. 1876), 82–97.

statement that led Smith to his denunciation of the 'scientific' idea of education.

> Severe strictures have been recently passed on the School of Moral Philosophy as too showy, ambitious, and vaguely comprehensive. The authors of these strictures, however, seem to have in view some intensely scientific and coldly critical idea of education, the superiority of which, I venture to think, is not established; . . . I can only say of the Philosophy School that it has produced many men able in the estimation not only of philosophers but of statesmen; and if a portion of the talent which it has trained has been taken up by the public journals, this is deplorable and discreditable to the University only on the theory that we are a community of intellectual monks, to whom it is degrading and contaminating to do anything in the world without.[85]

The traditional platitudes which had served to recommend the union of teaching and research clearly were dissolving under the pressure of conflicts between the proponents of rival ideals of academic life. Goldwin Smith, who had fought for 'reform' and suffered ostracism in Oxford for his 'progressive' views, was understandably bitter to find himself portrayed by a group of university reformers as a villain who had destroyed Oxford as a place for study and had resurrected it as a mere 'examining machine' and 'boarding-school for adults'.

Even those reformers of the 1850s whose views ought to have been more acceptable to the 'endowment of research' party were often forgotten in their general repugnance for the 'reforms' of this period. H. H. Vaughan wrote in 1872 from his retirement in Wales to Mark Pattison protesting against the insufficient tribute paid by Pattison in a public address to Vaughan's earlier efforts to establish a research-orientated professoriate in Oxford.[86] Pattison replied politely acknowledging Vaughan's contribution and excusing his failure to mention it since 'time did not permit of my reading the extract [from Vaughan's evidence submitted to the Royal Commission] I had prepared'.[87] Although Pattison assured

---

[85] *The Reorganization of the University of Oxford,* 27.
[86] Cited in E. G. W. Bill, *University Reform in Nineteenth-Century Oxford: A Study of Henry Halford Vaughan 1811–1885* (Oxford, 1973), 148–9.
[87] Ibid. 149.

Vaughan that 'if you ever looked at my book on Academical Organization you would see that I refer to your pamphlet *Oxford Reform*',[88] he certainly did not give Vaughan's theories a very prominent place in that work, nor did he ever rectify this neglect in his later writings. Vaughan's failure to complete the ambitious study of 'the causes of man's moral nature' undoubtedly contributed also to the neglect of his writings in favour of research ideals.[89] Similarly, L. R. Farnell, a young protégé of the 'endowment of research' party, described Bonamy Price as one of the 'morbid products' of 'the conversational art'. Price was another enthusiast for research ideals whose own scholarly writing had never matched his protestations. Farnell remarked contemptuously, after dining in college with Price, that his conversation was 'like a gentle brook that flowed on for ever and went on rippling, even though a mountain fell in it'.[90]

Although Mark Pattison had always disapproved of the 'professorial system' as a form of education,[91] the adoption of professorial modes of lecturing by the combined lecturers[92] probably served to discredit this theory of university reform more effectively with the 'endowment of research' party as a whole. Their experience of the little benefit to the cause of learning which had been obtained either from the moderate expansion in the professoriate since 1854 or from the requirement that at least six members of the Hebdomadal Council be professors also convinced many that the 'professorial system' had been tried already and had been proved a failure. Although Vaughan and the other supporters of a scholarly ideal of the 'professorial system' had gone farthest toward affirming that research ought to be the highest duty of the university professor, by the late 1860s, the emerging 'endowment of research' party was unwilling to claim intellectual kinship with these earlier reformers.

This was true despite the fact that, initially, the advocates

---

[88] Loc. cit.

[89] For an account of Vaughan's abortive work, see ibid. 239–47.

[90] *An Oxonian Looks Back* (London, 1934), 113.

[91] See Pattison's evidence submitted to the royal commissioners, in *Oxford Univ. Comm.* (1852), Evidence, 45–8.

[92] See above, Ch. II, pp. 84–5

of the 'endowment of research' did not go much beyond these earlier reformers in demanding the recognition of the advancement of learning as an important obligation of the university. In 1868 Mark Pattison still seemed to view teaching as a lowly function only when divorced from advanced study and active scholarly work. 'We have known no higher level of knowledge than so much as sufficed for teaching', he argued. 'Hence, education among us has sunk into a trade, and like trading sophists, we have not cared to keep on hand a larger stock than we could dispose of in the season.'[93] The implication was that teaching only became a 'trade' when knowledge was not cultivated by the teacher beyond that which was needed to prepare students for examinations. This implication was supported by Pattison's conception of the academic profession at this stage in his thought about university reform. 'It is a principle . . . held in view throughout these suggestions, to erect teaching and learning, inseparably united, into a life-profession . . . A new profession . . . which on its theoretical side has some specific branch of science for its matter, and on its practical side has teaching for its business, being erected, the candidate for its rewards and honours must see before him at least as good a prospect as if he were entering one of the old professions or any branch of the public service.'[94] Although the reference to teaching as the 'practical' and 'businesss' aspect and research as the 'theoretical' aspect of the 'new profession' made an invidious distinction between the two functions, the conclusion was still that they must be 'inseparably united'.

By 1876, however, Pattison and other members of the 'endowment of research' party were more willing to see the functions of teaching and research separated. 'We are beginning to see, that science and letters are a vocation, that they have a value in themselves and. are not merely useful as teaching material . . . that universities have other functions than that of educating youth', Pattison asserted in 1876.[95] In

---

[93] *Suggestions on Academical Organization* (Edinburgh, 1868), 167.
[94] Ibid. 204–5. On this subject see also V. H. H. Green, *Oxford Common Room* (London, 1957) and John Sparrow, *Mark Pattison and the Idea of a University* (Cambridge, 1967), esp. chs. iii and iv.
[95] 'Review of the Situation', in *Essays on the Endowment of Research* (London, 1876), 22.

a sense this view had been dictated by his earlier insistence
that this 'new profession' not only match the older professions
in 'rewards and honours' but also that it match their formal
characteristics as well; '. . . in order to make the profession of
learning and science a profession, it must be organized on the
same footing as any other profession'.[96] In both Law and
Medicine, the 'business' and the 'theoretical' aspects had long
been separated into the distinct careers of solicitor and
apothecary and the distinct professions of barrister and
physician.[97] Only the latter were considered proper models
for academics in Pattison's view since only they were high-
status, learned professions rather than mere 'businesses'. The
logic of this argument alone led to the view that the higher
and the lower aspects of this 'new profession' ought to be
separated as they were in its traditional models. Although
Pattison never fully developed this argument in his own
writings, there were some among the 'endowment of research'
party who were willing to carry their ideas to a more extreme
conclusion than their leader.[98] They argued that teaching
interfered with research by making it a mere 'hobby' rather
than a serious pursuit. Therefore, they ought to be separate
occupations entrusted to different types of people.[99] This
was an extreme view but it was clearly the direction in which
the advocates of the 'endowment of research' moved as
collegiate teaching and the examination system grew in
importance in 'reformed' Oxford.

[96] *Suggestions on Academical Organization,* 203-4.
[97] When surgeons began to discontinue mixing and selling drugs; i.e. when they
left off 'business', they gradually came to be recognized as a profession as well.
The son of one old-fashioned surgeon who refused to give up this practice implied
in his memoirs that status considerations were responsible for this 'change for the
worse'. He sarcastically noted that the younger surgeon has a 'disposition to
regard the multifarious services of the pharmacy as matters beneath his scientific
consideration, — as duties to be performed by a mere tradesman'. See John
Cordy Jeaffreson, *A Book of Recollections* (London, 1894), i. 23-6, citations
from pp. 24 and 25. George Eliot portrayed this attitude of the new professional
man more sympathetically in the character of Lydgate in *Middlemarch* (1872).
Lydgate is portrayed as a 'gentleman' of good birth who refused to sell medicine
because he considered it mercenary and degrading, thus arousing the ire of the
older practitioners.
[98] See below, pp. 138-9; also pp. 147-9.
[99] See Henry Clifton Sorby, 'Unencumbered Research: A Personal Experience',
in *Essays on the Endowment of Research,* 149-75.

By the mid-1870s, the advocates of the 'endowment of research' knew that the supporters of the 'tutorial profession' were their most powerful enemies in Oxford. They also knew quite accurately what this enemy wanted. The unsympathetic attitude of the 'endowment of research' party toward the tutors' grievances was expressed strongly by J. S. Cotton, a former fellow and lecturer of Queen's. Although Cotton had vacated his fellowship to marry after only three years in 1873, his brief residence had convinced him that the college tutors were a conscious interest group with plans directly contrary to his own:

... some of the residents of Oxford and Cambridge have begun to show signs of uneasiness. They commenced by making the notable discovery that despite the apparent bounty of *Alma Mater*, her own *alumni* are very poorly off. The substance of their complaint is, that while they bear the burden of teaching, the larger proportion of the endowments falls to alien hands. In short, the University affords them no career ... [T] his complaint forms the basis of a comprehensive scheme of reform which demands attention. The present generation of residents have hit upon a second discovery, equally valuable with the former, that fellowships were never intended to be carried away to London or elsewhere, and that non-resident fellows are a modern abuse. Teaching, they say, (and they are themselves tutors), is the proper function of a University, and therefore the one proper object of academical endowments; the incomes of the non-residents, which are now wasted will supply us with precisely the career that we need.[100]

These remarks illustrate strikingly Cotton's understanding of the revolution which had occurred since 1854: the growing consciousness of common interest among the college tutors, their desire for life-careers in Oxford, their increasing animosity toward prize fellowships, their emphasis on the primary importance of educational work. Cotton's intention was clearly to discredit the tutors as merely another self-seeking group crying out for a share of the university's rich endowment fund. He remarked condescendingly that the tutors' argument 'contains, no doubt, elements of truth, which have been worked up into a large grievance by that peculiar spirit of discontent which seems to be characteristic

[100] 'The Intentions of the Founders of Fellowships', in *Essays on the Endowment of Research*, 34-5.

of all confined societies'.[101]   For Cotton, prize fellowships
and tutorial fellowships were equally misuses of endowment
income. 'Sinecure fellows and college tutors may be both
alike historical abuses and economical blunders, but', he
noted sarcastically, 'they may yet have their place in a country
which can afford to indulge its taste for anomalies.'[102]

Cotton concluded that both these uses for college fellowships were contrary to 'founders' wills' and to economic law
as well. He argued that 'the general intention of the founders
of colleges was not to endow university teachers, any more
than to endow barristers, or schoolmasters, or clergymen'.[103]
It was of greater importance, however, that this use for
endowment income, especially to augment the salaries of
college tutors, was wrong-headed from the standpoint of
classical economic theory.

> [T]he proposed scheme to augment from fellowships the incomes of
> college tutors has special dangers of its own. From the point of view
> of political economy, it is just as mischievous as the creation of sine-
> cures. And in practical working, it would be expanded to far greater
> abuses. The unendowed teachers of the kingdom would have just
> ground for complaint that a few persons, arbitrarily selected, not pre-
> suming to the character of professors; but merely preparing candidates
> for examination, should be thus artificially protected against all fear
> of competition.[104]

This argument was significant because its case against tutorial
fellowships on the basis of classical economic theory and its
evident contempt for 'merely preparing candidates for examination' were both to become important themes in the
writings of the advocates of the 'endowment of research'.

Cotton concluded that the support of scholars was the
only use for collegiate endowment income which was sanctioned by both founders' wills and enlightened conceptions
of the proper functions of the university. By freeing some of
them from the degrading task of ordinary teaching, the
universities of England might again fulfil their obligations
toward the advancement of knowledge.

[101] Ibid. 34.   [102] Ibid. 62.
[103] Ibid. 36.   [104] Ibid. 36–7.

The money should be devoted to study, and to study alone; enforced as a duty, and protected by adequate guarantees, but unencumbered by any obligation to impart common instruction. By this one bold and necessary reform the Universities of Oxford and Cambridge may once again pick up the torch of intellectual progress, which has for a while fallen from their hands; and at the same time England, in fulfilling the designs of the great patrons of learning, may regain her place among the nations as the chosen home of literary erudition and scientific inquiry.[105]

E. The 'Endowment of Research' vs. The Examination System

One important aspect of the 'endowment of research' party's position and one of its chief indirect methods of attacking the 'tutorial profession', was to criticize the proliferation of examinations in post-1854 Oxford. They denounced the examination system as hostile to the spirit of true learning, both for the student and for the teacher. Although there had been much criticism previously of the new examinations established in 1850, the nature of the complaints altered drastically in the 1870s. Earlier critics had concentrated on the unfairness to students of the new system, while the new critics emphasized its unfairness to the teachers, especially to those who wished to have time for research and writing. The questioning of the role of examinations became one of the fundamental methods whereby the advocates of the 'endowment of research' defined their position *vis-à-vis* the proponents of the 'tutorial profession'. Even those college tutors who were discontented with the erosion of their learned status and sympathetic to the more moderate claims of the 'endowment of research' party had to perceive this new complaint as an attack on themselves since the increasing difficulty of the examination system had been the chief vehicle for the tutors growing importance in Oxford.

Under the system established in 1850, all students, both candidates for honours and passmen, were required to take four separate examinations to graduate BA. There were two examinations in the elements of Latin and Greek ('Responsions' and 'Moderations'), the final school of *Literae*

[105] Ibid. 63.

Humaniores, and one other final school from among those in Mathematics, Natural Science, or Law and Modern History. This was an increase of one final school over the pre-1850 system. The requirement to take an extra examination was attacked as an unfair burden on students.[106] Some were critical of the additional residence and consequent increased cost of obtaining a degree.[107] Others argued that the new system did not allow the student sufficient time to prepare for the second final school.[108] This complaint was made most vigorously by supporters of the primacy of *Literae Humaniores* who pleaded the hardship of the first-class classicist who might be 'plucked' in his second school. However, this same grievance was also voiced by proponents of the newer schools who considered the existing arrangements degrading to their subjects.[109] This issue created an unlikely alliance between these disparate malcontents to press for the abolition of the requirement to take two final schools.[110]

These complaints had a special urgency in the 1850s since matriculations were declining throughout this decade.[111] It was felt that the proliferation of examinations was leading students to prefer Cambridge to Oxford.[112] At Cambridge, the new examination system established in 1848 allowed an honours candidate to take only one 'tripos' or final school.[113] All students previously had been required to do mathematics before attempting any of the others. The Cambridge system since 1848 also provided a separate syllabus for passmen with only one final examination. The problem became especially

---

[106] [Montagu Burrows,] *Is Educational Reform Required in Oxford and What?* (Oxford, 1859). I owe this identification to Ward, 390 n. 54.

[107] See W. W. Shirley, *Ought our Honours to be Given Without Limit of Age* (Oxford, 1865).

[108] See J. P. Tweed, *The Least Change Which Suffices, Best* (Oxford, 1859).

[109] See Ward, 221. Ward also noted that the demand for 'full equality of the schools' was advanced by 'the more resolute liberals led by Goldwin Smith and supported by the scientists' (p. 222).

[110] A memorial to the Hebdomadal Council advocating this course in 1862 was signed by eight-two members of Congregation, mostly tutors and professors. See Bodl. G. A. Oxon. c. 78 (341), cited in Ward, 221.

[111] See Stone, Table IA, p. 91.

[112] See above, pamphlets by Tweed and Shirley, nn. 107-8.

[113] For an account of the Cambridge examination statutes of 1848, see D. A. Winstanley, *Early Victorian Cambridge* (Cambridge, 1940), 207-13.

acute after 1859 when Cambridge increased its comparative advantage by reducing the number of terms of residence necessary before a student could take a degree.[114]

This grievance against the examination system was eliminated gradually in the 1860s owing to the pressures created by falling enrolments, Cambridge's example, and the complaints of many academic residents against the unfairness of the Oxford system to students. In 1865, after several years of heated debate, honours candidates were allowed to delete the second final school. It was not until 1871, however, that a similar privilege was extended to the majority of Oxford students who were passmen. At this time, Oxford also followed Cambridge's example by establishing a single, comprehensive pass school to replace the previous 'pass' and 'class' options for each final school. It was probably to some degree because of the elimination of these complaints that matriculations began to rise again in the 1860s and continued to rise through the 1870s.[115] The type of criticism of the examination system that came to characterize Oxford in the 1870s was markedly different. While reform suggestions previously had been limited and melioristic in intention, the critics of the 1870s, motivated by the desire for the 'endowment of research' and by hostility to the 'tutorial profession', began to suggest more radical and destructive measures of reform. It was argued that the obsession with the honours examinations since 1854 had produced an atmosphere hostile to the spirit of learning itself.

This new type of criticism was expressed strongly by A. H. Sayce of Queen's, who argued that the examination system at Oxford encouraged a vicious process of cramming. It succeeded only in effectively stifling all genuine love of learning as well as the desire to pursue knowledge for its own sake.

The extinction of disinterested study is a necessary consequence of the encouragement of cram . . . The grown man is what he has been taught to be, and out of cram may come many pages of examination answers, or even a fellowship, but not original research and the love of knowledge

[114] This point was made in Ward, 220. Also see D. A. Winstanley, *Later Victorian Cambridge* (Cambridge, 1947), 147–8.

[115] In fact enrolments continued to rise through the early twentieth century. See Stone, Table IA, p. 91.

for its own sake. The specialist at the universities finds himself a marked man, with a wisp of hay upon his horns; he is looked upon with mingled feelings of suspicion and pity, or else regarded as aiming at a sinecure professorship. That there can be any knowledge outside the curriculum of the university, or if there is that it is of any value, is seldom dreamed of . . . The specialist who pleads on behalf of another kind of learning is considered a fanatic, out of harmony with the spirit of our English universities, and unappreciative of their merits. 'We don't want original researchers,' I have not infrequently heard it said, 'but good all-round men,' that is to say, the best specimens of the crammer who have a smattering of many things but know nothing well. But how can it be otherwise? Men whose whole attention has been given to discovering what will pay in the schools are not likely, when they have gained their reward and a sinecure annuity, to devote themselves to disinterested study.[116]

Although Sayce criticized the particular Oxford honours examinations as geared to reward those who had succeeded in cramming the largest quantity of second-hand theories, he did not believe that any melioristic changes in the system could alleviate the problem. For Sayce, who had studied briefly at Leipzig,[117] more fundamental changes were needed if Oxford was ever to see 'the crowded lecture-rooms and eager students of a German university'.[118]

Although Sayce disliked the effects of the examination system on students, his greatest concern was its influence on the teachers. 'It is painful to see men wasting their strength and talents which might otherwise have increased the knowledge of mankind, or helped forward the civilization of posterity, over piles of examination-papers, confessing that only the prospect of pay, and the necessity of a livelihood, would have induced them to undertake the dreary task.'[119] His blunt conclusion was that 'competitive examinations and original research are incompatible terms'.[120] Sayce's solution simply was to abolish the honours schools entirely. He proposed, instead, that all students take the pass examinations which he considered a wholesome introduction to university studies. The value of this type of examination

---

[116] 'The Results of the Examination System at Oxford', in *Fortnight. Rev.* (June 1875) reprinted in *Essays on the Endowment of Research*, 137–9.

[117] See A. H. Sayce, *Reminiscences* (London, 1923), 56–7.

[118] 'The Results of the Examination System', in *Essays on the Endowment of Research*, 133.   [119] Ibid. 145.   [120] Ibid. 139.

would also be enhanced if all students were required to take it much sooner than was often the case in 1875. In this way the majority could leave to begin their professional education at a more reasonable age and the university would be left to students and scholars who had a genuine love for the advancement of learning.

Although Sayce's position was, admittedly, an extreme view, there were many academic residents who began in the 1870s to share his concern. Sayce's attitude hardly surpassed the bitterness of Mark Pattison, who stated flatly that the examination system was 'an instrument of mere torture which has made education impossible and crushed the very desire of learning'.[121] It was not, however, only the extreme members of the 'endowment of research' party who disapproved of the dominance of examinations in the life of the university. James Bryce, who was only a moderate supporter of the party, also came to admit, in a more restrained form, the same essential criticisms. When the second university commission was appointed in 1876, he wrote that its purpose would be 'qualifying . . . [Oxford] to discharge that duty of furthering science and learning which it has forgotten in the restless hurry of examinations'.[122]

Although the attack on the examination system by the 'endowment of research' party clearly displayed a strong animus against the college tutors, there were many of them whose discontent with their position as mere 'teaching drudges' had made them sympathetic to the more moderate expressions of the party's viewpoint. These reformers had a difficult task since any attack on the basic rationale of competitive examinations was perceived in Oxford as an attempt to denigrate the work of the tutors. In a specific reply to the criticisms of the examination system made by 'Mr Pattison and Mr Sayce', Thomas Fowler of Lincoln, a moderate supporters of the 'endowment of research', dealt skilfully with this difficulty. He specifically commended the college tutors and, implicitly, criticized Pattison and Sayce

---

[121] *Memoirs* (London, 1885), 303.
[122] 'A Few Words on the Oxford University Bill', *Fortnight. Rev.*, New Series, xix, no. 113 (1876), 772.

for their hostility. Fowler wrote feelingly of

. . . the zeal and sense of duty which, in recent times, have inspired successive generations of tutors, impelling them to sacrifice their time, and in many cases, their prospects to the interests of their pupils. The college tutor, in fact, some years ago, voluntarily superadded the functions of the private tutor [coach] to his own. This may have been a mistaken course, and mistaken in the tutor's own interests it undoubtedly was, but at least it demands sympathy and admiration, even though, in some respects, the consequences may have been of doubtful service to learning and education.[123]

Fowler argued that the examination system, not the tutors, had robbed Oxford of its role as a home for the advancement of knowledge. The college tutor was exonerated from responsibility for this unfortunate situation since 'when the preponderating motive in the mind of the teacher is, and, for the nature of the circumstances must be, the success of his pupils in the class-lists, as the phrase sometimes runs, "getting classes for the college," we can hardly expect much enthusiasm for learning, or any very exalted ideal of education.'[124] Fowler's conclusion was 'that the Oxford tutor has become the slave of the examinations, that he has little time for his own studies and, as a natural result, that his intellectual stock of facts and ideas is often (though to this there are many conspicuous exceptions) not much greater than that which he imparts to his pupils'.[125]

The solution to the problem, according to Fowler, was not the total destruction of honours examinations. He advocated, instead, specific reforms which would make the examinations less susceptible to 'cramming'. He also argued that college fellowships, which previously had been given merely for success in the final schools, ought in the future to be awarded largely on the basis of the quality of research work submitted for this purpose. The only other reform which Fowler considered necessary to make Oxford a centre for both education and learning was 'the provision of a career for the teachers, which shall enable them to regard Oxford as their

[123] 'On Examinations', *Fortnight. Rev.*, New Series, xix, no. 111 (1876), 428.
[124] Ibid. 429.　　　　　　　　　　　　　　　　　　　[125] Ibid. 428.

permanent home'. Fowler concluded that, if these reforms were made, they would 'create . . . [in Oxford] an asylum for education, literature and science, of which the nation, in future years, will have no occasion to be ashamed'.[126]

It was unlikely however, that despite Fowler's more diplomatic tone, his substantive position would be acceptable to most college tutors as an account of their role in the university. His pity for the tutor as a 'slave of the examination system' whose 'intellectual stock . . . is often . . . not much greater than that which he imparts to his pupils' was dangerously close to being merely a less insulting version of Pattison's denunciation of the tutors as 'trading sophists . . . [who] have not cared to keep on hand a larger stock [of knowledge] than could [be] dispose[d] of in the season'.[127] Although Fowler clearly hoped that by avoiding extreme statements the advocates of the 'tutorial profession' and the 'endowment of research' party could present a united front to the new university commission, their basic disagreements about the purposes of the university and the nature of academic life made unified action impossible.

F. An Impasse: The 'Endowment of Research' vs. the 'Endowment of Teaching'

Among the more uncompromising advocates of the 'endowment of research', a critical point was to establish as a basic principle of university reform that endowment income ought not to be used to subsidize education. This was an essential step in their argument that this income should be devoted to the support of scholarly research. The 'endowment of research' party argued that it was both practically feasible and theoretically desirable for college tutors to be paid exclusively through students' fees. This argument, which was made largely on the basis of classical economic theory, was a prominent aspect of their comprehensive attack on the ascendancy of the college tutors. Although various compromises were suggested, none could have resolved the issues dividing these rivals. Another university commission came to be viewed as

---

[126] Ibid. 429.   [127] *Suggestions on Academical Organization*, 167.

the only method of overcoming the impasse which had been reached by the 1870s.

The argument against the 'endowment of teaching' from the standpoint of classical economic theory was made most explicitly by Charles Appleton of St. John's, the editor of *The Academy*. In a closely reasoned article in 1875,[128] Appleton argued by analogy to Adam Smith's *Wealth of Nations*, against the principle of tutorial fellowships. He insisted that education was a commodity from which the possessor derived large economic rewards, either directly through the learning of a specific skill or more generally through the better opinion held by society of the abilities of a well-educated person. In either case, from a purely economic point of view, investment in education was a worthwhile expenditure. Therefore, Appleton asserted that even if there were no endowments for education, sufficient demand still would exist to support the full economic cost of educational institutions and teachers. He concluded that endowments employed for education were a wasteful al-location of capital which could better be used for more productive and necessary purposes. In fact, they were worse than merely wasteful in the case of tutorial fellowships since, like any other use of subsidies in an otherwise free market, their major effect was artificially to preserve inef-ficient producers.

Appleton did make a weak attempt to engage the interests of the tutors in his plan for the elimination of educational endowments. 'What, then, would be the effect of withdrawing the old endowments of study and research which during the decay of learning have generally been appropriated to edu-cation?' he asked rhetorically.

Obviously this. The wages of the university teacher would at once rise to the level to which they are now brought by endowments; and we have shown that it is the *pecuniary* interest of the parent to pay this advance in the price. But the wages of the most eminent instructors would rise far above this level, owing to the same causes which raise the emoluments in the higher grades of any other profession . . . The

[128] 'The Economical Character of Subsidies to Education', *Theological Review* (1 Jan. 1875), reprinted in *Essays on the Endowment of Research*, 64–85.

employment of the academical teacher would become *a recognized profession,* able to compete with other liberal professions; able to attract and, what is impossible now, to *retain* permanently its fair share of the best minds of the country.[129]

This grand prospect would be unlikely to appeal greatly to the college tutor. The maintenance of the fellowship system was considered crucial for the establishment of an academic profession which would satisfy their aspirations. As one former tutor protested in reply to an argument similar to Appleton's advanced by Mark Pattison, 'Their [the college tutor's] income already depends largely on fees. But to lose their fellowships and "to be paid wholly out of fees, or if necessary, to have a small stipend in aid of fees" [quoted from Pattison's *Suggestions on Academical Organization* (1868)] would be for them a step down toward the position now occupied by private tutors [coaches].'[130] Aside from status considerations, the material prospects of the coach, in Oxford at least,[131] were not such as would lead the college tutor to desire to exchange places with him. As Robert Lowe, who had worked as a coach in Oxford, had written, 'There is nothing more hopeless than the career of a private tutor [coach] at present. He has nothing to look forward to from his occupation but endless labour, leading to no result; and with much more labour and higher attainments is not so well paid as a country schoolmaster.'[132] Few college tutors would have been as confident as Appleton that if endowments for collegiate teachers were removed, Adam Smith's dictum would be proved correct and rates of pay would rise.[133]

Appleton also used economic theory to answer the further question of what should be done with the endowment income of the colleges, arguing that the endowment of research was

---

[129] Ibid. 76-7.

[130] Charles Stuart Parker, *Academical Endowments* (London, 1875), 11.

[131] The situation was quite different in Cambridge. Perhaps because the 'tripos' which listed 'wranglers' in order of merit was more competitive than the Oxford system in which Firsts were listed alphabetically, the most successful Cambridge coaches were said to earn large incomes, albeit for very long hours of work. See D. A. Winstanley, *Early Victorian Cambridge* (Cambridge, 1940), 411-12. [132] *Oxford Univ. Comm.* (1852), Evidence, 13.

[133] Adam Smith's argument, in *Wealth of Nations*, Bk. I, ch. 10, was cited extensively and approvingly by J. S. Mill in his popular text, *The Principles of Political Economy* (London, 1848), Bk. I, ch. 14.

both justified and necessary on economic grounds.[134] He noted that the traditional modes of supporting the 'production' of knowledge in England had been to employ scholars either as clergymen, as Church dignitaries, as teachers in the universities, or as researchers for commercial enterprises. Appleton argued that the first three of these methods had proved increasingly unsatisfactory as these institutions had come to take their pastoral, administrative, and educational duties more seriously. The fourth method had the disadvantages that it would only be relevant to a limited range of scientific research and the utilitarian spirit inescapable in a commercial enterprise would unquestionably interfere with the disinterested pursuit of knowledge. Although some scholars were fortunate enough to possess independent means, this mode of support could not hope to compete with the effect of regular institutions, such as the research institutes of Germany and France.

Appleton argued that research differed from other 'commodities' since it was not capable of supporting itself even though it was of economic value to society. In order to maintain the consistency of his purely 'economic' viewpoint, Appleton was forced to use a rather tortuous mode of argument. The most obvious argument for the economic productivity of research, its role in stimulating invention and applied technology, was unsatisfactory for his purpose since it could justify only a very limited range of research, primarily in the natural and physical sciences. Appleton surmounted this difficulty by defining 'economic' in its broadest possible sense as concerning the production of 'goods' other than only material ones, including 'the Good' itself. Research was 'economically productive', therefore, because it was conducive to the 'enjoyment' of mankind.

Finally, Appleton had to confront the problem of why, if research was conducive to the 'enjoyment' of mankind, people were not willing to pay enough to support it. He argued that this situation was the result of the peculiarities of research as a 'commodity'. The sale of books embodying research could not support the scholars who had written

---

[134] 'The Endowment of Research a Productive Form of Expenditure', *Fortnight. Rev.* (Oct. 1874), reprinted in *Essays on the Endowment of Research*, 86–123.

them because these books often required many years of work;
yet, they could be bought for comparatively small sums and
only few people would be willing to buy them. The difficulty
was that, although research contributed to the 'enjoyment'
of mankind, 'buyers' would find it necessary to labour themselves to 'enjoy' research while 'sellers' could not lose their
product by selling it. Appleton concluded that since indirect
means of supporting research had proved ineffective and
because research, unlike education, was not a 'commodity'
which could be left to the operation of the free market, the
'endowment of research' was both justified and essential on
economic grounds.

Appleton's economic argument was not received with
much enthusiasm outside the 'endowment of research' party.
His views were attacked by *The Times* when his articles were
published.[135] Although they received a good deal of publicity
in the battle of letters which ensued, little of this public
notice was favourable.[136] One historian has concluded that
'Appleton did not get much credit for his ventures into political economy. His arguments were too doctrinaire for the
English taste.'[137] None the less, Appleton's work was of great
importance because it placed the cause of the 'endowment
of research' insistently before the public. His position was
notable also as the most extreme attempt to harmonize the
goals of his party with the dictates of classical economic
theory, 'the master science of the age', as D. P. Chase had
called it.[138]

The ideas of the 'endowment of research' party also aroused
much resentment in Oxford. The researcher's 'scientific'
notions of the proper functions of universities were rejected.
Their admiration for foreign, especially German, scholarship

[135] 28 Dec. 1874, p. 7, cols. 4-6.
[136] Appleton replied in *The Times*, 31 Dec. 1874, p. 11, cols. 2-3. He was also
attacked in a letter to *The Times* by J. G. Greenwood of Owen's College, Manchester, since Appleton had previously criticized this institution as an example of
a college catering only to the lowest form of commercial education because it had
no endowments to protect it from this fate. Greenwood's letter was printed on
6 Jan. 1875 (p. 7, col. 4) and Appleton replied on 13 Jan. 1875 (p. 5, cols. 5-6).
[137] Diderik Roll-Hanson, *The Academy, 1869-1879, Victorian Intellectuals in
Revolt* (Copenhagen, 1957), 82.
[138] *The Voluntary System Applied to Academical Instruction* (Oxford, 1859), 9.

was resented. The party's demands were viewed as simply the effect of the presumption and greed of a small clique. C. L. Dodgson gave this attitude an enduring expression in 'Fame's Penny Trumpet', written in 1876, and 'affectionately dedicated to all "original researchers" who pant for "endowment".' The strongest animosity had replaced the light wit which generally characterized Dodgson's verse.

> Blow, blow your trumpets till they crack,
> Ye little men of little souls! . . .
> Fill all the aire with hungry wails —
> 'Reward us, ere we think or write!
> Without your Gold mere Knowledge fails
> To sate the swinish appetite! . . .
> Go, throng each other's drawing rooms,
> Ye idols of a petty clique:
> Strut your brief hour in borrowed plumes
> And make your penny-trumpet squeek:
> Deck your dull talk with pilfered shreds
> Of learning from a nobler time,
> And oil each other's little heads
> With mutual Flattery's golden slime:[139]

In a somewhat lighter vein, Dodgson ridiculed the admiration which the 'endowment of research' party often expressed for German scholarship. In *The Vision of the Three T's*, written in 1873, a professor asserts that 'nowadays, all that is good comes from the German. Ask our men of science: they will tell you that any German book must needs surpass any English book. Aye, and even an English book, worth naught in its native dress, shall become, when rendered into German, a valuable contribution to Science.'[140]

---

[139] Reprinted in *The Complete Works of the Lewis Carroll* (London, 1939), 807–8.

[140] Ibid. 1040. A 'Sinecure Fellow' expressed a similar distaste for German scholarship with greater seriousness. 'What a learned and methodical person writes is sure to be useful, and such a person, if industrious, can write a great deal, if he will only write upon the German conditions,' he argued, 'if he will consent to be often trite and often rash, to conceive many things crudely and to express most things heavily, to say much that the reader would have said for himself, and sometimes, rather than say nothing, resign himself to say what is unmeaning.' In

The personal characters and scholarly attainments of the leaders of the 'endowment of research' party were also open to question, even by those with considerable sympathy for their goals. Mandell Creighton, for example,[141] wrote in 1872 to his friend J. R. Thursfield of Jesus, who was studying in Germany,

> I fear . . . our present University reforms in the interest of research don't make out a very good case in the eyes of the ordinary Briton in favour of research. Mark Pattison is undoubtedly a researcher, so are we all; but one Essay and Review and one edition of Pope's 'Essay on Man' scarcely justify to the Philistine a large endowment; nor can it be urged that abject poverty and hard work have prevented production . . . I could wish the academic cause were maintained by some men who had borne more of the burden and heat of the day. However, we must make the best of it, and protest as loudly as we can for the interests of learning.[142]

Creighton's reservations were common to many college tutors at this time. Although they wished to re-establish their learned status, they were well aware of the dangers of too close commitment to the position of the 'endowment of research' party.

This was the situation which led in the 1870s to the uneasy alliance between the advocates of the 'tutorial profession' and the 'endowment of research' for the purposes of demanding a second university commission. J. E. Thorold Rogers, a former Professor of Political Economy and a belligerent critic of the college tutors' power over the examination system, expressed his distaste for this alliance when he noted in 1879 that 'the peculiar function, it seems, of the new Commission', the re-distribution of the colleges' endowment income, 'is hailed with suspicious eagerness by most of those who are at present engaged in college work'.[143] Rogers' fear was that the college tutors and the advocates of the 'endowment of

---

contrast, 'few Oxford men would write on a subject on which they could not write better'. See 'Strike, But Hear', *Macmillan's Mag.* xxv, no. 148 (1872), 306.

[141] For Creighton's basic sympathy with the goals of the party, see his article, 'The Endowment of Research', *Macmillan's Mag.* xxxiv (June 1876), 186-92.

[142] *Life and Letters of Mandell Creighton*, i. 135.

[143] 'Reforms in the University of Oxford', *Brit. Quart. Rev.* lxx, no. 139 (1879), 90.

research' would be able to use the commission to divide the spoils quietly among themselves, while ignoring the crucial issue of undue tutorial influence over the examination system. Although Rogers was correct in predicting that his favourite issue would be of little interest to the Commission,[144] he was wrong in assuming that the redistribution of endowment income between the supporters of the 'tutorial profession' and the 'endowment of research' would be an amicable process.

The impossibility of a quiet division of the spoils can be demonstrated through an analysis of one compromise plan which attempted to satisfy the aspirations of both college tutors and the 'endowment of research' party while at the same time defending prize fellowships and financing 'university extension' outside Oxford as well. The plan was proposed in 1875 by C. S. Parker, an MP who had been a fellow and tutor of University College.[145] Parker began by defending the prize fellows, especially against the attacks of the 'endowment of research' party. 'To underrate the influence for good that such university men have in their professions, in public life, through the press, and not least in connecting the universities and colleges to the outer world', Parker argued, 'may be to take a narrow and one-sided view even of the interests of learning.'[146] He conceded, however, that the system as it existed was 'too lavish'. Parker concluded that an equitable compromise would be to reduce the number of fellowships from 400 to 200. He estimated correctly that about 100 of them were needed for college tutors,[147] while the other 100 might continue to serve as prizes. Parker also suggested that the celibacy restriction be abolished. Tutorial fellowships would be held for life instead and prize fellowships would be tenable for seven or, perhaps, ten years.[148]

According to Parker's plan, the endowment income freed

---

[144] In 1889–90, Rogers was still complaining of this same problem. See 'Oxford Professors and Oxford Tutors', *Contemp. Rev.* lvi (Dec. 1889), 926–36. This argument drew an angry reply from W. L. Courtney of New College, in 'Oxford Tutors and their Professorial Critic', *Fortnight. Rev.*, New Series, no. 278 (Feb. 1890), 294–6. Rogers replied in 'The Oxford History Examiners', *Contemp. Rev.* lvii (Mar. 1890), 454–6.

[145] *Academical Endowments* (London, 1875).   [146] Ibid. 12.

[147] There were, in fact, ninety-eight tutorial fellows in 1874. See below, Appendix 8, p. 292   [148] *Academical Endowments* (London, 1875), 12.

through these reforms would be used for two purposes, 'university extension' and the 'endowment of research'. Some would subsidize the salaries of professors in university colleges to be established in other cities in England. Each professor would receive the value of one fellowship. The city would be required to augment this salary and to provide all necessary facilities for teaching. The 'endowment of research' would be provided by the establishment in Oxford of additional professorships and readerships at salaries of £1,000 p.a. and £400 p.a. respectively. The primary qualification for these positions would be scholarly achievement and research would be their major duty. Parker suggested that Oxford could usefully fill about twenty-five positions of this type immediately, although he expected that eventually double this number might be established.

Due to its comprehensiveness, Parker's plan was a rather skilful compromise. It provided some relief for all malcontents while dealing gently with vested interests. College tutors would be allowed to marry and the advocates of the 'endowment of research' would be provided with additional funds. Prize fellowships were not to be eliminated entirely and some income even remained to satisfy the demands for 'university extension' to 'populous towns'. However, the virtues of Parker's plan only serve to emphasize the impossibility of compromise at this time.

The concessions to the prize fellows certainly would fail to win their favour. As Archbishop Whately had pointed out in 1852, the value of the fellowship would be diminished immeasurably if tenure were reduced to a term of years.[149] Prize fellows also would view a reduction of their numbers by two-thirds as making an invidious distinction between themselves and the tutorial fellows. Defenders of the system hardly could be expected to accept gratefully this spoliation. However, simply because Parker's plan would provoke the antipathy of the prize fellows was no reason to suppose that it would be viewed with any more sympathy by either of the rival groups of malcontents.

The supporters of the 'endowment of research' would feel

---

[149] *Oxford Univ. Comm.* (1852), Evidence, 24–7.

that a sop was being thrown to them. Instead of having virtually all the endowment income of the colleges used to support research, they would gain only a limited expansion of the professoriate. Instead of totally eliminating prize fellowships, there would be ten to fourteen awarded per year. Instead of having the college tutors exclusively dependent on fees, tutorial fellowships tenable for life would become the accepted system in Oxford. This compromise clearly would be unacceptable to all but the most half-hearted supporters of the 'endowment of research'.

However, the college tutors would be no more enthusiastic about Parker's compromise than would the prize fellows or the 'endowment of research' party. They would gain one important improvement in their position by the elimination of the celibacy restriction, but they might well feel that the cost had been too high. The suppression of a large number of prize fellowships would have been viewed favourably by the college tutors; however, by Parker's plan, the tutors would not benefit. Instead of using the endowment income for augmenting their incomes or providing them with retiring pensions, it was to be devoted entirely to increasing the university professoriate and endowing professorships at colleges in other cities.

Finally, the impracticality of Parker's entire compromise solution was underscored by his insistence that all alterations in the uses of collegiate endowments had to be accomplished with the full consent of the colleges. 'It may be a matter of regret that some part of the superfluous wealth of the colleges does not belong to the universities', he wrote. 'But any proposal to treat the property of so many distinct corporations as a common fund would be legitimately, stoutly and successfully resisted. The most that is proposed in this direction, is, that the colleges should tax themselves, in some fair proportion to their wealth, to form a fund for university purposes. And this could only be done by general consent.'[150] If this plan had to wait for the 'general consent' of the colleges, clearly it would have no hopes for success.

---

[150] *Academical Endowments* (London, 1875), 16.

Neither the 'endowment of research' party nor the college tutors would have been willing to accept any compromise solution, even one as comprehensive and skilful as Parker's in 1875. Furthermore, the distribution of power in both the colleges and the university made the prospect of acceptable melioristic change completely visionary. In this situation, the advocates of the 'endowment of research' came to look upon the prospect of a second university commission as their only hope for attaining their goals. Although the events of 1850 to 1858 had taught them the danger of commissions, their experience of 'reformed' Oxford had convinced them that the tendency of the times, if unchecked by outside intervention, was toward increasing power for the college tutors and increasing concentration on the tasks of education and examination. They saw that eventually the endowment income of the colleges would be appropriated largely for these purposes. Since the college tutors had grievances as well with 'reformed' Oxford, they were willing to join in the call for a second university commission. They hoped those aspects of the 'endowment of research' programme which could be adapted to their needs could be appropriated, while those plans which would effect adversely their power or status could be foiled successfully.

Chapter IV

THE 1877 COMMISSION AND THE PLAN
FOR A 'TUTORIAL PROFESSION'

The Commission of 1877 was created amidst great expectations
by the advocates of the 'tutorial profession', the 'endowment
of research' party and even the Church party that each could
use this external visitation for the accomplishment of those
goals which they could not achieve internally. The proponents
of the 'tutorial profession' wished to eliminate the causes
of their grievances with the settlement of the 1850s. They
especially wanted collegiate teaching recognized as the primary
function of a new academic profession. The 'endowment of
research' party hoped that, through the Commission, they
could halt the tendency toward the appropriation of collegiate
external income for the 'endowment of teaching'. They
wanted research accepted as the primary function of the
university and a separate profession created for researchers.
The Church party derived confidence from the fact that the
Commission had been proposed by a Tory government
sympathetic to the interests of the Church. They wanted the
manifest trend of the previous twenty years toward the
diminution of clerical influence at Oxford halted and even
reversed.

The new Commission was the logical outgrowth of the
Cleveland Commission of 1871, which had condemned
implicitly the distribution of collegiate income. The fact that
the Privy Council had refused to approve any alterations in
collegiate statutes since 1871 clearly indicated that the
government had conceived of the financial inquiry as a
preliminary step to a general reform of the colleges and
university.[1] On 1 February 1875, Dean Liddell of Christ

---

[1] *Hansard's Parliamentary Debates*, 3rd Series, ccxvi, 1871, p. 10-13, cited in
Ward, 299. The following account of the calling of the 1877 Commission is based
on the more detailed narrative in Ward, 299-302.

Church convened a meeting representing a wide spectrum of university opinion which communicated to Lord Salisbury, the Chancellor of the University, its resolution that the government appoint a commission to 'direct its attention ... to the tenure of headships, fellowships and professorships; and the appropriation of funds at the disposal of the university and colleges, and also to the encouragement of learning and research in connexion with the university and colleges'.[2] Lord Salisbury replied favourably to this overture[3] and Benjamin Disraeli announced in Parliament before the end of February the official view that 'no government can exist which for a moment maintains that the consideration of University reform, and consequently legislation of some kind, will not form part of its duty.[4] Conflict in the cabinet over the provisions of the proposed legislation, however, delayed the introduction of the bill until March 1876, and further conflict in Parliament prevented its passage until 10 August 1877.[5]

In keeping with its origins, the primary function of the new Commission was to be the re-allocation of collegiate income. The preamble to the act stated that 'it is ... expedient that provision be made for enabling or requiring the Colleges in each University to contribute more largely out of their revenues to University purposes'.[6] For this reason, a set of commissioners was empowered to write entirely new statutes for each of the colleges and certain new statutes for the university as well. In preparation for this task, they were to hold extensive public hearings in which evidence could be taken from witnesses representing the entire spectrum of Oxford opinion. The commissioners were expected to seek compromises with collegiate interests in the framing of new statutes; but, in contrast to the Executive Commission of 1855-8, they were granted sufficient power to insist on the acceptance of their own views if the colleges proved intransigent.

[2] Christ Church Salisbury MSS, H. G. Liddell to Lord Salisbury, 1 Feb. 1875; *The Times*, 6 Feb. 1875, p. 9, cited in Ward, 299.
[3] Bodl. MS Acland d. 74 fos. 46-7, cited in Ward, 299.
[4] *The Times*, 20 Feb. 1875, p. 9, cited in Ward, 299.
[5] Liddon House MS Liddon Diary, 23 Mar. 1876; *Guardian*, 1876, 204, cited in Ward, 299, see also Ward, 200-2 for the passage of the bill through Parliament.
[6] 40 and 41 Vict. cap. 48, reprinted in Shadwell iv. 65.

It was obvious that in this task of statute-writing all three prominent interest groups could not be given everything they wanted since their more extreme desires were mutually exclusive. The commissioners chose to support primarily the ideals of the 'tutorial profession'. The college tutors were the single largest bloc among the academic residents. Their dedication to collegiate work and their achievements of the past half century in taking this task upon themselves entitled their views to careful consideration. The college tutors' emphasis on the importance of educational obligations was certain to appeal to a governmental body concerned with the social responsibilities of the university. The commissioners were emboldened by the sanguine financial predictions of the Cleveland Commission, however, to hope that they also could achieve much toward the reconciliation and satisfaction of other interests as well.

A. The Reform of the Fellowship System

The establishment of a comprehensive plan providing for the marriage of tutorial fellows was an issue of the first priority for the Commission. When the bill was still being debated in Parliament, it was already assumed that the commissioners would use their powers to relax the celibacy restriction in favour of certain college officials. In the debate in Commons of 4 June 1877, H. Fawcett, MP for Hackney, was reported as mentioning in passing that 'it was contemplated by the Bill that those who were doing educational work in the University and the Colleges, such as Tutors and Lecturers, were to continue to hold their Fellowships, even though they became married men'.[7] No member of the government rose to deny this assumption, nor did this issue occasion any further debate.

In Oxford also it was generally understood that the Commission would use its powers to permit married tutorial fellows. In 1879, before the commissioners had completed any of their new statutes, an astute university politician like the Master of Balliol was able to assure A. L. Smith, the college's young history lecturer, that he would be elected to a tutorial fellowship as soon as married men were permitted to

---

[7] *Hansard's Parl. Debates*, 3rd Series, ccxxxiv, 1877, p. 1273.

hold such positions.[8] Jowett certainly would not have encouraged his protégé to vacate through marriage his prize fellowship at Trinity unless he was quite confident of this outcome.

The assumption that the Commission would relax the celibacy restriction in favour of college officers was probably the reason why this issue was virtually ignored in the evidence. Neither the witnesses nor the commissioners felt that general statements of principle or expressions of personal views would serve a useful purpose any longer. The crucial questions which remained concerned the precise ways in which college statutes regarding eligibility for fellowships would be altered and this matter could be approached only through detailed negotiations.

By the act of Parliament creating the Commission, it was determined that every college would receive a complete set of new statutes instead of merely revising their existing ones. The committee established for this purpose in each college consisted of the seven commissioners, including the chairman, with an additional three collegiate representatives.[9] The governing body did not have the right, which it had possessed in the 1855-8 negotiations, to exercise a veto over the statutes framed by the committee. The commissioners would be able to carry any point on which they were united but since the collegiate representatives were more familiar with the traditions and requirements of the particular college, their opinions would carry greater weight than their numbers alone indicated.

The effects of this balance of power were apparent in the college statutes written in 1880 and 1881. The commissioners attempted to establish a uniform standard regarding the conditions under which college officials would be permitted to marry while retaining their fellowships. However, the variations in ideals and material circumstances among the colleges and the fact that the commissioners had to bargain with each separately insured that complete uniformity would not be attained. A general policy was established but a large

[8] See Above, Ch. III, p. 110
[9] 40 and 41 Vict. cap. 48, clause 36, in Shadwell iv. 82.

degree of variation was accepted as well. In practice, this compromise meant that the restrictions affecting the marriage of fellows differed considerably from one college to another.

A broad distinction was drawn among the fellowships, corresponding roughly to the difference between the resident college officers and the generally non-resident prize fellows. Tutors and some other office-holders were eligible for 'official fellowships' tenable by married men and renewable until retirement. Official fellowships were limited to a fixed maximum. The number permitted to marry was further restricted by the provision that a certain number of official fellows had to be unmarried and resident in college. The remaining 'ordinary fellowships' were to serve primarily as prizes for success in the undergraduate examinations. They differed, however, from prize fellowships under the old system in that their tenure was limited to seven years and the celibacy restriction generally was eliminated.

In those colleges most sympathetic to the concept of the 'tutorial profession', such as Balliol and New College, the right to marry was granted to all official fellows who had served the college for seven years or more, provided that the minimum number of unmarried resident official fellows was maintained.[10] Any official fellow of less than seven years standing vacated his fellowship by marriage, although he was eligible for immediate re-election. At Magdalen, a similar effect was achieved by permitting all official fellows to marry, except for the proviso that if the number of tutors and other college officers wishing to marry at any one time would jeopardize the maintenance of the minimum number of residents, then 'seniority in date of appointment to offices shall determine the order in which the privilege of so marrying shall be conceded'.[11]

By either of these regulations, a college tutor or other official in most cases was completely free of the celibacy restriction by his early thirties. His situation was, therefore, comparable to that of other professional men outside the

---

[10] See Balliol, Statute III, Clause 16(e), p. 15. Also New College, III, 11, p. 136 (PP 1882, li).

[11] IV, 27(b), p. 110, in ibid.

university who rarely were financially secure enough to marry before this age. Certainly the official fellow at one of these colleges was in as favourable a position regarding marriage as the clerical fellow had been under the traditional system. In fact, if the clerical fellow had to base his expectations of preferment solely on the college livings, he probably would have waited longer than the seven years normally expected of the don under these new statutes.

Most other colleges, however, were not as generous as Balliol, Magdalen, and New College in framing statutes allowing their official fellows to marry. At some, a vote of a majority, or even a two-thirds majority, of the governing body was required regardless of how long they had served the college.[12] A few colleges were able to obtain even greater statutory restrictions on marriage. For example, of the nine or ten official fellows at Queen's, only the three most senior tutors or lecturers and the senior bursar were permitted to marry. Even if they chose not to marry, this privilege could not be granted instead to one of the younger fellows.[13] This meant that there would be at least five or six, and probably more, unmarried official fellows resident in college at all times. Except for very large colleges, the general rule was for the minimum number of unmarried residents to be set at three or four. One college even emerged from the work of the 1877 Commission with no provision at all for married fellows. Pembroke was able to convince the commissioners that because of the extreme poverty of its foundation it could not afford to establish the pension fund which would be needed if college tutors and other officers were permitted to marry.[14] For the unmarried fellow, it was considered sufficient to allow him as a retirement income after thirty years' service the proceeds of an ordinary fellowship which could be temporarily suppressed for this purpose. Since the entire set of new statutes at Lincoln were rejected by the Privy Council, they continued under the old ones which allowed the two chaplains to marry but not the college tutors.[15]

---

[12] See, for example, Brasenose, III, 15(a), p. 30, in ibid.
[13] See II, 19, p. 179, in ibid.   [14] See III, 7–8, p. 166, in ibid.
[15] Pressure had been put on the Privy Council by the Bishop of Lincoln,

The settlement regarding pensions followed the pattern established on the basic issue of relaxing the celibacy restriction itself. A broad general policy was accepted which inevitably yielded a considerable degree of variation when applied in each college. It was agreed as a general principle that since tutors and other officials were to be permitted to marry and view their positions in Oxford as permanent careers, some provision for retirement incomes was necessary. The writing of complete new statutes for each college enabled the commissioners to avoid unsatisfactory situations such as had occurred previously at University College, where the Privy Council had accepted the college's proposed statute revision allowing a certain number of college officers to marry but rejected the pension scheme which had formed an integral part of the total plan.[16] Some provision for the retirement of official fellows was made in all colleges, although both the methods used and the amount of the pension varied considerably. In a few colleges, pensions were created simply by allowing the college temporarily to suppress ordinary fellowships for the benefit of retired official fellows.[17] In most colleges, however, separate pension funds were established instead, since it was considered undesirable to reduce still further the number of ordinary fellowships which would be available in the future as prizes.

Because of the differing needs, attitudes, and wealth of the colleges, these pension funds varied greatly in projected size, modes of accumulation, and individual benefits. In general, the richer colleges provided for maximum pensions of £400

---

whose traditional right as Visitor to nominate one fellow had been eliminated under the new statutes. See V. H. H. Green, *Oxford Common Room* (London, 1957), 253-60.

[16] See above, Ch. II, pp. 72-4.

[17] Both Pembroke and Worcester were permitted to employ this method because of their poverty, while Jesus used a similar plan, although its benefits were augmented due to the greater wealth of the foundation. For Pembroke, see above, n. 14; for Worcester, where the provisions were the same as Pembroke's despite the fact that its tutors and other officers were permitted to marry, see III, 10, p. 237; for Jesus, see IV, 30, p. 94; all in ibid. Jesus allowed retirement after twenty-eight years of service, while the others required thirty years. Also, the retired official fellow received £300 p.a. (the value of an ordinary fellowship plus £100 p.a. from general corporate revenues) instead of only £200 p.a. as at Pembroke and Worcester.

p.a. after about thirty years of service,[18] while poorer colleges, or those less sympathetic to the 'tutorial profession', were less generous.[19] Similarly, the amount which the colleges were to pay annually into the pension fund and the methods of obtaining that sum varied considerably. The most common ruling was to allow the college to apply to the capital or income of the pension fund the proceeds from the sale of advowsons, up to 10 per cent of the tuition fund and an annual payment from general corporate revenues.[20] However, there were several colleges which made no provision for the sale of advowsons[21] and some who either did not allow or discouraged strongly the use of money taken from the tuition fund.[22] The largest variation, of course, was in the annual payments permitted by the statutes. They ranged from £1,000 p.a. in rich colleges[23] to only £200 p.a.[24] or £250 p.a.[25] in poor ones.

Another important difference among the colleges was whether an official fellow was given a right to a certain pension after serving for a specified number of years or, whether the college only had the option of granting it. The precise wording of the statute indicated more the attitude of the governing body toward the 'tutorial profession' than the wealth of the foundation. At the most career-orientated colleges,[26] the statute read that the retiring official was 'entitled' to a pension. At colleges which were less enthusiastic

[18] See Merton, V, (b), 5, p. 126, and Magdalen, VIII, 1(a), p. 112, both in ibid.

[19] Oriel was only able to allow a maximum of £300 p.a. for thirty years service. See VII, 3, p. 157. At Trinity, no pension was to exceed £250 p.a. See VI, 2, p. 197, both in ibid.

[20] See Pension Funds at Balliol, 'Schedule (C.)', 2-5, p. 25; at Brasenose, XII, 1-4, p. 37; at Corpus Christi, 'Pension Fund', 54, p. 67; at Exeter, VII, 2, p. 83 and XIII, pp. 84-5; at Queens, XIII, 1-2, p. 183; at Trinity, VI, 1, p. 197; and at St. John's, XV, 1, pp. 14-15; all in ibid.

[21] See, for examples, Christ Church, XI, p. 45; Magdalen, VIII, p. 112; New College, XV, pp. 142-3; and Oriel, VII, p. 157, all in ibid.

[22] No provision was made for this type of augmentation of the pension fund at University College, while at Wadham it was only allowed if the Tuition Fund 'be unnecessarily large'. For University College, see 'Schedule of Pension Scheme', I, pp. 217-18; for Wadham, see IX, i, p. 230, both in ibid.

[23] See, for example, New College, XV, p. 142, in ibid.

[24] See Wadham, XI, p. 231, in ibid.

[25] See Trinity, VI, 1, p. 197, in ibid.

[26] See, for example, Balliol, III, 18(a), in ibid.

about academic careers[27] it only read that the governing body 'may grant' such a pension. This distinction could be crucial since it determined the extent to which college officers would be at the mercy of their colleagues when they retired.

In framing statutes for the new 'ordinary fellowships', the commissioners were able to obtain a greater degree of uniformity than had been possible regarding official fellowships. In all colleges, ordinary fellowships were fixed in value at £200 p.a. for seven years, with an option for extension only for a maximum of two years spent as a college tutor or lecturer. The major purpose of these new awards was to preserve the legitimate purposes of the old prize fellowships while eliminating their abuses. Undergraduate examination successes would be rewarded with a moderate independent income during the first difficult years of professional study and practice while the possibility of excessive income or tenure would be eliminated.

The secondary purpose of these ordinary fellowships was to strengthen the linkage between university teaching and the colleges and also to provide some funding for the 'endowment of research'. Virtually every college had a clause in their new statutes enabling them to elect to ordinary fellowships 'any Professors or Public Readers within the University of Oxford' and 'any person whose attainments in Literature, Science or Art, shall . . . qualify him for election as a Fellow, and who shall undertake, if required, to perform any definite literary or scientific work . . . which work shall be specified in the Resolution by which he is elected'.[28] These awards could be made without public notice of a vacancy and by nomination rather than examination. Precautions were taken, however, that only a small number of fellowships would be used for these secondary purposes. Either a fixed maximum, generally between two and four, was placed on them,[29] or the votes of two-thirds or three-quarters of the

---

[27] See, for example, Magdalen, VIII, 1, pp. 112–13, in ibid.

[28] This was the most common wording of this clause, although there were several small verbal differences. This wording was taken from the new statutes of Exeter, III, 24(a) and 24(b), p. 76, in ibid. Christ Church was the only college to successfully resist the inclusion of clauses of this type in their new statutes.

[29] See, for example, the new statutes of Corpus Christi, where no more than

governing body were required for election while only a simple majority was needed for filling vacancies after competitive examination.[30] The effect of these restraints was to insure that most ordinary fellowships would be awarded as prizes to young BAs.

The commissioners were less successful in attaining the uniformity they desired concerning those aspects of the ordinary fellowships other than their basic purposes, income, and length of tenure. In regard to the property or outside income disqualification of £500 p.a. which previously had been applied to all fellowships, most colleges preserved it for ordinary fellowships (excepting those given by nomination to professors, readers, or researchers) while eliminating it for official fellowships. Two colleges, however, were permitted different regulations on this issue.[31] Similarly, on the question of whether married men ought to be eligible for ordinary fellowships, the majority of colleges were willing to have no celibacy restriction for these awards. A substantial minority of five, however, retained this restriction.[32] There were also large differences in the ratio of ordinary to official fellows in each college. The richer a college, and the less sympathetic its governing body to a 'tutorial profession', the larger the number of ordinary fellows which were permitted.[33] However, in all colleges, the number of possible official fellowships was larger than the number which actually were filled by college officers.

In writing these new statutes concerning ordinary fellowships, the commissioners seem to have been guided by the views expressed by the academic residents. Only one witness, H. P. Richards of Wadham, defended the existing system

---

three fellowships could be awarded under these clauses while ten to fourteen could be given as prizes. See 'The Fellows', 22(a) and 23(a), p. 62, in ibid.

[30] See, for example, Exeter, III, 24, p. 76, in ibid. where a majority of three-quarters was required.

[31] Balliol was able to convince the commissioners to accept a clause abolishing this financial disqualification completely. See III, 5, p. 13. All Souls was allowed to retain fellows possessed of over £500 p.a. although they would be ineligible to receive the income from their fellowships. See III, 3, p. 3; both in ibid.

[32] See Christ Church, XVI, 2, p. 47; Magdalen, IV, 3, p. 107; Queen's, II, 4, p. 177; Trinity, II, 6, p. 192; and University College, III, 2, p. 205; all in ibid.

[33] At one extreme was Magdalen which allowed a maximum of only eleven

unequivocally.[34] All others were critical to some degree. There were considerable differences, however, about how the system ought to be reorganized and what purposes it ought to fulfil. Some began with the premise that non-resident fellowships were an abuse of academic endowments. One opinion was that this income ought to be used to augment the tuition funds of the colleges and to enhance the financial position of the college officers.[35] Another view was that it should be either apportioned among the various faculties[36] or given to a university-wide board of examiners[37] to establish awards for promising researchers. All witnesses except Dr Appleton[38] argued that they ought to be terminal and given only for specific pieces of work to guard against sinecurism. The commissioners gave some weight to these opinions since they provided that scholars engaged on definite projects could be elected to ordinary fellowships. Collegiate interests, however, were protected since these awards were to be made by the colleges and not by the faculties or university boards. The fact that the number of fellowships which would be available in the future for college officers was raised above existing needs at the expense of those which would be available as prizes indicated that the commissioners also gave some credence to the spokesman for tutorial interests on this issue. There were those, however, who denied the premises that non-resident fellowships were unsound in principle. It was argued that the only modification needed was for awards to be given only for a fixed term of years.[39] In this way, the legitimate functions of rewarding success in the examination schools and connecting the university with the professions would be maintained while the admitted evils of sinecurism

official fellowships out of a total of thirty to forty fellowships. See IV, 1, p. 107 and IV, 22, p. 109. At the other extreme was Brasenose where as many as nine of the twelve fellowships could be official. See III, 1, p. 28 and III, 7, pp. 28–9; both in ibid. [34] PP 1881, lvi. 332.

[35] See 'G.E. Thorley, Esq., MA (Fellow of Wadham College), examined', ibid. 133 (no. 2178).

[36] See 'Robert Bellamy Clifton, Esq., MA (Professor of Experimental Philosophy), examined', ibid. 27 (no. 489–99).

[37] See 'J. L. Strachan Davidson, Esq., MA (Fellow of Balliol College), examined', ibid. 237–9 (no. 3861–79). [38] Ibid. 29–36.

[39] See 'The Rev. Benjamin Jowett, MA (Master of Balliol College), examined', ibid. 158–9 (no. 2698–705).

would be avoided. It was clear from the statutes written in 1880-1 that this opinion was the one which the commissioners accepted. Although some concessions were made to the advocates of both tutorial careers and research, it was firmly decided that prize fellowships, in a new form with their most prominent abuses removed, would continue to have an important claim on collegiate endowments.

Considering the alterations in the fellowship system as a whole, it was apparent that the advocates of the tutorial profession had achieved a substantial victory. The celibacy restriction had been largely eliminated and retirement pensions supplied. These essential prerequisites for the establishment of a profession had been attained in practically every college. The lack of uniformity in college statutes, however, meant that the desirability of this new profession would vary greatly from one college to another. The claims of the 'endowment of research' party were recognized only to a limited extent. The small number of terminal fellowships for researchers which the new statutes sanctioned could hardly be considered a satisfactory embodiment of their plans. Essentially, when the commissioners accepted the view that the basic principle of prize fellowships was sound, at least the more grandiose of the plans for the support of research became financially impossible. Neither the commissioners nor most of the colleges were positively hostile to research ideals; however, they proved unwilling to sacrifice the entire prize system for this end.

B. *The Boards of Faculties and the Reform of the Combination System*

The reform of the combination system was also a task which required the legislative efforts of the Commission. The system had grown and prospered on an informal basis but its full potential for eliminating needless duplication of elementary lectures, for providing increased opportunities for specialization by college tutors, and for integrating professorial and collegiate teaching had not been realized.[40] These benefits

---

[40] See above, Ch. II, pp. 81-93, for a discussion of the achievements and deficiencies of the combination system.

could not be attained so long as combinations were merely private arrangements among individual tutors or colleges. An official system with statutory powers was required if all college and university teaching was to be successfully co-ordinated. Although it was feared that such powers might interfere unduly with the autonomy of the colleges or of the individual lecturers or professors, the commissioners and most of their witnesses agreed that the potential benefits were great enough to justify this risk. None the less, the framing of statutes which were strong enough to be effective but which contained sufficient safeguards against the abuse of official power would be a task of considerable delicacy. The creation of Boards of Faculties with powers over university teaching and examination was the commissioners' attempt to achieve this goal.

The only approach which had been made to university-wide faculty organization prior to the Commission was the establishment of Boards of Studies in 1872. There were separate boards for each university examination; three for Moderations and seven more for the final schools (one for each of the six honour schools and one for the pass school). Each board consisted of those professors whose fields were included among the subjects of the particular examination, all those who had served as examiners during the past two years, and sometimes a certain number of co-opted members as well. The boards were meant to provide an informal check on the powers of the examiners in any given year. Although they had no statutory powers, it was hoped that their over-seeing of the examination system would tend to eliminate the complaints which had become prevalent in the 1860s that standards varied from year to year with changes in intellectual fashions and in the pet theories of individual examiners.[41] The Boards of Studies also served to appease, to a limited extent, the professors' dissatisfaction because they had been excluded from control of the examination system. Professorial representation on all the boards was meant to compensate them for their lack of direct power over the administration of the schools. Care was taken,

[41] See above, Ch. III, pp. 116-17, nn. 33-35.

however, that professors were far outnumbered by examiners and other members to insure that this innovation would not infringe on the independence of the colleges. Although the Boards of Studies had no powers over college or university teaching, they were the model from which the commissioners' plan for Boards of Faculties later emerged.

In the questioning of witnesses, the commissioners revealed their hostility to the combination system as a method for organizing public lectures. Several dons were asked to defend the actions of the combinations of which they were members but none accomplished this task with much persuasiveness. For instance, the commissioners demanded aggressively of J. R. Thursfield of Jesus why there were three separate lectures at the same time in different colleges on Aristotle's *Ethics* and why lectures on Plato's *Republic* were scheduled for the same time as those of the Professor of Logic.[42] On the first point, Thursfield could only agree that such an arrangement was wasteful. He added lamely that it 'is what one might call a remnant of the old college system'. On the second point, his only defence was that the meeting of lecturers held every term attempted to reduce such inconveniences to a minimum. Even the secretary of another *Literae Humaniores* combination, T. L. Papillon of New College, had to admit that lack of organization and needless duplication of lectures were endemic problems under existing conditions.[43] Papillon was also questioned closely about the hostility of the combinations to professorial lectures. Although he denied this charge, when confronted with two sets of professorial lectures on relevant topics which were not included in his list, he could only reply weakly that in one case the omission was an 'oversight' and in the other the lectures were announced too late to be included. The only conclusion which could be drawn was that, although the combination system had initiated the methods by which the colleges could improve the organization of university teaching, the existing informal methods had proved inadequate for eliminating anomalies.

On this issue of reforming the combination system, the greatest impact on the commissioners was made by the

[42] PP 1881, liv. 120, esp. no. 1997.   [43] Ibid. 233–4.

carefully prepared plan submitted jointly by W. W. Jackson and H. F. Pelham, both of Exeter College.[44] They recommended the establishment of a central board in each subject to co-ordinate all college and university teaching in its field. Each board would have the responsibility for organizing the list of public lectures open to all members of the university, including courses offered by both professors and combined lecturers. The plan was that in every field the board ought to be composed of all professors and readers in related subjects and, in addition, at least an equal number of members elected from among the educational staffs of the colleges. The Jackson–Pelham scheme was intended to strike a delicate balance between the need for organization and for autonomy, and between the interests of the 'tutorial profession' and the 'endowment of research'.

The prospective advantages of this scheme would be (1) an authoritative organization of the teaching, by which waste of power would be avoided, and the present unequal pressure on individual teachers would be relieved; (2) college teaching would be connected with the higher instruction given by professors and readers; (3) special study of particular subjects would be encouraged, and ambition raised by the prospect of a recognized position and a larger audience; (4) greater freedom and variety as well as a higher standard of excellence would be secured. Negatively, it would not preclude, but rather facilitate, individual supervision in the separate colleges, while also the union of a professorial element in the controlling board would be beneficial to both, checking on the one hand a tendency to make the teaching an official monopoly, and on the other preventing the teaching from sinking to too low a level, or becoming too entirely divorced from research.[45]

The statutes written by the commissioners for the new Boards of Faculties[46] were virtually identical to the plan recommended by Jackson and Pelham. These new institutions differed from the earlier Boards of Studies in that there no longer would be a separate board for each university examination. Instead, one board was established for each subject recognized by a final honour school. As in the Jackson–Pelham plan, all professors and readers in related fields were given *ex*

---

[44] Ibid. 300-1.   [45] Ibid. 300, no. 4594.
[46] See 'A Statute . . . concerning Boards of Faculties', 70-3 (PP 1881, lxxiii).

officio membership. On collegiate representatives the commissioners diverged slightly from the Jackson–Pelham plan by deciding that each board would be free to include any number of college tutors or lecturers so long as this number was not greater than the total of professors and readers holding *ex officio* membership.[47] Jackson and Pelham had suggested that the number of collegiate representatives ought to be 'at least' equal to the number of university teachers. Provision was also included for extra co-opted members, but in practice this clause was not used since the principle was soon accepted that college tutors and lecturers always would exactly equal the total of university professors and readers on each board.[48] These collegiate representatives were to be elected by all tutors and lecturers certified by the head of a college or hall to be teaching subjects related to the particular faculty.[49]

The main purpose of the Boards of Faculties was to prepare and print each term a list of the public lectures by university professors, readers, and combined lecturers. All college and university teachers were required to submit to their boards the subjects of the public lectures they proposed to deliver during the next term and the times they wished to give them. The boards were expected to alter these individual plans so each would contribute most effectively to the efficiency of the faculty as a whole. The Boards of Faculties were not, however, given statutory powers to compel any teacher to change his lecturing plans to suit the requirements of the university. The boards were forced to rely largely on persuasion to accomplish their goals. In the case of a professor or reader who refused to agree to alterations which were thought to be essential, the board could only report his recalcitrant behaviour to the Vice-Chancellor. In the case of a collegiate teacher, the board could retaliate only by removing his lectures from their official published list.[50] The statutes did not specify what practical effect these actions would have. The result was that the old system of persuasion continued much

[47] Ibid. 71, no. 6.
[48] See below, Ch. V. pp. 235-7 for the results of these decisions concerning representation.
[49] Op. cit. 72, no. 11 (ii).   [50] Ibid. no. 18, p. 73.

as before.[51] It was clear that the often expressed fears of the colleges and their teachers that an official system would infringe on their independence had been allowed to influence strongly the commissioners. This was also the reason why more extensive powers over university teaching were not granted to the boards. For example, it had been proposed that they ought to be given a significant voice in the appointment of combined lecturers as well as in the organization of public lectures.[52] The commissioners, however, decided to heed instead Pelham's warning that university teaching should not be confined to an 'official monopoly'.

The appointment of examiners was the one area in which the new statutes gave the Boards of Faculties concrete powers while reducing the influence of the colleges. These offices previously had been the patronage of the Vice-Chancellor and the two proctors. The traditional practice was for examinerships to be given to members of the same college as the proctors. The new statute reduced the power of the proctors and, by extension, of the colleges and increased to a corresponding extent the powers of the Boards of Faculties. The nominating board for each examinership was to consist of six members of whom three would be the Vice-Chancellor and the two proctors while the remaining three would be appointed by the Board of Faculty in the subject in which the examination was to be held.[53] This statute was intended to augment the influence of the professors in an area in which they had often resented bitterly their powerlessness.

[51] A very well-documented instance of the type of conflict which could occur in this situation can be found in the Pusey-Liddon correspondence. In 1879/80 Dr Pusey had a long and acrimonious correspondence with William Ince, the Regius Professor of Divinity and the chairman of the new Faculty Board in Theology. The issue was Pusey's anger at college tutors lecturing on the same topics or at the same time as himself. In the end, Pusey refused to lecture when he could not obtain satisfaction from the board. In this case, the issue was much clouded by theological and political differences. Ince was no friend to High Churchmen and was clearly taking the opportunity to do them an ill turn. The fact that Archibald Sayce was one of the offending college lecturers did not help matters either. See Pusey House MS letters, HPL to EBP, ii, no. 77, 80-3, 93, 95, 98. Also EBP to HPL, ii, nos. 268-9 and iii, nos. 3-5, 38.

[52] 'Sir Henry J. S. Maine, KCSI, Hon. DCL, Corpus Professor of Jurisprudence, examined', 370-3 (PP 1881, lvi).

[53] See 'A Statute . . . concerning the nomination of examiners', 4-5, no. 2 and no. 5 (PP 1882, li).

Although college tutors would have a significant voice in the appointment of examiners, this power would be theirs as members of a faculty board rather than as fellows of a particular college.

In framing statutes for the Boards of Faculties, the commissioners had compromised between the desire for improved organization and the need to safeguard the autonomy of the colleges and their teachers. Whenever possible, reliance on persuasion had been preferred to the granting of statutory powers. None the less, the new boards were considerably better adapted than the old system for eliminating the most glaring flaws in the combination system. To the extent that these reforms were successful in reducing the duplication of elementary lectures and the poor scheduling of college versus university lecturers, they would tend to ameliorate the tutors' complaints of 'teaching drudgery', the professors' complaints of collegiate hostility, and the researchers' complaints of insufficient opportunities for specialized teaching.

C. The Commission and the Decline of the Church

The Commission of 1877 continued the trend toward the diminution of Church influence at Oxford. The Church party had hoped that by supporting the demands of both the tutors and the researchers, they would be able to use the new Commission, at the least, to halt permanently the erosion of their interests. These hopes, however, were to be cruelly disappointed. The commissioners chose instead to move toward the virtual elimination of both clerical fellowships and clerical headships.

As soon as it became clear that a new university commission was to be established, the Church party organized quickly to attempt to utilize the influence they could be expected to have with a Tory government to mould it for their own purposes. They met regularly at Keble, beginning in February 1875, and soon were able to forward a petition to Lord Salisbury which shrewdly combined their own goals with those of both the tutors and the researchers. This intention was apparent in W. R. Ward's summary of their petition:

they called for the immediate appointment of an executive commission to transfer college funds to the university for the purposes of enlarging the professoriate, for remunerating resident teachers more adequately, and supporting others engaged in study and learning. Funds should be reserved for the assistance of poor students. The powers of colleges to change their constitutions should be restricted. Non-resident fellowships should be reduced in number and limited in tenure to a term of years. Finally clerical fellowships should be retained in their present proportion to the whole, and candidates for them should be required to take Holy Orders not later than a year after their election.[54]

When the bill was first published in March 1876, the Church party took credit for it[55] and the opponents of clerical interests became alarmed. Lyulph Stanley saw it as a plot to preserve and extend the influence of the Church under the guise of university reform. 'It enables the Commissioners to reimpose clerical tests on offices now free from them', he angrily asserted. 'It enables them to direct funds to found new clerical offices . . . And it enables the Commissioners by the wholesale suppression of lay fellowships and the preservation of clerical fellowships to revolutionize the governing bodies of the colleges in the interest of the sacerdotal party. . . . [B]y keeping the heads out of the bill it preserves their clerical restrictions . . .[56] The interests of the Church suffered an important tactical defeat, however, in the selection of the members of the Commission itself. J. W. Burgon of Oriel, an indefatigable High Church polemicist, originally was chosen by Lord Salisbury to represent collegiate interests. His appointment, however, aroused so much opposition that it was withdrawn when the bill was revised.[57] The Church party later suffered a second tactical defeat when the chairman, Lord Selborne, became Lord Chancellor and had to resign from the Commission. Selborne always had been a firm supporter of the Church and was known to be sympathetic to

[54] Ward, 300, cited from Christ Church Salisbury MSS Petition of Resident Members of Congregation to Lord Salisbury, 17 Mar. 1875. The following account of the machinations of the Church party and the way in which their plans were foiled is based on the more detailed narrative in Ward, 300–3.

[55] *Church Quarterly Review*, xii, 211 (cf. *Guardian* 1880, p. 817); cited in Ward, 299–300.

[56] Cited in Ward, 300. Ward does not provide a reference for this quotation but he does cite Stanley writing to the *Nonconformist* and to Mark Pattison in the same vein. See p. 412, nn. 47 and 48.

[57] See Ward, 300 and 302 for a discussion of this point.

the principle of clerical fellowships. He was replaced as chairman by Montague Bernard, Chichele Professor of International Law, who had no such sympathy for the Church party. Lord Selborne's place on the Commission was filled by G. G. Bradley, who was antipathetic to both clerical fellowships and the High Church views which characterized the Church party in Oxford.[58]

The evidence before the Commission contained virtually no mention of the claims of the Church. Dr Pusey was the only witness to speak out for the maintenance of clerical fellowships.[59] The reason for this silence, however, was not that the Church had no supporters in Oxford, but simply that the public hearings of the Commission were an inappropriate forum. Since the battle would involve the alteration of college statutes concerning eligibility for fellowships, the private meetings between the commissioners and the representatives of each college were considered to be the most effective setting for the discussion of this issue.

Although Church sentiment varied widely among the colleges and the commissioners had to negotiate with each separately, a remarkable degree of uniformity was attained in statutes concerning clerical fellowships. It was apparent that the Commission chose to exercise its statutory powers to the fullest, especially after the departure of Lord Selborne. The basic principle was established in virtually all colleges that fellowships restricted to those in holy orders were justified only by the need to fulfil religious obligations. The statute which was accepted by the majority of colleges stated that only one fellow in holy orders was required to serve as chaplain.[60] This fellow could be elected by nomination rather than examination. Beyond this minimum, the governing body was allowed to elect a second clerical fellow without examination,[61] but no more than two fellows elected under this

---

[58] Ibid. 312. [59] PP 1881, liv. 295-300.

[60] A few colleges with strongly anti-clerical governing bodies attempted to eliminate even the one clerical fellow. H. P. Liddon wrote to Dr Pusey on 10 Dec. 1879, 'I hear that Oriel & Balliol are each to have only *one* clergyman among their fellows. Monro & the Oriel fellows wished to have *none* & to "pay a chaplain to read prayers": but the Commissioners insisted on their having *one*.' Pusey House MS letters, ii, n. 110.

[61] For examples of this statute, see Balliol, III, 22, p. 16; and Brasenose, III,

clause were permitted. Colleges were free, of course, to elect more clergymen to any of their other ordinary or official fellowships, but they would have to compete with laymen on equal terms. The commissioners had firmly rejected the traditional view that fellowships existed largely to serve the interests of the Church.

Only a few colleges emerged with more than one obligatory clerical fellow under their new statutes. These exceptions were explained by either the special religious needs of the college or the special obduracy of the governing body. At Magdalen, the statutory minimum was set at two[62] since the governing body was extremely insistent. In their initial draft statutes, they had provided that fully half of their fellowships were to be restricted to clergy. After Lord Selborne had been replaced by Bradley, the Commission no longer was willing to accept this draft.[63] In the case of Christ Church, the Church supporters could argue persuasively that its structure as part college and part cathedral required more clerical fellows simply to fulfil the needs of the institution. Perhaps the commissioners also were influenced by Dr Pusey's argument that the virtual elimination of clerical studentships would be unfair and even dishonest since some had been created only twenty years before by the suppression of two canonries. Pusey insisted that the chapter had only agreed to their abolition on the understanding that the studentships to be created would be restricted to clergymen.[64] The commissioners originally agreed to six clerical senior students[65] but after the departure of Lord Selborne the governing body was able to reduce this number to three and to insist that they be elected by examination rather than nomination.[66] These small concessions were the only instances in which the commissioners were persuaded to depart from their basic rule regarding clerical fellowships.

The Church party also suffered a defeat on the issue of the remaining clerical headships. By the Act of 1871, the specific requirement that the head be in holy orders had been

9, p. 29 (P.P. 1882, li).
[63] See Ward, 312.
[65] See Pusey House MS letters, H. P. Liddon to E. B. Pusey, 10 Dec. 1879, ii, no. 110.
[62] IV, 24, op. 109–10; in ibid.
[64] See above, n. 59, p. 175.
[66] XVI, 12, p. 48 (PP 1882, li).

abolished in most college. However, a few colleges still remained in which the headship was tied to a clerical office, generally a cathedral canonry. A large part of the income was often derived from this preferment. In one case, the canonry of Rochester attached to the provostship of Oriel, the commissioners decided to eliminate the connection. This move was opposed strenuously by Provost Hawkins, but it was supported by many of the fellows led by D. B. Monro, the most probable direct beneficiary of this change.[67] The bitterness of this defeat for clerical interests was lessened somewhat by the fact that the severed canonry was attached to the professorship of exegesis held by H. P. Liddon. The commissioners left only two headships in Oxford which were tenable by clergymen alone. The Dean of Christ Church was left as head of the college since any change would have required a complete reconstruction of the institution. The only other college to escape with a clerical head was Pembroke, where a canonry of Gloucester was attached to the mastership. The college was able to argue that it was too poor to provide an adequate stipend without this income.

One only had to look back twenty-five years to before the first university commission to gauge the losses which had been suffered by the Church and the revolutionary suddenness of the change. In 1850, Oxford was a predominantly clerical society. All the heads of colleges, with the one exception of the Warden of Merton, were clergymen. The vast majority of fellowships were not tenable beyond a short term of years except by those in holy orders. Virtually all tutors were clergymen. All undergraduates were members of the Church and about 80 per cent of them were destined to be clergymen themselves. The Commission of 1877 continued the work of dismantling this ecclesiastical society, leaving to the Church only two headships and perhaps thirty reserved fellowships in the entire university.

The Commission left the supporters of clerical interests in Oxford in a mood of anger and despair. Francis Paget of Christ Church caught this feeling in a letter to his sister on 2 December 1878. 'And the Commission have been dealing

[67] In fact, Monro did become Provost when Hawkins died in 1882.

very roughly with us, so that it is hard to feel very hopeful about the future', Paget wrote. 'Liddon is almost desperate and Dr Pusey most sadly prophetic'.[68] Even though J. W. Burgon could still assert belligerently in 1883 that 'the Colleges are, without exception, *Ecclesiastical foundations*, openly and avowedly endowed for the sustentation of the Clergy',[69] he had to recognize that this view had been decisively rejected by the government. He denounced the first Royal Commission as 'a moral and constitutional wrong;'

a needless invasion of the liberties of the University and the Colleges, as well as a shameful perversion of the known intention of Founders and Benefactors . . . In open defiance of Right, the Clerical tenure of fellowships was reduced within certain arbitrary limits: by which act of injustice to Founders and to the Church, a fatal precedent was established for a yet more sweeping act of confiscation at the end of less than 20 years.[70]

The work of the Executive Commission and the 1877 Commission, as well as the abolition of religious tests, were also strongly condemned. 'Disastrous as had been the Legislation of 1854-7, there remained in Oxford far too much of its ancient Religious constitution and character to satisfy the secularist party', Burgon bitterly complained.

A heavy blow was inflicted in 1871 by the 'Universities Tests' Act,' — subsequently to the passing of which, no declaration of Religious belief was any longer allowed to be made at the taking of any degree other than degrees in Divinity. In this way, the door was set wide open for the *Secularization of University teaching* . . . In 1876, a fresh 'Oxford University Commission' having been appointed, it became the one object of the enemies of the Church to oust the Clergy from their endowments and to de-Christianize the Colleges. The *animus* of the proposed Legislation no one could mistake.[71]

One need hardly wonder at the hysterical tone adopted by the supporters of the Church considering both the suddenness and the extent of their losses.

---

[68] Stephen Paget and J. M. C. Crum, *Francis Paget, Bishop of Oxford* (London, 1912), 52.
[69] 'Rev. Edward Hawkins, DD, Provost of Oriel College, Oxford', *Quart. Rev.* clvi, no. 312 (1883), 345.
[70] Ibid. 331.　　　　　　　　　　　　　　　　　　　　　[71] Ibid. 344.

D. University Readerships and the
Need for Progressive Careers

Plans for the establishment of 'university readerships' below the professors in rank but above the college tutorial fellows was perhaps the most characteristic and energetically debated of the schemes placed before the commissioners. In fact, however, the establishment of readerships cannot be considered as one unified scheme since there were three separate plans which involved the creation of these offices. Each had a distinct rationale and each had its supporters and its enemies. In forming their statutes the commissioners attempted to satisfy the needs of all the advocates while quieting the fears of the opponents of these various plans.

The view which received the most support among the witnesses was that readerships could be used as promotions for college tutors who had been successful as combination lecturers. These offices would provide a method for giving them extra income for their university lectures. In this way, they would have a possibility for progressive careers which merely allowing official fellows to marry could not supply in itself. Thomas Fowler expressed this view forcefully. '[I] f a man obtains a tutorship, say, at the age of 23 or 24, practically speaking, he has little else to look forward to', he complained.

[I] f he stays in Oxford the probability is that he will go on as a tutor for the rest of the time that he remains. We find, practically, that at the age of 40 or 45 men throw up a tutorship and get tired of the work. If there were, as I propose, a graduated scale of teachers beginning with the college tutor and going on to the university reader, and culminating in the university professor, there would be an object for a man's ambition, and an incitement to his exertions.[72]

Several other witnesses identified this same problem. Bonamy Price, who had complained of the lack of progressive careers in Oxford as early as 1850,[73] reiterated this point to the commissioners. '[T]here is no academical motive for the teachers to advance and improve after they have once become

---

[72] PP 1881, liv. 96, no. 1567. Fowler's own ambition had been satisfied since he had recently become Professor of Logic and given up his Lincoln tutorship, though not his fellowship.   [73] See above, Ch. I, pp. 30–3.

tutors', he bluntly asserted. 'The Oxford tutor begins at his best, in point of reward, — at the age of 25'.[74] Similarly, Alfred Robinson of New College complained that 'the man who is on the tutorial staff of the college feels that he has no career, or that after three or four years his position is as good as it is ever likely to be, and he is discontented, and does not improve'.[75]

A few colleges attempted to ameliorate this problem by introducing an element of progressive increase into the distribution of their tuition funds. At Balliol, the new statutes of 1882 provided that the tutors would receive, in addition to their fellowships of £250 p.a., a graduated increment from the tuition fund of at least £100 p.a. in the first year of teaching, rising by £15 p.a. for sixteen years to a maximum of £340 p.a.[76] This would make a minimum scale for tutorial fellows of £350 p.a. rising to at least £590 p.a.[77] The problem with this solution was that small, regular, and automatic increments would not provide much incitement to ambition. It was also unlikely that many college tutors would view with enthusiasm a plan which created progressive careers largely by lowering the stipends of junior tutorial fellows.

The plan for university readerships was presented as the ideal solution to this problem. Benjamin Jowett argued that readerships ought to be created because 'there should be a reward for a distinguished college tutor'.[78] Dean Liddell of Christ Church also informed the commissioners, 'The proposition of creating university readers was made with a view to providing some university offices for those gentlemen who have done their duty well in the colleges, and shown that they could do good service to the university.'[79] The most widely accepted view, and the one which received the support of the Hebdomadal Council, was that readerships should be worth £400 p.a. or £500 p.a. and that the teaching duties required ought not to be significantly greater than those already performed by the college tutor who served also as a

---

[74] PP 1881, lvi. 121, no. 2016. [75] Ibid. 149, no. 2559.
[76] V, 1(b), p. 18 (PP 1882, li).
[77] It was clear that if there was enough money in the tuition fund, the tutorial fellows could be given larger incomes. See V, 1(c), p. 18, in ibid.
[78] PP 1881, lvi. 156, no. 2664. [79] Ibid. 16, no. 360.

combined lecturer. A readership could be held, therefore, with an official fellowship and would simply mean a significant rise in income.

Some witnesses, however, suggested that when college tutors were promoted to university readerships they could use this opportunity to give up some portion of their college teaching work. According to this plan, the reader still would be rewarded with some increase in total income but also would have more time for advanced study and writing. As J. L. Strachan-Davidson of Balliol remarked enthusiastically, the creation of university readerships would provide college tutors with the chance that 'they might attain a position in which, with an augmentation of pay and dignity, they would be relieved from some of the most laborious and least interesting of their duties, and gain leisure for more advanced learning'.[80] Although Strachan-Davidson mentioned the value of this plan as an encouragement for research, the point was almost an afterthought among the more substantial advantages of his readership plan: a larger income, higher status, and fewer duties.

There were others, however, who saw the creation of readerships primarily as a way to advance the cause of learning and research. T. H. Green, for example, recommended a plan which was directed specifically toward this goal.[81] It differed in certain respects from the scheme which had obtained the endorsement of the Hebdomadal Council. Green argued that the quality of a candidate's research and writing, as well as lecturing ability, ought to be considered especially in awarding these posts. He suggested that the new readerships ought to be worth £400 p.a. but that they should be tenable only with a college fellowship, not with a tutorship. According to this plan, readers would not receive incomes significantly greater than those of college tutors. The main advantage of this new position was that they no longer would have to confine their teaching to the level of the undergraduate examinations and would also have more leisure to pursue scholarly interests. The majority of the reader's class would consist of BAs preparing for fellowship examinations, though a few advanced

---

[80] Ibid. 235, no. 3828.   [81] Ibid. 200-5.

undergraduates doing a special subject in the reader's field or motivated by pure desire for knowledge might also attend. The advantages of readerships for the encouragement of research were clearly much more important for Green than they were for Strachan-Davidson.

There was also a third viewpoint from which the establishment of readerships was recommended. A few witnesses, mostly professors, considered that it would be desirable to introduce more hierarchical organization into university teaching.[82] John Earle, Professor of Anglo-Saxon, suggested that it would be useful to have a reader in Anglo-Saxon to analyse documents with historical students, leaving him free to pursue the higher subjects.[83] Similarly, J. O. Westwood, Professor of Zoology, suggested that a readership be established in vertebrate zoology and his own professorship be restricted to invertebrate zoology since the Hope collection of which he had charge was too large and diverse for one person to manage successfully.[84] In this case, the desire for hierarchy was only implied by the fact that Westwood asked for a readership rather than for another professorship. M. A. Lawson, Professor of Botany and Rural Economy, also suggested that his subject be divided into two positions, one a professorship and the other a readership, the distribution between botany and rural economy to be determined by the relative eminence of the particular individuals available for the posts.[85] Although Lawson denied that his intention was to place himself at the head of a hierarchy of university teachers, his insistence that the professor and reader be allowed to select the demonstrators in their fields without examination seemed to imply some desire for empire-building.

Only one college tutor, R. L. Nettleship of Balliol, recommended the establishment of readerships as a method of

[82] Henry Acland, Regius Professor of Medicine, argued the similar position that he ought to be the executive head of his department. Although he did not recommend readerships for this purpose, he did suggest that the other teachers of subjects related to medicine ought to be subordinates of the regius professor. Acland was enough in touch with Oxford opinion, however, to recognize that the younger scientists would object to this view. The commissioners also showed marked hostility toward this conception of the regius professor's function. See ibid. 181-95.

[83] Ibid. 217-19.   [84] Ibid. 195-7.   [85] Ibid. 328-30.

introducing hierarchy into university teaching. Nettleship asserted that the existing position of the college tutor was defective since 'he is cut off from healthy subordination to his superiors . . . The natural authorities to whom he should turn for guidance are the professors of the university; but except personal friendship there is nothing to bring him into relations with them, nor any organization provided by which he can naturally approach them.'[86] For Nettleship, the creation of university readerships had the advantage of repairing this defect, although it may safely be assumed that this was an eccentric view for one in his position.

Since there were three separate types of plans for university readerships, the opposing arguments were equally diverse. Each of the specific advantages attributed to the scheme; the rewarding of college tutors, the encouragement of research, and the improvement in the organization of university instruction, were strenuously denied by other witnesses. A general objection to all readership plans also was made on the ground that the creation of new teaching posts in the university for any purpose was unnecessary and wasteful.

Several witnesses denied that college tutors needed opportunities for promotion. Edwin Palmer, Corpus Professor of Latin, bluntly asserted that there was no need to give them either extra financial rewards or more leisure for research.[87] He explictly denied that academic life ought to be able to compete with the more lucrative professions and he suggested that the Long Vacation already provided ample time for those who wished to do research. This denial of the material aspirations of the tutors was heavily seconded by Max Müller, Professor of Comparative Philology. Müller made an invidious comparison between Oxford and Germany where 'the professors are not expected to live as a banker lives. They still know the meaning of *laeta paupertas.*'[88]

Other witnesses, while accepting the desirability of rewarding college tutors, denied that the creation of university readerships toward which they could aspire would achieve this end. H. P. Richards of Wadham suggested instead that this goal could be attained more directly by establishing pay scales

---

[86] Ibid. 224, no. 3627.   [87] Ibid. 97–102.   [88] Ibid. 215, no. 3481.

for college tutors which were steeply graduated, with a longer ascent and a higher maximum than characterized any existing arrangements.[89] George Thorley of Wadham also disapproved of readerships as a method for promoting college tutors. He recommended instead that readerships ought to be created as collegiate appointments which would rank below the position of a tutorial fellow.[90] In this way, progressive careers would be obtained for college tutors, not by creating offices toward which they could strive, but by establishing posts subordinate to their own.

No member of the 'endowment of research' party supported any plan for the creation of university readerships. They had their own schemes and probably felt that the 'leisure for advanced learning' which other witnesses saw as a specific advantage of readerships was only a platitude. Neither Mark Pattison nor Archibald Sayce chose to discuss this issue at all, while Dr Appleton argued strongly against the establishment of readerships.[91] He insisted that such a plan would simply be a way of giving more money to combined lecturers under a new name. Readerships would be only another 'endowment of teaching' and might interfere with the creation of the 'studentships' for pure research which he hoped to see established.

The use of readerships to bring greater efficiency to university teaching through the introduction of hierarchy aroused little enthusiasm beyond the small number of professors who would have benefited by this plan. Despite the commissioners' desire to improve the organization of university instruction, they were markedly sceptical of the advantages of introducing subordination and clear lines of authority.[92] Few college tutors either could have been expected to echo R. L. Nettleship's enthusiasm for a position under the control of the professors. The plea that the establishment of readerships would bring better organization to university teaching by remedying the defects of the combination system also was strongly denied by H. P. Richards[93] and J. R. Thursfield.[94]

[89] Ibid. 332–3, nos. 5078–80.   [90] Ibid. 133, no. 2173 and 135, no. 2215.
[91] Ibid. 29–36.   [92] See above, p. 182, n. 82.
[93] PP 1881, lvi. 331, no. 5056.   [94] Ibid. 111–18.

Other witnesses condemned all schemes for readerships on the ground that any more provision of university teaching would be redundant. H. A. Pottinger of Worcester argued that there was no general need for readers from the viewpoint of teaching and, even in the new subjects where such a need did exist experience had shown that '[t] he appointments would probably be worse filled up . . . and the work would be more likely to be neglected' if the university rather than the colleges controlled these new teaching positions.[95] Similarly, William Ince of Exeter denied the desirability of establishing readerships on the ground that 'there is so much more intimate personal relationship with the men by personally superintending what they are doing than in a general lecture, . . . they are brought much more into living connexion with the teacher through the instrumentality of the college system'.[96] Fears clearly existed that readerships, like any other proposed university organization, might infringe on the independence of the colleges. The feeling also existed among many dons that professorial teaching already had been given a fair chance to show its value and had been found wanting. To create more posts for teachers who would lecture to practically empty rooms was considered to be merely wasteful.

The commissioners had a very difficult task in framing statutes concerning university readerships. There was a good deal of scepticism about each of the advantages which the system was supposed to secure and even its supporters clearly had widely differing conceptions of what goals these new positions ought to accomplish. The commissioners attempted to form a compromise which would satisfy all the proponents of readerships, especially the largest group interested in promotions for college tutors, while neutralizing the animosities

[95] Ibid. 266, no. 4271. Pottinger's hatred of university instruction was so strong that when Professor Bernard asked him, as a college law lecturer, whether the endowments of the law professors were too large, he replied bluntly, 'I think they are a great deal more than the work is worth, at the market value. The work is worse done than it is in the college, and it costs about twenty times more, and that is a state of things that I do not want to see extended.' (p. 265, no. 4255.)

[96] Ibid. 146, no. 2491. Ince also noted that 'nor would college tutors like thus to be turned into mere disciplinarians and deprived of teaching functions'. (p. 146, no. 2490.)

of all the opponents of these schemes. The commissioners decided that initially they would create seven readerships worth £300 p.a. each.[97] Readers were to be appointed by a committee comprised of the Vice-Chancellor, ten members of Convocation (five each appointed by the Hebdomadal Council and Congregation), and one representative of each Board of Faculty.[98]

The new statutes did not specify which college offices could be held along with university readerships. The intent was to sanction the entire range of recommendations which had been proposed to the Commission. Readers were permitted to hold college fellowships alone without tutorships, as T. H. Green had suggested.[99] In fact, virtually every college had a clause in their statutes explicitly allowing them to elect university readers to ordinary fellowships.[100] If the colleges would permit this option, a readership also could be held with a fellowship and partial tutorship, as Strachan-Davidson had proposed.[101] The new statutes permitted as well the tenure of a university readership with a full tutorial fellowship. Finally, a readership could be held without any college office.

The commissioners probably intended, however, that the holding of a readership together with a full official fellowship would be the option most often used. The new statutes required readers to give a minimum of two lectures and two periods of 'informal instruction' a week during at least seven weeks of each term.[102] Only the 'informal instruction' with students outside their own colleges might have represented an increase in teaching duties for college tutors who already gave combination lectures. For the college tutor who was not a combination lecturer, the office would entail a large increase in teaching duties. If the reader held no college office, the position would offer only a pitifully small income. The issue of research was completely ignored by the statutes. They

---

[97] See 'A Statute . . . concerning University Readers', 69, no. 2 (PP 1881, lxxiii).   [98] Ibid. 69, no. 3.

[99] See above, p. 181, n. 81.

[100] For an example, see for Brasenose, III, 19, pp. 30-1, in PP 1882, li.

[101] See above, p. 181, n. 80.

[102] See 'A Statute . . . concerning University Readers', 69-70, no. 4(d), (PP 1881, lxxiii).

stated only, 'It shall be the duty of every Reader to lecture and give instruction on the subject or branch of study for which he is appointed.'[103] In contrast, all professors were enjoined, in addition to their teaching duties, to 'assist the pursuit of knowledge and contribute to the advancement of it'.[104] Although readers were not prohibited from using their positions to reduce, or even eliminate, collegiate teaching obligations in the interests of advanced study and writing, these statutes clearly offered no encouragement to this view of the office.

The commissioners made no effort in their new statutes to subordinate readers to the professors. The only slight hint of a hierarchic relation between these two orders of university teacher was the vague admonition to the reader that 'it shall be his duty to have regard to the arrangements made or proposed to be made by the Professors, if any, lecturing in the same department of study'.[105] Since a corresponding obligation was not imposed on the professors, it might be inferred that readers were expected to defer, to some unspecified degree, to the professors in their field. None the less, the statutes as a whole could hardly be viewed as a real threat to the reader's autonomy. The commissioners had placed their hopes for the more efficient organization of university instruction on the creation of the Boards of Faculties, not on the introduction of clear lines of authority among university teachers.

The major apparent defect in the statutes concerning university readerships was that the creation of seven new offices could not provide about one hundred collegiate teachers with realistic expectations for promotion. However, it was the clear intention of the commissioners that these seven only represented the beginning of the programme. Readers were to be paid from a Common University Fund which was expected to grow considerably over the next twenty years, thereby providing more money for this purpose. This fund was established through progressive taxation of the

---

[103] Ibid. 70, no. 5.   [104] Ibid. 65, no. 1.   [105] Ibid. 70, no. 5.
[106] See 'A Statute ... concerning college contributions for University Purposes', 2, n. 4 (PP 1882, li).

endowment incomes of the colleges, rising from 2 per cent for colleges with external incomes under £5,000 p.a. to 35 per cent on external incomes over £20,000 p.a.[106] The colleges were given a considerable grace period for adjusting to this new demand on their resources. Until 1889, colleges were required only to pay one-quarter of the contribution which the statutes ultimately would demand. One-half of their total statutory obligation would be expected from 1890 to 1894, three-quarters from 1895 to 1899 and the full amount beginning only in 1900. Since one-quarter of the total contribution could finance seven readerships, funds would be available by 1900 for the support of twenty-eight of these positions. This was, furthermore, only a minimum calculation since the commissioners also assumed that collegiate external income would rise during this period by the one-third which had been confidently predicted by the Cleveland Commission in 1874. With the possibility of thirty or more university readerships by 1900, college tutors could look forward realistically to the possibility that they would be able to attain this promotion by mid-career.

This statute concerning university readerships was a skilful compromise which incorporated a wide spectrum of opinion. If the commissioners' financial calculations had been correct and if a few loopholes which enabled colleges to evade their contributions to the Common University Fund had been removed,[107] this plan would have been the solution to the college tutors' complaint that they lacked the prospect of a progressive career in Oxford. Those readers who were motivated toward research also could have used their extra income to ameliorate the 'teaching drudgery' of which they had complained. Unfortunately, the agricultural depression was to upset these calculations and destroy these plans beyond repair.[108]

E. The Commission and the 'Endowment of Research'

The 'endowment of research' party had little cause to be satisfied with the outcome of the 1877 Commission. Their

---

[106] See 'A Statute . . . concerning college contributions for University Purposes', 2, no. 4 (PP 1882, li).

[107] See below, Ch. V, pp. 246-7.　　　　[108] See below, Ch. V, pp. 245-8.

plans for the devotion of a substantial proportion of university resources to the establishment of pure research positions unconnected with teaching found little favour with witnesses outside their own coterie. Many were sympathetic to research ideals but few looked with any enthusiasm on this particular plan. The commissioners also revealed their own antipathy to the ideas of the 'endowment of research' party, both in their questioning of witnesses and in their writing of statutes. The result was that, although the party was wholly defeated, the obligation to support learned research was accepted as a secondary function of the university, legitimate but subordinate to its primary educational duties.

Dr Appleton was the only witness to present a comprehensive scheme embodying the ideals of the 'endowment of research' party.[109] He suggested that prize fellowships be curtailed drastically and the income used for the support of those who wished to make 'learning their profession'.[110] He asserted that £30,000 p.a. from collegiate endowments could be diverted easily to establish a fund for this purpose administered by a committee composed of representatives of each faculty board. Grants would be made to individuals at first only for specific research projects and for short periods of time. If the work was performed satisfactorily, however, the grants could be renewed. Appleton argued that the committee would have sufficient evidence by the time scholars reached the age of thirty-five to decide whether they were suited for a life of pure research. The committee could award permanent 'studentships', not restricted to specific projects or periodic renewal, to those it considered to be qualified. Dr Appleton suggested that salaries ought to be on a graduated scale, rising eventually to £700 or £800 p.a. With £30,000 p.a. at its disposal, the committee probably would be able to support at least fifty or sixty of these 'students'.

Neither Archibald Sayce nor Mark Pattison, the only other 'endowment of research' essayists to address the Commission, recommended Dr Appleton's plan or suggested concrete plans of their own for the establishment of research as a profession. Apart from proposing that professors be

[109] PP 1881, lvi. 29–36.   [110] Ibid. 29, no. 522.

placed on the governing bodies of the colleges, Sayce confined himself to recommending 'the establishment of a few professorships or sub-professorships or readerships in oriental studies.[111] The interests of research were clearly uppermost in Sayce's mind since the only reason he advanced for creating these offices was as 'an inducement to a student to pursue his studies while he is still young and vigorous, in the hopes that after he has done good work he might eventually find a maintenance for the rest of his life, or at least for the rest of his working life'.[112] Even though Sayce admitted that few students would attend the lectures of these additional teachers, he was not so bold as to suggest that they ought to be relieved of their lecturing obligations.

Mark Pattison strayed even farther in his testimony from the recommendation of specific plans for the support of research.[113] He devoted most of his evidence to the reaffirmation of his belief in 'liberal education' as opposed to the 'professorial system' which he had expounded so eloquently to the 1850 Commission[114] and to the condemnation of the effect of competitive examinations on this ideal.[115] He suggested vaguely that if some method could be devised which would ensure that fellowships were awarded to those devoted to the advancement of knowledge rather than to mere coaches who viewed their role only as enabling their pupils to pass examinations, Oxford's problems as a home for both research and education would be solved.[116] Pattison did not pursue this point to the extent of suggesting any concrete plan. Both Sayce and Pattison were probably so demoralized by the public reception of the *Essays on the Endowment of Research*,[117] or so intimidated by the hostility of the commissioners[118] that they were unable to present the views of their party in a coherent form. Pattison was also too old and ill to wish to become involved in any controversies. He had been prevailed upon to write this contribution to the *Essays* only with the greatest

---

[111] Ibid. 106–11, esp. 107, no. 1762.   [112] Ibid. 107, no. 1762.
[113] Ibid. 255–9.   [114] *Oxford Univ. Comm.* (1852), Evidence, 41–50.
[115] PP 1881, lvi. 256, no. 4115.   [116] Ibid. 256–7, no. 4116.
[117] See above, Ch. III, p. 149.
[118] See below, pp. 191–2, nn. 124–8.

difficulty.[119] Only the indefatigable Dr Appleton was able to rise above these difficulties.

Although no other witnesses proposed that research ought to be raised to the level of a separate profession, many suggested other schemes which recognized the obligations of the university as a home for advanced study. The Hebdomadal Council recommended the creation of a fund to finance worthwhile research projects and this plan was supported by D. B. Monro and R. L. Nettleship.[120] J. F. Bright of University College argued that this method of encouraging research would not be likely to degenerate into jobbery and sinecurism since funds would be provided only for well-defined projects and for limited periods of time.[121] The implication was that the more grandiose plan of Dr Appleton contained too few safeguards against this objection. This scheme even gained the grudging acceptance of some witnesses who were basically sceptical of the value of encouraging research at all. George Thorley, despite his primary concern for educational matters, was willing to sanction the creation of a small fund to give 'occasional' grants as an experiment.[122] Even Benjamin Jowett, who believed so few people were capable of doing worthwhile research that any large-scale system of support was unnecessary, accepted the value of providing funds for 'any kind of study that has definite results in adding to knowledge' so long as this rationale was not used to finance 'mere unproductive study'.[123]

The commissioners showed their strong antipathy toward the 'endowment of research' party in their questioning of witnesses. They reacted with pronounced hostility when J. R. Thursfield chose to begin his testimony with a daring quotation from Pattison's writings in which it was asserted that Oxford had to decide whether it was to be a genuine university 'to which free science and liberal letters attract by

---

[119] The historian of *The Academy* has described vividly Pattison's attitude at this time. 'It needed a great number of persuasive letters to overcome Pattison's procrastination and secure his contribution. He tried to excuse himself and told Appleton that he was going abroad. But Appleton took no pity on the old Rector. "You will go abroad with a much freer mind", he wrote to him, "if you leave this behind you done."' See Diderik Roll-Hanson, *The Academy* (Copenhagen, 1957), 81-2.   [120] See PP 1881, lvi. 11 nos. 241-2 and 53-5.

[121] Ibid. 77-9.   [122] Ibid. 131-5.   [123] Ibid. 156, no. 2661.

their own lustre only such ingenious youth as have a true vocation, or . . . a great national lyceé through the routine of which we shall attempt to force willing and unwilling, apt and unapt, by the stimulus of emulation, of honours, prizes and rewards'.[124] Professor Bernard belligerently demanded in response, 'Are we bound to accept either the very broad or the very narrow view of the question?' To conciliate him, Thursfield was forced to admit that this extreme polarization was unfair and did not represent his own views.[125] Similarly, when J. R. Magrath of Queen's suggested that professorial duties ought to be defined exclusively in terms of research with no lecturing obligations, he was attacked aggressively by the commissioners. After asking Magrath sharply whether 'giving 24 lectures in a year can be pleaded as any excuse for a professor's not working at the advancement of his subject', Professor Henry Smith continued sarcastically, 'Do you not think it likely that a specialist who is, if I may say so, running over with his favourite subject, would not be able to discourse about it with great ease for that limited number of hours in the year?'[126]

The commissioners also displayed marked hostility in their interview with Mark Pattison. Despite the fact that he devoted his testimony almost entirely to discussing ideals of education, they accused Pattison of wishing to transform the university into a place of research alone. 'You are viewing the university in the main as a place for learned study in the remarks which you have made to us, leaving almost altogether out of sight the educational view of the university', Sir Mathew Ridley charged.[127] After repeated badgering by the commissioners on this point, Pattison finally burst out in exasperation, 'I am afraid that you would not attach much importance to any answer that I could give to that question.'[128]

Despite this antipathy to the 'endowment of research' party, the commissioners attempted to satisfy the widespread desire for a research fund while avoiding the dangers of sinecurism. Although the payment of university readers was

[124] Ibid. 111–12, no. 1842.
[125] Ibid. 112, no. 1844.
[126] Ibid. 142, nos. 2407 and 2409.
[127] Ibid. 257, no. 4132.
[128] Ibid. 258, no. 4134.

to be the first call on the resources of the Common University
Fund, provision was made also for 'making payments . . .
for . . . the conducting of investigations within the University
in any branch of learning or inquiry connected with the studies
of the University'.[129] It was also specified that the fund would
be applicable '[f]or providing . . . libraries, collections or
apparatus for any purpose connected . . . with research in
any art or science or other branch of learning, and for maintaining the same'.[130]

From the standpoint of the 'endowment of research' party,
of course, this provision was totally inadequate. The amount
was pitifully small compared to the £30,000 p.a. which Dr
Appleton had demanded. Initially, a maximum of only £900
p.a. would be available for these grants.[131] Even by 1900,
when the assumption was that the Common University
Fund would have grown four or fivefold, there was little
likelihood that more than £3,500 to £4,500 p.a. would be
devoted to this purpose. Furthermore, the fact that grants
were to be made available for 'the conducting of investigations'
rather than for the support of scholars implied strongly that
only specific projects would be financed and that the establishment of university careers for pure researchers would receive
no encouragement from this plan.

The commissioners' decision on the issue of who was to
control this research fund was also unlikely to give satisfaction
to the 'endowment of research' party. Dr Appleton had
recommended that these grants ought to be made by a
committee composed of members elected by each faculty
board. James Bryce, who sympathized with the goals of the
'endowment of research' party, suggested that the disburse-
ment of research funds should be entrusted 'in each subject'
to a board consisting of 'the professor and other persons
associated with him'.[132] The commissioners decided instead

[129] 40 and 41 Vict. cap. 48, XVI, 3; in Shadwell iv. 72.

[130] Ibid. XVI, 10, pp. 72-3; cited in 'A Statute . . . concerning the Common
University Fund', 14, no. 5(b), (PP 1881, lxxiii).

[131] The fund was to contain £3,000 p.a. initially of which £2,100 p.a. would
be needed to pay the seven university readers. See 'A Statute . . . concerning the
Common University Fund', 14, nos. 2(c) and 5(a), (PP 1881, lxxiii).

[132] PP 1881, lvi. 90, no. 1488.

to give the Boards of Faculties a distinctly subordinate role in the administration of this fund. Each of the six boards contributed only one representative to the seventeen-member committee which controlled the Common University Fund. It was apparent that the fear of giving too much power to the new Boards of Faculties had prevented their being given a larger voice even in the administration of a fund for the support of research.

The other major provision which the commissioners made for the encouragement of research was that they inserted a clause in the statutes of virtually every college permitting the election to an ordinary fellowship without examination of 'any person whose attainments in Literature, Science or Art shall . . . qualify him for election as a Fellow, and who shall undertake to perform any definite literary, scientific, or educational work in the College or the University, which work shall be specified in the Resolution by which he is elected'.[133] It was clear that 'mere unproductive study' was the major danger which this statute was meant to avoid. There was also a strong incentive for colleges to avail themselves of this permission, since any funds which they chose to spend in this way could be deducted from the sums, beyond the minimum 2 per cent contribution, they were required to pay into the Common University Fund.[134] Especially for the richer colleges who otherwise would have been forced to pay large amounts into the fund, the choice was between selecting for themselves the research purposes for which their money would be spent, or giving it to an external body to allocate as they chose. The only other encouragement to research written into the college statutes was that six colleges were permitted to extend the tenure of ordinary fellowships beyond the normal seven year limit if the fellow 'is engaged in the study of Literature or Science, and . . . his studies are likely to produce valuable results in published writings'.[135]

[133] See, for example, New College, III, 21, p. 137 (PP 1882, li). Words virtually identical to these were used in the statutes of every other college (except for Christ Church) although minor differences in election procedures and in payment were allowed.

[134] 'A Statute . . . concerning college contributions for university purposes', 2, no. 3 (PP 1882, li).

[135] The citation is from the statute of this type at Balliol. See III, 12(ii), p. 14.

Although the commissioners provided for the establishment of several new professorships and for the greatly increased endowment of many existing ones, especially in the natural and physical sciences, by attaching these offices to the richer colleges, the statutes regarding professorships did not give much encouragement to research ideals. Although many witnesses advocated more and better endowed professorships largely in the interests of research,[136] the commissioners laid greater emphasis on defining exactly the duties of professors in regard to teaching than on enforcing research obligations.[137] None the less, the professors' obligations to deliver a minimum of two lectures a week during term was not so heavy as to preclude advanced study and writing. Some professors objected very strongly to these obligations but their anger was directed more toward the implied attitude of suspicion than toward the onerousness of the duties themselves. When E. A. Freeman, Regius Professor of Modern History, complained that as a result of the 1877 Commission, '[t]he professors are put under every possible kind of fetter', he explained that '[i]t is the being ordered, the being distrusted, the being treated like an usher, and not like a man who is or ought to be at the head of his subject which is the grievance.'[138] The commissioners were clearly apprehensive that professors would seek to turn their offices into sinecures in the absence of strictly defined duties.

Research ideals might well have fared better in Oxford if the 'endowment of research' party had taken care to seem less of a clique. In all their actions concerning professors,

---

Statutes having the same effect were permitted at Magdalen, IV, 21, p. 109; at New College, III, 22, p. 137; at Christ Church, XVI, 16, p. 49; at Trinity, II, 3(b), pp. 190–1; and at University College, III, 12(c), p. 207; all in PP 1882, li.

[136] See 'Robert Bellamy Clifton, Esq., MA, (Professor of Experimental Philosophy) examined', p. 25, no. 457; 'The Rev. George Rawlinson, MA (Camden Professor of Ancient History) examined', p. 250; 'The Rev. Archibald H. Sayce, MA (Deputy Professor of Comparative Philology) examined', p. 107, no. 1762; and 'A Memorial to the University of Oxford Commission', advocating more professorial chairs in 'the more recondite dead languages', p. 376; all in PP 1881, lvi.

[137] 'A Statute . . . concerning the duties of Professors', 65, no. 3; 66, no. 1(b) and 67, no. 2(b), (PP 1881, lxxiii).

[138] 'Oxford After Forty Years', *Contemp. Rev.* li (May 1887), 621.

readers, and research in general, the commissioners betrayed an extreme degree of suspicion that there were people in the university who would completely eliminate students and teaching to devote all the resources of the colleges to the support of arcane learning unless restrained by the most explicit statutory inhibitions. Some evidence for the counter-productivity of the 'endowment of research' party is provided by the fact that the statutes written by the commissioners for Cambridge, where this party was less prominent, did not attempt to define each professors' minimum teaching obligations with the specificity which was the rule at Oxford.[139] Research was warily accepted as a legitimate function of the university by both the commissioners and the colleges, but the view that research ought to be raised to the level of a separate profession was firmly rejected.

F. The Commission and the Problem of University Government

The only one of the tutorial grievances which received no attention from the 1877 Commission was the problem of the domination of Convocation and Congregation by 'non-academical' persons. This grievance was completely ignored by both the witnesses and the commissioners. The statutes written in 1881 and 1882 left the constitution of these university legislatures unaltered. The political sympathies of the government, the commissioners' conception of their proper functions, and the changing composition of Congregation itself all contributed to this result.

One reason the reform of university government was not attempted was that the 1877 Commission, as an outgrowth of the Cleveland Commission, was expected to concentrate on the re-allocation of collegiate and university resources. Lord Salisbury was reported to have argued in his speech moving the second reading of the bill establishing the Commission,

---

[139] See 'A Statute made by the University of Cambridge Commissioners on the 15th March 1881, for the University, marked Statute B.' XI, 4-5, p. 11 (PP 1882, li).

They refused to pass beyond the actual requirements of the case — the actual disposal of the money of which the [Cleveland] Commission had indicated the existence for the purposes which the University felt to be necessary; and the limit which they specially imposed on themselves was that they declined to enter into the difficult fields of controversy connected either with the government of the University, or with the position of the Ecclesiastical Bodies within it.[140]

The reform of Convocation and Congregation was not one of the sixteen specific objectives eventually listed in the parliamentary act.[141] Although the seventeenth section was a general enabling clause giving the commissioners power '[f]or altering or repealing any statute, ordinance, or regulation of the University, and substituting or adding any statute for or to the same',[142] they clearly decided to confine their attention to the goals specifically enumerated for them.

Attempts had been made in Parliament to include the reform of university government within the jurisdiction of the Commission, but they were not supported by the government and were defeated. Sir Charles Dilke proposed in debate that the bill contain a specific clause giving the commissioners the power 'for altering the qualifications required for membership of congregation at Oxford, . . . and for limiting or abrogating the power of the convocation'.[143] Dilke was reported as protesting in the name of the academic residents against 'the thirty or forty curates at Oxford, who were locally known, he believed, as "the black dragoons", being even potentially a controlling element in the direction of the studies of the University'.[144] He specifically included, however, non-academic elements other than the local clergy in his denunciation of the existing Congregation. 'It was not only of the curates that they complained; but why, he asked, should the ordinary residents of an ordinary provincial town, who happened to have taken their ordinary degrees, the doctors, the solicitors, and the chief constable, able and estimable persons though they might be, have a voice in the administration of

---

[140] *Hansard's Parl. Debates*, 3rd Series, ccxxxv, 1877, p. 664.
[141] 40 and 41 Vict. cap. 48, no. 16 (1–16), in Shadwell iv. 72–3.
[142] Ibid. 73–4.   [143] Ibid. ccxxxiv, 1877, p. 285.
[144] Ibid. 286. This same complaint of clerical dominance had been made earlier in the House of Lords by the Earl of Morley. See ibid. ccxxvii, 1876, p. 1689.

affairs for which special qualifications and attention were needed?'[145]

Dilke's amendment aroused considerable debate, most of it hostile. Gathorne Hardy, the spokesman for both the government and the university, asserted incorrectly[146] that this reform was unnecessary since 'not twenty' members of Congregation 'were resident MAs not connected with the teaching of the University'.[147] Sir Thomas Acland argued that the existing voting qualification already placed 'too large a power in the hands of the tutorial interest, many of them being very young, acute, and subtle men, with a very moderate acquaintance with the general affairs of the world'.[148] This point was pursued by Mr C. Dalrymple, a Cambridge graduate, who protested against this amendment 'that the opinion of the outside world was often of great value'.[149] The final note was struck by Staveley Hill, himself a non-academic member of Congregation, who remarked blandly that 'he had never heard any dissatisfaction with the present state of things'.[150] When Dilke's amendment came to the vote, it was defeated 115 to 143.[151] An attempt was made later to revive this issue by introducing a clause restricting membership in Congregation to resident fellows of colleges, former fellows, and those holding college or university offices. This amendment was also defeated 108 to 136.[152]

The Conservative government clearly wished to avoid reforming the university legislatures. The parliamentary debates revealed that if they had included this issue within the jurisdiction of the Commission, the difficulty of passing the bill would have been greatly increased. Lord Salisbury was also notably sympathetic to clerical interests[153] and, since 'non-academical' membership in Congregation and Convocation meant in practical terms greater representation for the Church, he did not wish to disturb this situation. The well-known Tory politics of most good Churchmen in any

---

[145] Ibid. ccxxxiv, 1877, p. 286.
[146] See the figures for 1874 and 1881 in Appendix 4, below p. 289
[147] *Hansard's Parl. Debates*, 3rd Series, ccxxxiv, 1877, p. 291.
[148] Ibid. 295.   [149] Ibid. 296.   [150] Ibid. 295.
[151] Ibid. 296. For the entire debate, see 286–96.   [152] Ibid. 1240–2.
[153] See above, pp. 173–4 for Lord Salisbury's involvement with the Church party in Oxford.

case would have inclined the government to avoid an issue certain to alienate their supporters. Since most younger fellows of colleges were not Tories in the 1870s, George Brodrick was able to remark acidly that 'Lord Salisbury was no less motivated by a desire to prevent the government of the Colleges from passing into the hands of young Radicals, than by a genuine zeal for the benefit of science.'[154]

The fact that the witnesses did not protest the exclusion of questions of university government from the jurisdiction of the Commission also may be explained by changes in the distribution of power which were occurring spontaneously in Congregation at this time. A comparison of those qualified to vote in Congregation in 1874 and in 1881 would lead one to think that the problem of non-academic members was solving itself without the need for constitutional reforms.[155] The most significant change was the marked rise in the number of tutorial fellows and college lecturers and the corresponding decline in resident MAs not engaged in official academic work. It was reasonable to expect that this trend would continue since the effect of the commissioners' statutes was to increase both tutorial fellows and university teachers. It could easily have been assumed that the disproportionate number of non-academic members of Congregation in the 1860s and early 1870s had been the result of a short-lived period of religious enthusiasm which had attracted to Oxford many High Church clergy. Since the tone of the university was undoubtedly becoming less ecclesiastical, many dons may have thought that this attraction would continue to diminish in the future. Those who objected as a matter of principle to 'non-academical' voters in the university legislatures might have been persuaded that, as a matter of practical policy, it was wiser to leave this issue alone.

The Commission of 1877, therefore, left the constitutions of Congregation and Convocation totally unchanged. Although problems concerning the distribution of power in the university legislatures were to recur in an even more aggravated form

---

[154] *Memories and Impressions 1831–1900* (London, 1900), 182.
[155] See below, Appendix 4, p. 289.

within the next twenty years,[156] in 1881 there were probably few dons, beyond the extreme anti-clericals, who were much dismayed by the decision of the government and the Commission.

The Commission of 1877 took as its primary task the re-allocation of endowment income to establish an academic profession for college tutors. The modification of the celibacy restriction and the creation of pension funds enabled college teachers to view their offices as careers for life. Efforts were made to insure that in the future there would be reasonable opportunities for promotion to positions offering larger incomes and more dignified teaching obligations. The need for the more efficient organization of university instruction was recognized only to the extent that changes for this purpose would not interfere with the autonomy of either the colleges or the individual don. Research ideals also were accepted only to the degree that they were consistent with the interests of the college tutors. Prize fellowships and the interests of the Church were sacrificed ruthlessly when they interfered with the formulation of this plan. The principle of collegiate independence and the definition of this new academic profession primarily in terms of educational work within the colleges were also firmly established.

Unfortunately, the government chose a particularly inappropriate time for the creation of plans for the university. The implicit assumption behind all the commissioners' reforms was that the re-allocation of collegiate endowment income for greater public efficiency was the only major problem confronting Oxford. It was also assumed that the painfulness of this re-allocation would be eased considerably by the rise in external income expected on the basis of agricultural improvements and changes in the tenure of college property. Although the interests of the Church, the prize fellows, and the researchers were all subordinated to those of the tutors, resentment was diminished by the confident inclusion of measures for the satisfaction of these other groups as well. Although the future was to reveal a certain

---

[156] See below, Ch. V, 211–14 for a continuation of this theme.

number of internal flaws in the commissioner's plans, they were all small enough to be rectified through minor revisions. A wholly unexpected external event, however, the agricultural depression, was to damage their plan beyond minor repair since the funds necessary for its implementation were sharply reduced. Virtually every aspect of the commissioners' comprehensive scheme was affected and some were transformed beyond recognition.

Chapter V

THE AGRICULTURAL DEPRESSION AND THE FATE OF THE 1877 COMMISSION'S PLAN

A. Anatomy of a Financial Crisis

Any discussion of the fate of the 1877 Commission's plans must begin with the agricultural depression. This long-term decline in the value of agricultural land began in the mid-1870s and, despite some fluctuations, the trend continued into the twentieth century with no genuine remission. Since a large portion of collegiate investment was in agricultural land, the financial position of most colleges deteriorated seriously during this period. This financial problem had a profound effect on the ability of the colleges to implement the 1877 Commission's plan for the establishment of a 'tutorial profession' while at the same time preserving a substantial part of the prize fellowship system and accepting new obligations for the support of science and research as well.

The dimensions of the financial crisis can be outlined from a series of papers delivered before the Royal Statistical Society between 1892 and 1913[1] in which L. L. Price of Oriel College charted this phenomenon with as much statistical accuracy as the material would allow. He provided figures for aggregate collegiate income in 1883, 1893, and 1903. If his figures are compared with those compiled by the Cleveland Commission for 1871, a roughly accurate notion can be derived of the extent of the crisis.

Several caveats must be entered, however, concerning the value of Price's and the Cleveland Commission's aggregate

---

[1] See 'The recent depression in agriculture as shown in the accounts of an Oxford College, 1876–1890', *Journal of the Royal Statistical Soceity* lv (1892), 2–36; 'The colleges of Oxford and agricultural depression', *Jour. of the Royal Stat. Soc.* lvii (1895), 36–74; 'The accounts of the Colleges of Oxford, 1893–1903, with special reference to their agricultural revenues', *Jour. of the Royal Stat. Soc.* lxiv (1904), 585–660; and 'The Estates of the Colleges of Oxford and their Management', *Jour. of the Royal Stat. Soc.* lxxvi (1993), 787–90.

statistics. Accounting differences existed both between the 1871 statistics and the later figures and between the various colleges and all of the sample years. Despite Price's efforts to compensate for these differences and my attempts to mould the Cleveland Commission's figures into consistency with Prices's, some inaccuracy still must be assumed. Furthermore, the years for which statistical information is available are not ideal for charting the extent of the agricultural depression. Since the crisis began in the late 1870s, the figures for 1883 cannot be seen as the high point of prosperity and, therefore, the decline from 1883 to 1893 can represent only the minimum financial impact of the depression. Aggregate figures also are somewhat misleading since a few colleges experienced rises in external income during this period. Their presence in the totals tends to obscure the greater effect of the agricultural depression on most colleges. None the less, the broad trends were substantial enough to out-balance any reasonable allowance for error caused by imperfections in the statistical data.

Appendix 9 shows the trend in gross and net collegiate income in the four sample years from 1871 to 1903.[2] It reveals that net collegiate income rose during the last years of 'the golden age of English agriculture' in the 1870s, fell by at least 15 per cent in the 1880s and early 1890s, and recovered only about half its losses by the early twentieth century. Disappointed expectations also must be included in judging the extent of the financial losses sustained by the colleges. By 1895 they had to accept a loss of about £20,000 p.a. in net external income in place of the increase of approximately £100,000 p.a. which the Cleveland Commission had predicted. The fact that the colleges had practically recovered their 1871 positions by 1903 was, undoubtedly, a very small consolation.

The effects of this economic decline were intensified by the reforms which had been undertaken since 1858 under the authority of the series of Universities and College Estates Acts.[3] The traditional system of beneficial leases had been

[2] See below, p. 293.
[3] See 21 and 22 Vict. cap. 44 (1858), 23 and 24 Vict. cap. 59 (1860), 43 and

eliminated in favour of rack-rent, a system which in a period of agricultural depression gave the colleges as landlords the worst possible situation. They acquired a heavy burden of interest charges on debts necessitated by the costs of running out the old leases. They also were required to accept greatly expanded responsibilities for taxes, repairs, and improvements on their estates during a time when reliable tenants able to pay economic rents regularly were at a premium. These increased expenses insured that the decline in the colleges' net external income would be far greater than the decline in their gross external income.

The aggregate statistics, furthermore, underestimated the effect of the agricultural depression since most colleges suffered more than these figures indicated. Collegiate external income from house rents and urban property was included in these totals as well as receipts from agricultural land. These other types of property generally rose in value during the late nineteenth century. Merton, Magdalen, Brasenose, and St. John's; who were all lucky or astute enough to own a considerable amount of non-agricultural property, experienced an average rise in their net external incomes between 1883 and 1903 of 17 or 18 per cent.[4] The effect of the agricultural depression on those colleges which were not so fortunate was more severe than the total statistics would indicate. For example, Brasenose was able to raise its net external income from £7,400 in 1871[5] to £10,300 in 1903[6] despite some falling off in the 1880s. During the same period, Wadham, which had had in 1871 an external income almost identical to that of Brasenose, fell by two-thirds, from £7,300[7] to only £2,000.[8] As early as 1878 the combination of increased outlays on farm property, lowering of rents, arrears of rents, and too high increments to the fellows had forced Wadham to sell stock worth £4,796 to pay the stipends of the fellows

---

44 Vict. cap. 46 (1880), and 61 and 62 Vict. cap. 55 (1898) in Shadwell iii. 247–78, 301–11 and iv. 102–6, 206–20.

[4] *Jour. of the Royal Stat. Soc.* lxiv (1904), 589.

[5] See Return A. 18, p. 584 (PP 1873, xxxvii, part ii).

[6] *Jour. of the Royal Stat. Soc.* lxiv (1904), Table I, 588.

[7] See Return A.18, p. 815 (PP 1873, xxxvii, part ii).

[8] *Jour. of the Royal Stat. Soc.* lxiv (1904), Table I, 588.

and college officers.[9] In 1882 the college was simply unable to pay the Warden his last quarter's salary.[10] Price estimated that if the four fortunate colleges were omitted, the average loss sustained by the remaining colleges would be half again as great as the aggregate figures revealed.[11]

In the evidence of witnesses before the 1877 Commission there was little indication that the sanguine financial predictions of the Cleveland Commission were in need of drastic revision downward. The curators of the University Chest, when asked directly by the commissioners whether these figures were still accurate, indicated that they were.[12] Alfred Robinson, the bursar of New College and a man widely respected in Oxford for his business acumen, echoed the Cleveland Commission in assuring the commissioners that the colleges in aggregate could expect to increase their external income by £100,000 p.a. by 1895.[13] He confidently predicted that it would be possible to accept greatly increased expenditure for university purposes without diminishing the collegiate staffs or establishments at all.

By 1880-1, when the commissioners framed their new statutes, the hard times for agriculture had already begun. It was generally thought, however, that this was merely a short-term decline and that the upward trend would soon recommence. Both colleges and commissioners felt justified by expert testimony in making this optimistic assumption. Appendix 9 makes clear why some acute observers could have displayed this misguided confidence. Although the figures for 1883 certainly represented a decline from the peak period of the mid-1870s, they still showed a considerable advance since the early 1870s. Gross external income had risen by over 15 per cent despite the more recent bad years. Although the increased costs of ownership of estates let on rack-rent leases consumed two-thirds of this gain, it was not unreasonable in 1881 to assume that prosperity would return soon, the burden of debt would be erased quickly, and the colleges would be left to the full enjoyment of their increased incomes.

---

[9] Wadham MS Convention Book, p. 372. I owe this reference and the following one to Professor Lawrence Stone.   [10] Ibid. 373.

[11] *Jour. of the Royal Stat. Soc.* lxiv (1904), Table I, 589.

[12] PP 1881, lvi. 249.   [13] Ibid. 147.

There were some observers, however, who looked more deeply into current trends and saw a more disturbing future. One anonymous critic in 1881, writing his jeremiad under the pseudonym of 'Oxoniensis', accurately predicated the future course of decline in agricultural income. Oxoniensis argued that the abolition of the old system of beneficial leases would prove an unmitigated disaster for the colleges.[14] He complained that they were deeply in debt for 'improvements', at the mercy of rapacious tenants for every repair, and often unable even to collect their rents. 'Firmly believing that they were doing the right thing for their successors,' Oxoniensis lamented, 'the authorities have in many cases burdened their colleges with a load of debt which a fall in rents will soon make unbearable.'[15] He concluded bleakly that 'the Colleges have been most unfortunate in their efforts at reform. They have destroyed, beyond all hope of recovery, a long-established system of tenant-right, and it fails them just at the time when it is most urgently needed.'[16] Although the retention of beneficial leases certainly would not have saved the colleges from the long-term effects of the agricultural depression, Oxoniensis was undoubtedly correct in his contention that the expenses involved in the transfer to rack-rents exacerbated its effects. In this situation, Oxoniensis urged that 'the claims of University reform will have to be deferred indefinitely till things right themselves'.[17]

The commissioners probably would have dismissed Oxoniensis as an opponent of their plans, whose lugubrious predictions were merely convenient justifications for anti-reform sentiment. In an expansive mood engendered by agricultural prosperity, the commissioners had assumed that there would be enough money for all the new calls they had sanctioned on endowment income. It seemed that the needs of married tutors, the desire for more professors, the requirements of the natural and physical sciences, and the demands of research all could be satisfied without infringing on the traditional amenities and prerogatives of collegiate life or on the rights of the learned professions to academic subsidies.

---

[14] 'The Colleges as Landlords', *Fraser's Magazine* xxiii, n.s. no. 137 (1881), 590–600.   [15] Ibid. 594.   [16] Ibid. 597.   [17] Ibid. 595.

The witnesses before the Commission also had betrayed no consciousness that they were competing for shares of a limited, even a shrinking, endowment fund. The tacit assumption was that sums available for collegiate and university purposes were certain to expand markedly. The evidence was remarkable on the whole for the relative lack of animosity displayed by witnesses toward each other's proposals. Arguing persuasively for the desirability of one's own plans seemed more important than showing the disadvantages of alternative schemes.

The financial crisis, however, fundamentally transformed the nature of university reform in the 1880s and 1890s. When the happy predictions of the Cleveland Commission proved illusory, reform soon became a matter of increasingly strident and frustrated groups struggling desperately for a share of a diminishing endowment fund. Tradition would be no very persuasive argument for the allocation of resources in this situation. Nor would purposes which were considered desirable but not essential have much chance for funding. University reform could not be 'deferred indefinitely till things right themselves', as Oxoniensis had suggested, but the goals and priorities of the 1877 Commission's plan for the creation of an academic profession could be altered to meet the exigencies of a period in which relative scarcity instead of plenty became the norm in Oxford.

B. 'Young Oxford' Versus the 'Ageing Radicals'

The financial crisis caused by the agricultural depression had far-reaching effects on the attitudes of academic residents toward university reform. As year after year the external income of the colleges continued to fall, animosities developed between the 'ageing radicals' who had benefited from the changes introduced by the 1877 Commission and the new 'Young Oxford' whose aspirations no longer could be satisfied. The bitter conflicts of the 1880s and 1890s concerning the implementation of the commissioners' plans were fought along lines created by these animosities. The younger dons joined forces with the non-academic members of Congregation to thwart reforms of which they disapproved. This alliance tended to draw into an unlikely union all those who would have gained to any degree from the 1877 settlement: scientists, professors, and even researchers, as well as the older official fellows. The enduring conception of the nature and functions of the academic profession which emerged in Oxford was the result, to a large extent, of the clashing of these alliances in an emotional atmosphere heightened by the knowledge that the funds no longer existed to finance all worthwhile objects.

The mood of Young Oxford before the period of the 1877 Commission was confident, aggressive, and generally icono-clastic. J. R. Green noted indulgently of the young don in 1870, 'He is young in the intensity of his worships, in the precocity of his criticism . . . His youth breaks out in defiant heterodoxies and orthodoxies, in a fiery party-spirit, in a passionate loyalty to academical wire-pullers, in an abhorence of "caves" and moderation, in a preference for strict party votes.'[18] If observers had been asked to judge whether the 'defiant heterodoxies' or the 'defiant orthodoxies' predom-inated during this period, most would have emphasized the former. For example, another critic of 1870 argued that the chief vice of the college tutor was more often an irresponsible desire for change rather than a bigoted conservatism.[19] A more hostile commentator of this period condemned the 'slightly atheistic views' of the younger dons whose conver-sation he described as 'a jargon of Voltaire and Comte'.[20]

After 1885, although the 'fiery party spirit' remained, the balance of opinion among the younger dons shifted away from 'defiant heterodoxies' and toward 'defiant orthodoxies'. Young Oxford was characterized by the Non-Placet Society, which was founded at this time 'to criticize modern inno-vations' and to organize voters in the university legislatures against reforms of which they disapproved.[21] A. T. S. Good-rick, a young fellow of St. John's in the 1880s and a mem-ber of the Society, explicitly described this organization

---

[18] Mrs J. R. Green and Miss K. Norgate (eds.), *Oxford Studies* (London, 1901), 263. This quotation is from an article which appeared originally in the *Saturday Review* in 1870.

[19] 'College Tutors: the Old School and the New', *London Society* xvii, no. 100 (1870), 344.

[20] 'In the Common Room: An Oxford Sketch', *Belgravia* vi (Sept. 1868), 356.

[21] Sir Charles Oman, *Memories of Victorian Oxford* (London, 1941), 195.

as the result of conflict between the old radicals who had fought against clerical domination and for the marriage of tutors, and the young fellows whose own prospects were injured by the career aspirations of their seniors. 'The younger men when they came in found themselves side by side with old dons masquerading as youthful Radicals', he contemptuously observed.

On the strength of refusals to go to morning chapel twenty years before, these derelicts claimed to be considered as champions of liberty, while the young bloods persisted in regarding them as Whigs of a peculiarly malignant and self-seeking type. To this natural repulsion was in part at least due the origin of the once-famous Non-Placet Society . . . [T]here was . . . a consensus of opinion among the younger men against ill-considered and unnecessary legislation, and to this was added presently a strong feeling of protest against personal jobbery. For an era had now begun in which it was necessary to find a place for deserving politicians who either were married or desired to marry, and in some instances, offices were apparently created for the especial behoof of such persons.[22]

Goodrick related the hostility of the younger dons to their discontent with the settlement of the 1877 Commission. 'Every year young men of talent who a few years ago would have been gladly welcomed by their own colleges, after taking their degree, to fill up the gaps in the tutorial body which were continually occurring as the older men recognized (or were recommended to recognize) their advancing years and consequent diminution in energy, are now practically dismissed from the University', he complained.

They are presented with an annuity for seven years, and they go forth into the cold shade of the Civil Service or the Junior Bar, lest they should interfere with men who are no whit their superiors in talent and who have long enjoyed the sweets of office. The disinherited go to swell the ranks of the malcontents, and being by no means voiceless, their strictures must at times even flutter the comfortable dovecots of New Oxford. But the old men are fettered now in their places by family considerations.[23]

Goodrick concluded that 'people are beginning to ask whether the Nationalization of the Universities has after all meant the

---

[22] 'Congregation and Convocation', *Macmillan's Mag.* xc (July 1904), 225.
[23] Ibid. 223.

creation of a number of co-optative oligarchies whose members are like to be paralyzed by the possession of that bane of the Englishman, a modest competence'.[24]

The material basis for the transformation of Young Oxford from enthusiasm for reform in the 1870s to diehard opposition to 'modern innovations' in the 1880s and 1890s can be shown by comparing the size of the colleges' fellowship fund with total collegiate disbursements 'for university purposes' during the worst period of the agricultural depression. Since 'university purposes' were calculated to include only the funds used to pay the salaries of university professors and readers, to provide laboratories and equipment for scientific education, to finance improvements in the Bodleian Library, and to support research projects; the aggregate trend in this category of expenditure would be a good approximation of the amount of collegiate income used to carry out the plans of the 1877 Commission. Between 1883 and 1893, while the net external income of the colleges fell by 15 per cent, the amount spent on fellowships also declined by about 15 per cent, from £70,980 to £59,715.[25] However, during this same period, the collegiate contributions for university purposes rose by over 20 per cent, from £16,740 in 1883 to £20,570 in 1893.[26] With the aid of these figures, it will not be difficult to understand the growth in resentment among the younger dons toward science, research, and the career aspirations of the 'ageing radicals'. Although some resentment against the settlement of the 1877 Commission, especially against the married tutors who prevented younger fellows from succeeding to college offices, certainly would have existed even if the financial predictions of the Cleveland Commission had proved correct, the actual decline in collegiate income undoubtedly increased both the urgency and the bitterness of this resentment.

These sentiments on the part of Young Oxford were certain to elicit an enthusiastic response from the majority of the local clergy, professional men, and private coaches who

[24] Ibid. 224.
[25] *Jour. of the Royal Stat. Soc.* lviii (1895), Table X, 65.
[26] Ibid. Table IX, 64.

constituted the non-academic members of Congregation. They never had felt much sympathy for science or research ideals and they saw no particular value in allowing college tutors to view their positions as professional careers.[27] The plans formulated by the 1877 Commission were anathema to them. In contrast, Young Oxford had turned against these ideals only when it had become apparent that, in a period of declining endowment income, their implementation could be accomplished only if the young dons were ruthlessly sacrificed for the benefit of their seniors. None the less, it was found that, despite the different origins of their discontent, Young Oxford and the majority of the resident MAs who did not hold academic offices were able to join forces on virtually every specific issue before the university. Together they constituted a powerful alliance against 'modern innovations'.

The impact of this alliance was enhanced by the growth in the power of the non-academic elements in Congregation. The most striking change revealed by a comparison between the members of Congregation in 1881 and 1900 was the increase in the number of resident MAs not engaged in official academic work.[28] Although the number of university and collegiate teachers as well as other officials expanded during this period due to the provisions made by the 1877 Commission, the rise in matriculations,[29] and the proliferation of examinations; the significance of these tendencies was dwarfed by the growing power of the non-academic voters. This group, which had been the object of the especial hatred of Young Oxford in the 1860s, more than doubled between 1881 and 1900 to become again, as they had been in the early 1870s, the single largest category of voters in Congregation.

These new non-academic members of Congregation did not consist entirely of the clergymen and private coaches who previously had dominated this category. The number of resident clergymen who held no official collegiate or university offices only expanded sufficiently by 1900 to maintain the percentage of Congregation which these 'black dragoons' had

[27] See above Ch. III, pp. 118-21 for a discussion of the influence of the Church party among the majority of the non-academic members of Congregation.
[28] See below, Appendix 4, p. 289.
[29] Matriculations rose about 10 per cent, from 757 in 1882 to 839 in 1900.

represented in 1881.[30] It also was unlikely that private coaches accounted for any substantial increase in non-academic voters. Honour coaching had become virtually extinct in most fields by the late nineteenth century.[31] Although some indications existed that pass coaching may have grown to some degree because of the antipathy of college tutors to this work,[32] the diminishing ratio of passmen to honourmen[33] insured that no rise in the number of pass coaches could have accounted for the tripling of non-academic laymen in Congregation between 1881 and 1900.

The primary cause of the rise in the number of non-academic voters in Congregation in the late nineteenth century was that the university came to attract a growing population of 'genteel private families, who have selected Oxford as a desirable residence'.[34] One observer suggested that the educational advantages of Oxford had attracted these new residents. '[A] longside the academic race which peoples the outskirts of the University,' he noted, 'there is also a great influx of immigrants from other quarters, who have settled near Oxford for the sake of getting a cheaper University education for their sons'.[35] George Brodrick remarked spitefully that the presence of married tutors had created a society of educated people with small incomes which had attracted others in similar circumstances to Oxford. 'Nor

[30] See below, Appendix 10, p. 294.

[31] Law seems to have been an exception to this rule. See F. H. Lawson, *The Oxford Law School 1850–1965* (Oxford, 1968), 48.

[32] Several witnesses before the 1877 Commission had complained that passmen were being forced to go to private coaches because of the poor collegiate tuition. See 'The Rev. Edwin Hatch, MA (Vice-Principal of St. Mary's Hall), examined', 43–6 and 'Montague Burrows, Esq., MA (Chichele Professor of Modern History), examined', 46–53, both in PP 1881, lvi. George Brodrick later asserted that inter-collegiate lectures had not proved as satisfactory for pass education as the old catechetical system. See *Memories and Impressions 1831–1900* (London, 1900), 80. Several college tutors suggested in letters to *The Times* that pass-men ought to be removed totally from the university. P. A. Wright-Henderson of Wadham attacked this proposal in 'The Oxford Undergraduate, Past and Present', *Blackwood's Edin. Mag.* clxxxv, no. 621 (1909), 342.

[33] In 1881 about two-thirds of degree candidates (340 of 512) were honourmen. By 1900, this percentage had risen to three-fourths (428 of 558).

[34] T. E. K[ebbel], 'Oxford in the Long Vacation', *The Cornhill Magazine* xl, no. 237 (1879), 332.

[35] T. E. Kebbel, 'Old and New Oxford', *The National Review* ix, no. 52 (1887), 452.

does the general society of Oxford consist wholly or mainly of those actually engaged in teaching, with their families', he asserted. 'The increasing number of such families with limited incomes but refined tastes, has attracted from all parts of the country the same class of residents which has long frequented Bath, Cheltenham, and Leamington; indeed, it has been discovered that plain living and high thinking can be combined in Oxford more easily than in any other provincial town.'[36]

Lord Curzon, the Chancellor of the University, drew together all these explanations for his denunciation of the growth of non-academic voters in Congregation. He argued that modern conditions had expanded their numbers far beyond· the expectations of the mid-nineteenth-century framers of this legislative body. He complained that

the central position, the excellent railway connexions, the educational advantages (not of the University alone), and the perennial beauty of Oxford have attracted thither a large non-academic population, drawn from different classes and professions – the male members of which, including retired civil servants and clergy, military officers, doctors, solicitors, etc. – if they already possess or can take a MA degree, and happen to reside within the one and a half mile limit, become members of Congregation and have a direct voice in the legislation and internal government of the University.[37]

Curzon wished to check this proliferation of non-academic voters by altering the criteria for membership in Congregation from residence within one and a half miles of Carfax to the holding of an official collegiate or university office.

Although several attempts were made in the late nineteenth and early twentieth centuries to accomplish this reform, it was not achieved until 1913 and its practical effects were deferred even longer since the passage of this statute through the university legislatures was made possible only by large concessions to 'existing interests'.[38] Any resident MA who had been qualified by residence to vote in Congregation was permitted to retain this privilege so long as he continued to

[36] *Memories and Impressions 1831–1900* (London, 1900), 347–8.
[37] *Principles and Methods of University Reform* (Oxford, 1909), 29.
[38] See the draft statute approved by the Hebdomadal Council, II, 1, in *Report of the Hebdomadal Council* (Oxford, 1910), 8–10.

live within one and a half miles of Carfax. The result was that the power of the non-academic elements in Congregation remained largely intact until World War I. The fortuitous growth in the number of non-academical members of Congregation markedly enhanced the ability of Young Oxford and the other forces of opposition to 'modern innovations' to wage their many battles against the ' 'dvocates of science and the endowment of research.

This movement of Young Oxford into united action with those non-academic elements which had traditionally opposed university reform tended to encourage the creation of a counter-alliance between the older official fellows, the scientists, the professors, and the researchers for the purpose of saving the benefits which they had gained under the 1877 settlement. Goodrick asserted bitterly, 'There was apparently a tacit understanding between these folk ['the Museum vote', i.e. the scientists] and the literary Radical to the effect that if they lent aid in carrying his measures they should receive his support in all their own proposals.'[39] W. L. Courtney complained that this alliance was too powerful to be resisted successfully by Young Oxford. 'It is true that the most recent specimens of youthful College Fellows have betrayed a remarkable tendency towards orthodoxy and conservatism;' he noted, 'but it is no less true that the resident members of Convocation . . . can four times out of five, carry liberal measures, and that the management of the Colleges is vested in men, if not young in years, at all events youthful in their feverish energy and sometimes destructive ardour. The internal reform of Oxford has proceeded in recent years with unabated vigour: the claims of science have been upheld by men whose own learning has been exclusively classical . . .'[40]

Evidence for this generation conflict and for the alliance between literary and scientific 'radicals' which it engendered does not depend, however, solely on the testimony of hostile critics. One advocate of science at Oxford, in the course of a bitter attack on the way in which scientific education had been 'sabotaged' by the colleges, admitted nevertheless that

[39] 'Congregation and Convocation', *Macmillan's Mag.* xc (July 1908), 226.
[40] 'New Lamps for Old Ones', *Macmillan's Mag.* lv, no. 325 (1886), 49.

'there are many at Oxford who are classical to the core, yet would willingly do all that is required for the advancement of natural science'. He added pointedly, 'They are mostly to be found among the middle-aged, not among the younger graduates.'[41] Percy Gardner, Professor of Classical Archeology and an enthusiastic supporter of research ideals in classical studies, also displayed a graceful spirit of reciprocity by recognizing the claims of science. 'That the physical and biological sciences are far less cultivated and esteemed among us than they should be, I have no doubt', he remarked in the midst of an appeal for an expanded role for his own subject in the *Literae Humaniores* course.[42] Gardner also indicated that the attitudes of Young Oxford were the major obstacles to the acceptance of his scheme. 'Thrice, in 1890, 1898 and 1900, has a committee of senior members of the Board of *Literae Humaniores* reported in favour of giving Classical Archeology a place in the final examination. Thrice has a majority of the Board, consisting largely of its younger members, rejected the report of the committee and vetoed all change', he complained angrily.[43]

The proponents of research and science formed their own organization to counteract the influence of the Non-Placet Society. Its core was a 'militant dining club of thirty members' founded in 1889 by L. R. Farnell of Exeter and Sidney Ball of St. John's.[44] The club included older supporters of research such as Ingram Bywater, Reader in Greek, who had been one of Mark Pattison's close friends, as well as scientists such as Ray Lankester of Exeter. 'Its aim was mainly to maintain and develop the character of the University as a home of learning and science and for this purpose to place the interests of the University as a whole above those of the separate college', Farnell argued: 'to strengthen the influence of the professoriate and to diffuse the ideal of research throughout the college teaching-staffs; to encourage new subjects of study, but to keep the examination system within bounds and to exorcise the examination-spirit; to act on academical, not

[41] 'The Position of Science at Oxford', *Nature* liv, no. 1393 (1896), 228.
[42] *Oxford at the Crossroads* (London, 1903), 19. [43] Ibid. viii.
[44] See Lewis R. Farnell, *An Oxonian Looks Back* (London, 1934), 270. See also Oona H. Ball, *Sidney Ball: Memories and Impressions* (n.p., 1923), 192.

political, grounds in elections to Council and other University bodies: finally to safeguard the Bodleian Library as a centre of mature study'.[45] Farnell frankly asserted that 'in the many conflicts in Congregation where the interests of the Museum were involved, we generally fought on their side; in return their *personnel* could be called up to assist us where the controversy was between the University and the separate college-interest'.[46]

These alliances of literary and scientific 'radicals' against Young Oxford and their non-academic supporters were to be crucial factors in each of the battles concerning the implementation of the 1877 commissioners' plan for the creation of an academic profession in Oxford. Although each side insisted that it was the virtually helpless victim of its enemies, both these assertions must be viewed with a considerable degree of scepticism. Scientists, researchers, professors, and older dons complained that their plans constantly were spoiled by the intransigence and ill-will of 'the younger graduates'. Young Oxford felt equally justified in lamenting that the alliance of 'literary radicals' with the 'Museum vote' insured their triumph over the colleges, the tutorial system, and the ideals of 'liberal education' itself. Extravagent complaints of both these contradictory types were expressed plentifully in each of the major conflicts which aroused Oxford opinion in the late nineteenth century: the quarrels about 'compulsory Greek' and the position of scientific education, the continued battles concerning research and the introduction of more 'specialist' studies into the honours schools, the struggles caused by attempts to carry out the commissioners' plan for 'progressive careers' despite declining endowment income, and the renewed confrontations over the presence of non-academic voters in Congregation. Since several of these conflicts raged at intervals for almost forty years before a final decision was reached, one must conclude that the sides were more evenly matched than either was willing to admit.

45 Ibid. 270.
46 Ibid. 271.

C. *The Agricultural Depression and the Growth of Hostility to Science*

The crisis caused by the agricultural depression was an important factor in the growth of hostility to science in Oxford. The 1877 Commission had revealed in their writing of new statutes a strong desire to enlarge and improve the facilities for teaching the natural and physical sciences. Although the commissioners were far from advocating the introduction of technical education in Oxford, they were certainly desirous of emulating the well-publicized German successes in harnessing university science in both its educational and research aspects for technological innovation in industry. These plans had been accepted in Oxford with acquiescence, if not with enthusiasm. In the lean years of the 1880s and 1890s, however, the attempts to implement or extend the commissioners' plans aroused the bitter resentment of Young Oxford and their non-academic allies. Although the expansion of scientific education certainly would have aroused hostility among non-scientists even under optimal financial conditions, the coincidence of the increasing demands of the scientists and the deteriorating economic position of the colleges served to intensify this hostility. In the late nineteenth century, virulent animosity toward science became fixed as one of the principal hallmarks of collegiate loyalty among the younger dons, while Oxford scientists developed a deep reciprocal hatred for the entire collegiate system.[47]

The 1877 commissioners' plans for the enlargement and better endowment of the professoriate operated to a large extent for the benefit of the scientist. Many of the new chairs

[47] G. L. Geison has attacked the argument on this point in my thesis in his *Michael Foster and the Cambridge School of Physiology* (Princeton, 1978), 114-15. He asserts that the agricultural depression could not have been as important as I suggest in shaping Oxford attitudes toward science since Cambridge suffered at least as much yet was still willing to disburse the large sums needed to establish a successful research school of physiology. My argument is not, however, that the agricultural depression was responsible for Oxford's relatively poor showing in scientific teaching and research between 1870 and 1900, but that the mutual hostility of scientists and the colleges was exacerbated and fixed by the financial constraints of this period. Although the agricultural depression bred similar animosities in Cambridge, stronger scientific traditions and the greater power of the university in relation to the colleges prevented their interfering with the plans of the scientists.

which they established were in scientific subjects, while the existing science professors had the most to gain financially from the commissioners' efforts to raise all professorial salaries to about £900 p.a. In order to accomplish this goal, funds were diverted on a large scale from the colleges. Most professorial chairs became permanently attached to fellowships at the richer colleges. Often the colleges were obliged to accept the entire financial responsibility for the professors' salaries. Magdalen, for example, was charged with the expense of approximately £4,000 p.a. to maintain six university professorships, five of which were to be held by scientists or mathematicians.[48] New College also was expected to contribute £2,100 p.a. toward the support of five professors, three of whom were scientists or mathematicians.[49]

Provisions were also made in some colleges to insure that a certain number of scholarships and ordinary fellowships would be awarded to scientists. At Magdalen, for instance, one out of every fourteen ordinary fellowships (one every seven years) was to be given for either natural science or medicine, and another was reserved for mathematics.[50] The statutory distribution of ordinary fellowships at New College was virtually identical to the effect of Magdalen's regulation.[51] At Balliol and Brasenose, there was a general rule that three of every ten fellowships were to be given in fields other than *Literae Humaniores*.[52] Although Queen's had no requirement to award a fixed number of fellowships to scientists, they were obligated to give at least one of their five annual scholarships for proficiency in science or mathematics if a qualified candidate applied.[53]

These encouragements for scientific education were accomplished with virtually no hostile criticism from the vast majority of Oxford dons. Charles Neate, the cantankerous senior fellow of Oriel, was the only witness who attacked the plans for the expansion of science. 'I think that a great

[48] See VI, 1–3, p. 111 (PP 1882, li).
[49] See III, 2–4, p. 135; and XXI, 1, p. 145; in ibid.
[50] See IV, 14, p. 108; in ibid.
[51] See III, 16, pp. 136–7; in ibid.
[52] For Balliol, see III, 6(b), p. 13; for Brasenose, see III, 4, p. 28; both in ibid.
[53] See III, 4, p. 180; in ibid.

accession of physical science students would be a very undesirable thing . . . I do not think it is desirable to encourage people who come here for the sake of getting employment at Manchester or elsewhere', he explained.[54] By drawing the traditional Oxford connection between science, technical education, and low utilitarian motivations,[55] Neate struck directly at the hope that the university ought to serve the needs of industry. The fact that this traditional line of reasoning was not pursued by more non-scientists in their testimony was the result of the buoyant mood of the 1870s, nurtured by the optimistic financial predictions of the Cleveland Commission. College tutors could view complacently the creation of new science chairs, secure in the knowledge that the general expansion of the professoriate also would satisfy their own career aspirations. Enthusiasts of linguistic and historical research could recognize that they shared with scientific researchers a common concept of the proper functions of universities. Even those who had no respect for the educational or scholarly value of science saw no pressing need to attack its pretensions since it was generally believed that the scientists' goals could be accomplished without infringing on the traditional studies of the university or on the principles of collegiate and tutorial autonomy.

In the absence of external criticism, the scientists who gave evidence were able to concentrate on elaborating their own plans and conducting their own internecine struggles. Most scientists recommended an increase in the number of professors and readers in their fields.[56] While the commissioners sometimes baulked at the plans for the expansion of the professoriate made by other dons,[57] the scientists' proposals always were received with respectful attention. In fact, when

[54] PP 1881, lvi 286, no. 4499.

[55] See above Ch. I, pp. 27-30 for the rejection of the ideal of professional education at Oxford in the period before the Royal Commission.

[56] See, for examples, 'Robert Bellamy Clifton, Esq., MA (Professor of Experimental Philosophy), examined', 25; 'William Odling, Esq., MA (Waynflete Professor of Chemistry), examined', 171-6; 'Henry W. Acland, Esq., DM (Regius Professor of Medicine), examined', 181-95; and 'George Rolleston, Esq. DM (Linacre Professor of Physiology), examined', 269-73. All in PP 1881, li.

[57] The commissioners attacked Canon Liddon's call for more theological chairs (pp. 290-5) and R. L. Nettleship's call for new chairs in Teutonic and Romance philology (pp. 53-5). In ibid.

the Professor of Geology neglected to volunteer suggestions leading to an enlarged role for his subject, the commissioners pointedly urged him to rectify this omission.[58] A few scientists also suggested that the Honour School of Natural Science be divided into several more specialized schools.[59] These recommendations also were received politely by the Commission although they were not enacted, probably because the commissioners had decided to leave all curricular reform to the university authorities.

The issue which caused the most controversy among scientists was whether Oxford ought to undertake professional medical education. Although several witnesses advocated the establishment of a medical school,[60] others argued that the university would fulfil its scientific mission more effectively through research and pre-professional education.[61] It was apparent from their plans that the commissioners were convinced by the arguments against an Oxford medical school. They accepted Sir James Paget's view that the duty of universities toward the medical profession was fulfilled best through 'the educating young men to be gentlemen and men of science, who may elsewhere be educated to be physicians and surgeons of the highest social and professional rank'.[62] Greatly enlarged provisions were made for the teaching of science and for scientific research, but no recommendation was made for the establishment of a medical school.

[58] See 'Joseph Prestwich, Esq., MA (Professor of Geology), examined', ibid. 313–15.

[59] See, for example, 'M. A. Lawson, Esq., MA (Professor of Botany and Rural Economy), examined', ibid. 328–30, in which it was suggested that botany ought to be a separate examination school.

[60] See 'J. F. Payne, BA, BM (Fellow of Magdalen College; Assistant Physician to St. Thomas's Hospital, London; Examiner in the Medical Faculty of the University of Edinburgh), examined', 346–52; 'E. R. Lankester, Esq., MA (Fellow of Exeter College), examined', 341–6; and 'No. 15' (a letter from Horatio Donkin, MA, BM (Oxon.)), 381–3. All in ibid.

[61] See 'Henry W. Acland, Esq., DM (Regius Professor of Medicine), examined', 181–95; 'No. 16' (a letter from the President of the Royal College of Physicians), 383–4; 'No. 17' (a letter from the President of the Royal College of Surgeons), 384; 'No. 18' (a letter from Sir William W. Gull, bart.), 384–5; 'No. 19' (a letter from Sir James Paget, bart.), 385–6; 'No. 20' (a letter from William Turner, MD, FRS, Professor of Medicine at the University of Edinburgh), 386–8; and 'No. 21' (a letter from thirty Oxford medical graduates), 388. All in ibid.

[62] Cited approvingly from a letter, by Professor Acland; ibid. 182, no. 3107.

In the late nineteenth century, the battle of Young Oxford against 'modern innovations' became in large part a struggle against the demands of the scientists for changes in the examination system, new appointments, and more funds. Financial pressures ensured that these controversies were conducted with great bitterness and personal animosity. This mood and its causes can be seen in A. T. S. Goodrick's denunciation of the work of Jowett's vice-chancellorship in the late 1880s which he argued 'was principally directed to the advancement of the cause of scientific and technical education at the expense of the literary side'. He continued bitterly, ·

it was quickly perceived . . . that every step gained in that direction rendered the next more easy. The innumerable pigeon-holes of natural science offered facilities for the introduction into them of innumerable teachers, and as these were promptly created Masters of Arts, every such appointment meant a fresh vote gained; and it was by means of such appointments that the genuine internal development of opposition . . . was met. For such new appointments facilities were afforded partly by the action of the Commission, which had light-heartedly appropriated for the purpose large sums from the prospective agricultural increments of the incomes of the colleges, and partly by alienating the very slender funds of the University itself. Hardly a term passed without the allocation of large sums to the support, or rather establishment, of a study for which Oxford, as many thought, offered no natural facilities, – an adventitious and artificial growth.[63]

The argument that Oxford was inherently uncongenial to science was echoed by many other young dons in the 1880s. W. L. Courtney, noting the 'very large sums' which had already been spent on the development of scientific education at Oxford and 'the enormous sums which they ['our scientific professors'] so unblushingly demand',[64] concluded that 'after all, despite its efforts, Science in Oxford is not so successfully taught as in the American scientific schools, and the natural deduction to be drawn is not that it ought in consequence to have larger opportunities allowed to it in comparison with the classical education, but rather that the Oxford soil is not wholly congenial to this modern growth.'[65] Another young

[63] 'Congregation and Convocation', *Macmillan's Mag.* xc (July 1904), 226.
[64] 'New Lamps for Old Ones', *Macmillan's Mag.* lv (Nov. 1886), 54.
[65] Ibid. 53.

don went so far as to argue that each English university, aside from the basic and minimal requirements of general education, ought to specialize for the purposes of research on a few closely-related disciplines.[66] The scientific community recognized fully that the intention behind this suggestion was to remove all science from Oxford.[67]

The major issue between the scientists and the young dons (and both their allies) was why science had failed to establish itself in Oxford. In the early 1870s there was considerable hopefulness among the scientists that, with the erection of the new Museum, Oxford had begun a new era in which their legitimate claims would be fully recognized. As one supporter of scientific education noted confidently, 'The progress which Natural Science has made at Oxford within the last few years has far exceeded the anticipations of even the most sanguine of its promoters . . . When the position taken by Natural Science at a university which has commonly been condemned for neglecting this very subject is fully recognized outside its own walls, there can be no doubt that a far greater number than at present will come up to Oxford to pursue their science studies there.'[68] The plans formulated by the 1877 Commission could only have enhanced these expectations. None the less, by the 1890s it was clear that these early hopes had been premature. Despite the large sums which had been spent on the establishment of science at Oxford, it was undeniable that the results had been disappointing.

The basic premiss that science had failed to establish itself at Oxford despite lavish financial support was stated forcefully in 1896 by an article in *Nature*. 'Whilst the study of natural science has been progressing rapidly in other universities and colleges during the past ten or fifteen years, it is a matter of common knowledge that it has progressed very slowly indeed in the University of Oxford', the author argued.

It must be understood at the outset that the University, considered as a body separate from the colleges which compose it, has not dealt

---

[66] [H. H. Henson,] 'Oxford and its Professors', *Edin. Rev.* clxx, no. 348 (1889), 303–27.

[67] See the reply to Henson's article, 'Oxford and its Professors', *Nature* xl (1889), 637.

[68] J. P. Earwaker, 'Natural Science at Oxford', *Nature* iii (1870), 170.

ungenerously with science. The staff of professors, and the emoluments attached to their chairs, compare favourably with those of any other university in Great Britain; and Oxford actually set the example, at great cost to itself of building a museum and equipping laboratories for educational purposes. Moreover, the opportunities of scientific study in Oxford are greatly enhanced by the existence of a first-rate scientific library, such as is not possessed by any other college or university in the kingdom. It is a strange thing that when it has so many advantages, Oxford has allowed itself to be completely outstripped in this particular path of intellectual progress.[69]

The growth in the number of science students lured to Oxford by these advantages was not rapid; the well-paid professors often lectured to virtually empty lecture halls. Even more disturbing was the fact that the existence of scholarships and fellowships reserved for scientists did not always call forth an adequate supply of qualified candidates. Often these prizes were not awarded because no qualified candidate appeared. The status of the Honour School of Natural Science remained low. These facts were accepted by both supporters and opponents of science. The crucial question, however, was why this was the case.

For the opponents of science, the reasons for this failure were quite easy to understand. They argued that it was simply a waste of effort and money to attempt to force this study on the university.[70] They also assumed that it was natural for the more intelligent students to choose the greater rigour and intellectual discipline offered by classical studies rather than to accept the mere useful information provided by 'stinks'. For Young Oxford and their allies the solution to this problem of scientific education was equally obvious: give up the futile attempt to impose an unsuitable and inferior discipline on the Oxford environment.

For the scientists and their supporters, the explanation for the dismal condition of science at Oxford after twenty years of lavish support was to be found in the basic hostility of the colleges.[71] They argued that the efforts of the 1877 commissioners to establish science at Oxford on a solid basis

[69] 'The Position of Science at Oxford', *Nature* liv, no. 1393 (1896). 225.
[70] See above, pp. 221-2, nn. 63-6.
[71] Op. cit. 225-8, for this entire argument.

had been sabotaged purposely by the colleges to discredit the cause of scientific education. The fact that most tutors were classicists who encouraged all the best students to read their own subject was alleged by the scientists as one cause of their poor showing despite generous financial support. However, they argued that the Greek required of all undergraduates at Responsions was the chief reason why science had failed to establish itself. The university regulation was that this examination must be passed by the end of an undergraduate's first year of residence, but most of the better colleges insisted on the fulfilment of this requirement before matriculation. Since those grammar and day schools which most emphasized scientific education often did not teach Greek at all, if their graduates wished to attend an Oxford college, they had to waste several months in expensive cramming for Responsions. This expense was beyond the financial means of most science students who were generally of lower social origins than the public school graduates who comprised the majority of Oxford students. According to the advocates of science, this injustice was compounded by the fact that candidates for admission were not required to know any science. They argued that the natural and intended result of this situation was to discourage those who had studied science from competing for Oxford awards. They implied that a desire to maintain the social exclusiveness of the university was at the root of its opposition to scientific education.

The issue of 'compulsory Greek' was, however, much more complicated than the scientists allowed. A crucial reason for the maintenance of this requirement was its importance to candidates for holy orders. As Canon Liddon wrote to Dr Pusey when this issue arose at a meeting of the Hebdomadal Council in 1873,

The physical science professors' proposal to substitute German for Greek is, for the present, shelved. They contemptuously rejected our offer of a BS degree; they *would* have the BA without Greek. My deepest objection to their demand is that such a modification of the studies of the Univ.^{y} would certainly diminish the candidates for Holy Orders; & make a wish to take H.O. more difficult of accomplishment — when the language of the N.T. had to be learnt *ab initio*. [72]

[72] Pusey House MS letters, HPL to EBP, Lady Day 1873, i, no. 141.

It was indicative of the diminished influence of Church interests in university government in the 1870s that Liddon continued, 'But I have not thought it well to mention this in Council; and so fought the question on the ground of the historical idea of studies represented by the BA — since the Renaissance, at any rate.' This concern for clerical interests explains a good deal of the passionate commitment of some of those holding the pro-'compulsory Greek' position.

The controversies over 'compulsory Greek' and the endowment of science at Oxford eventually reached levels of considerable animosity, especially among those who adhered closely to strict party divisions. It was indicative of the polarization of Oxford opinion that only those professors and researchers who could not support their scientific allies in calling for the abolition of compulsory Greek[73] and those college tutors who were unable to accept Young Oxford's insistence on the maintenance of the Greek requirement[74] who expressed their opinions without resorting to personal abuse. Those controversialists, whether scientists or young dons, who represented orthodox party views proved unwilling or unable to avoid expressing the deep rancour which they felt.

Among the scientists, a low point in the level of controversial argument was reached in 1903 when *Nature* saw fit to reprint the text of a harangue delivered by John Perry, Professor of Engineering in the University of London, to an audience in Oxford. Professor Perry asked his listeners insultingly, 'Are you learned misers going for ever to gloat in secret over your learning or to edit for ever the same Greek texts, or for ever to spin new metaphysical philosophies out of your inner consciousnesses.'[75] He referred to 'compulsory Latin and Greek for the average youth at Oxford' as 'the

---

[73] See, for example, Edward A. Freeman, 'Greek in the Universities', *Contemp. Rev.* lx (1891), 663–71. Freeman was not generally know for the temperance of his statements on university issues. See above, Ch. IV, p. 195, n. 138 and also below, this chapter, p. 237, nn. 129–30.

[74] See, for example, P. A. Wright-Henderson, 'Schoolmasters in Council', *Macmillan's Mag.* lxiv (May 1891), 61–8. Wright-Henderson was an examiner for 'pass Greek' who argued diplomatically that the requirement ought to be abolished since its maintenance contributed nothing to the diffusion of classical culture.

[75] 'Oxford and Science', *Nature* lxix, no. 1783 (1903), 209.

worship of mumbo-jumbo'.[76] He dismissed Plato as 'pretentious and shallow' and Aristotle as 'so unscientific as to be maudlin', having read them in translation.[77] Perry argued that hostility to science at Oxford was the result of a conscious and crafty plan, 'Oxford has not merely induced neglect of science; she has been its active enemy pretending friendship.'[78] He concluded by addressing to Oxford men an impassioned peroration in which he implied a connection between the study of classical literature and lack of manliness.

Give up this mere absorption of other men's ideas, whether old classics or in quarterly and monthly reviews, this collecting of ready-made opinions on all subjects whatsoever. Are you for ever to hang to the apron-strings of the ancients? Is your manhood worth so little that you cannot exist without worshipping men who were creatures like yourselves? . . . When you insist upon your classical texts you spoil our whole scheme of study, and you are merely acting as brigards, you are only taking that sort of *advantage* which all mean people take when they have official positions.[79]

Perry was probably not incorrect in asserting that Oxford men would denounce the 'impudence' of his arguments[80] and consider him 'a man of little culture'.[81] His speech certainly provided ammunition for those who wished to view all scientists as 'Philistines' and 'low mechanical persons'.[82]

Among the proponents of compulsory Greek, an equally low level of invective was reached by W. L. Courtney. He condemned 'the Scientist' as 'a pushing creature' because 'he labours without ceasing to enable the scientific student to get through his academic course without learning an ancient language'.[83] He also could not resist the temptation to retell the probably apocryphal story that the scientists had been unwilling to put the traditional Oxford motto *Dominus Illuminatio Mea* over their new physiological laboratory.

[76] Ibid. 213.
[77] Ibid. 212.
[78] Ibid. 211.
[79] Loc. cit.
[80] Loc. cit.
[81] Ibid. 212.
[82] Ibid. 209.
[83] 'New Lamps for Old Ones', *Macmillan's Mag.* lv, no. 325 (1886), 53.

Courtney spitefully suggested that they ought to have chosen instead *Scientia et Vivisectio Sua.*[84]

Similar animosities were expressed in the controversy concerning 'Oxford Colleges and Natural Science' which raged in the *Saturday Review* in 1900. The main contestants were George Brodrick, Warden of Merton, and E. Ray Lankester, Linacre Professor of Physiology.[85] Brodrick was an accomplished Liberal polemicist who found himself drawn increasingly into alliance with conservative Young Oxford by their common hostility to the carrying out of the plans of the 1877 Commission. Lankester's Oxford career had been filled with controversy and in 1888 he had suffered the humiliation of being removed as an examiner for the Honour School of Natural Science.[86] Neither of the major contestants chose to avoid bitter invective and personal recriminations in their statements. In fact, these letters were Lankester's angry farewell to Oxford since he resigned his professorship in the midst of this correspondence.

Brodrick began the exchange with a letter to the editor of the *Saturday Review* denouncing Lankester's demand that two-thirds of the endowment income of the colleges ought to be devoted to the support of the sciences.[87] Brodrick argued

[84] Ibid. 54. Anti-vivisectionist sentiment often was used in the battles against science. See E. B. Nicolson's correspondence of 1883-5 on the founding of the Oxford Physiological Laboratory, Bodl. MS Top. Oxon. c. 182. On this subject, see also Richard D. French, *Antivivisection and Medical Science in Victorian Society* (Princeton, 1975).

[85] The correspondence was also entered by J. K. Fotheringham of Magdalen supporting Brodrick, see *Saturday Review* lxxxix, no. 2323 (1900), 559 and no. 2326 (1900), 651. Lankester was supported by P. Chalmers Mitchell, in no. 2324 (1900), 586.

[86] See the letters, 'The Vice-Chancellor and Professor Ray Lankester', in the *Oxford Magazine* vi (1888), 153-6, 246 and 247 for this earlier controversy. Lankester was evidently an abrasive character. A student remarked in his diary in 1890, 'He is a very clever and energetic man, but I think he is no gentleman . . . Lankester has managed to pick quarrels with nearly everybody, through his determined effort to raise the standard of the morphology prelim . . . Burdon Sanderson [Waynflete Professor of Physiology] is at loggerheads with him on this point . . . Lankester has offended Vines [Sheridian Professor of Botany] for the deliberately arranged his lectures to clash with the botany classes.' See Balliol MS 443, 'Autobiography of Sydney J. Cole, MA, MD (Oxon.)', p. 44.

[87] Lankester made this demand in the preface of his *Linacre Reports* (Oxford, 1900) iv, a collection of the papers published in scientific journals by his pupils and assistants during the previous year. This work was reviewed in the *Saturday Rev.* lxxxix, no. 2312 (1900), 208.

that despite financial hardship, the university and the colleges had been extremely generous toward natural science. '[L]avish grants of money — such as no other class of teachers would dare to ask', he asserted, 'are now constantly made, on the requisition of a scientific Professor'.[88] He concluded bitterly, 'The truth is that having been grievously neglected for many generations, Natural Science has become the spoiled child of the University.'[89] Later in the correspondence, Brodrick suggested that his description of science as a 'spoiled child' who 'gets everything for which it cries' could also apply to Professor Lankester. Brodrick implied that his opponent had been guilty of personal ingratitude to an institution which always had treated him generously. He remarked pointedly, 'I remember that he obtained a vote of £6,000 or £7,000 after the briefest possible debate, for the extension of the Morphological Department, just before his resignation.'[90]

Lankester replied that although the 1877 Commission had done much for science, the colleges had done everything in their power to stifle the advancement of these studies. He pointed out that the funds devoted by the colleges to the payment of science professors and the equipping of laboratories 'had been taken from them forcibly by Act of Parliament'.[91] He insisted that the colleges 'have always resisted and where possible evaded their enforced contributions'.[92] For Lankester, the real test of collegiate encouragement for science was the number of fellowships not restricted to particular subjects devoted to this purpose. He asserted that only 12 of the 250 available were held by scientists, a figure which he considered grossly inadequate. Lankester later argued that at least half of the college fellowships ought to be given to scientists.[93] The best construction that J. F. Fotheringham of Magdalen, one of the defenders of the colleges, was able to place on the existing situation was that, including restricted fellowships, 32 of 297 were held by scientists.[94] The gap between the supporters and the opponents of science was well illustrated by the fact that,

[88] *Saturday Rev.* lxxxix, no. 2312 (1900), 332.
[89] Ibid. 332.
[90] Ibid., no. 2320 (1900), 459-60.
[91] Ibid. no. 2318 (1900), 394.
[92] Loc. cit.
[93] Ibid. no. 2322 (1900), 527-8.
[94] Ibid. no. 2323 (1900), 559.

while Lankester demanded at least half the fellowships, Fotheringham considered 10 per cent a just proportion.

Lankester's argument quickly reached the same level of personal invective as Brodrick's. He denounced the collegiate system in terms of calculated insult; 'a boarding-house keeper's scheme for securing a lucrative monopoly (fees to the amount of sixty thousand pounds a year) to themselves'.[95] Later he broadened his attack to include a contemptuous dismissal of tutorial instruction as well. 'I have no wish to see the Natural Sciences made to any large extent the subjects of college competitions and college teaching in Oxford', he asserted. 'I should fear that were this done the pursuit of these sciences might become as unproductive as that of Historical and Philological Science has become under college auspices.'[96] Lankester repayed Brodrick's personal reference to his ingratitude by condemning the *Literae Humaniores* course as valuable only for 'nurturing the journalists of the future'.[97] Brodrick had been a leader-writer for *The Times* before his election to the wardenship of Merton.

Despite their energetic campaigns against the interests of science, Young Oxford was never able to undo to any great extent the work of the 1877 Commission. Although all colleges had a clause in their statutes enabling them to forgo financial obligations they could no longer afford,[98] these powers were used only sparingly. Essentially, the problem was that with the increasing number of older married college tutors and the expanded number of science professors created by the commissioners, Young Oxford no longer dominated the university in 1900 as it had in 1870. Between 1874 and 1900, the percentage of college tutors over the age of forty-five rose from only 10 per cent to almost 35 per cent, while the percentage under thirty fell from 42 per cent to only 12 per cent.[99] Largely as a result of this situation, the alliance of scientists and 'ageing radicals' was able to achieve many of their goals. Even Lankester had to admit that those sympathetic to science 'are able to carry important votes in

[95] Ibid. no. 2318 (1900), 395.
[96] Ibid. no. 2322 (1900), 528.   [97] Loc. cit.
[98] For an example, see the statute at Balliol, VII, 3, p. 20 (PP 1882, li).
[99] See below, Appendix 11, p. 294.

the University legislature, and to construct a costly and magnificent machine for the promotion of study in Natural Science'.[100] On the issue of compulsory Greek, however, the young dons were able to mobilize enough support in Congregation to keep this requirement until 1920, despite repeated attempts to abolish it. Even the forcefully-expressed opposition after 1909 of Lord Curzon proved ineffective.[101] It was only the abolition of the Greek requirement for the 'Previous Examination' at Cambridge in 1919 which finally pressured Oxford into changing its rule as well. Although young dons no longer ruled Oxford as they had in 1870, it was apparent that they still had considerable power to delay, at least, undesirable 'modern innovations'.

D. The Agricultural Depression and the 'Endowment of Research'

The hostility of Young Oxford to the claims of natural science was combined with an equal alienation from the 'endowment of research'. This cause, which in the 1870s often had seemed useful for the amelioration of the tutors' 'teaching drudgery' and their lack of 'progressive careers', in the hard times of the 1880s and 1890s appeared as simply another financial drain. Young Oxford was, however, more successful in inhibiting the growth of research than in halting the advancement of science. Although the advocates of research could rely on the support of the scientists on those issues decided in the university legislatures, this powerful aid obviously was unavailable to them in the individual Boards of Faculties where several of the most important struggles concerning the interests of research were fought.

The agricultural depression had a significant influence in determining the issues on which the advocates of research concentrated their energies. It was apparent that, in the straitened circumstances of the 1880s and 1890s, any attempt to obtain new funding for the creation of pure research offices on a large scale would be completely futile. Therefore, the

---

[100] *Saturday Rev.* lxxxix, no. 2322 (1900), 527.
[101] *Principles and Methods of University Reform* (Oxford, 1909), 101-14. A large mass of occasional writings on the issue are collected in G. A. Oxon. b. 141 (181c-331).

researchers began to direct their attention toward goals which did not require direct endowment. Their efforts were directed largely toward obtaining alterations in the examination system to aid the cause of research by drawing a closer connection between a don's tutorial work and his advanced studies. The major issues involving the 'endowment of research' in the 1880s and 1890s were the controversy over the introduction of 'specialism' into the *Literae Humaniores* course, and the question of whether the new Honour School of English would be primarily an examination in philology or in literature. Although these issues did not range Young Oxford and their allies against the 'literary and scientific radicals' as consistently as directly financial issues would have done; none the less the structure of alliances insured that they were fought along similar lines to those of the battles over the advancement of science.

Young Oxford's attack on science was often combined with hostility toward the encouragement of research. H. H. Henson, who had suggested that scientific research ought to be removed from Oxford,[102] expressed in the same article his animosity toward professors, readers, and research ideals. He made an explicit connection between these animosities and the financial strain which the university and colleges were experiencing. 'It is not unnatural that in times of severe agricultural depression, academic economists should regard with suspicion and resentment the secure and comfortable stipends of the professors and readers;' he argued, 'nor is it surprising that in face of a public attention by no means friendly, when trenchant criticisms are heard from outside on the meagre educational results of heavily-endowed Oxford, busy college tutors and lecturers should chafe against the existence of well-paid professors, whose lectures nobody attends, and whose researches nobody cares about, as a costly and burdensome encumbrance, at once useless and indefensible.[103] W. L. Courtney, who had suggested that Oxford was not a congenial spiritual environment for scientific education,[104] in the same article scornfully characterized the

[102] See above, pp. 221-2, n. 66.
[103] 'Oxford and its Professors', *Edin. Rev.* clxx, no. 348 (1889), 318.
[104] See above, p. 221, nn. 64-5.

'Original Researcher' as 'one who burrows in the ancient literature with the instincts of a mole; who adds to his Latin and Greek a knowledge of Sanskrit as an indispensible auxiliary and does his best to convert Philology into an exact science . . . He knows the value of Inscriptions and Monumentary Evidence, and he studies manuscripts in foreign libraries.'[105] Max Müller and Archibald Sayce would not have been slow to recognize the oblique personal references in this characterization.

The proponents of research also identified their enemies in terms remarkably similar to those used by the advocates of science. Scientists like Ray Lankester and John Perry had denounced the collegiate and tutorial systems as the major obstacles to the advancement of scientific education at Oxford.[106] Percy Gardner, the most prominent advocate of 'specialism' in the *Literae Humaniores* course, also considered that these institutions were detrimental to the cause of research. Gardner employed a more diplomatic tone than the scientists, perhaps because he was neither an outsider to Oxford nor on the point of resignation, but his complaints were substantially the same as theirs. Even though he recognized that any major changes in the existing college system were unlikely, he could not resist adding that 'an excess of collegiate feeling or too great control by college tutors may tend to mar the freedom and breath of university education'.[107] Gardner also insisted that the tutorial system was, at best, a mixed blessing. Although the personal relation between tutor and pupil was often of value to the student, it tended to inhibit 'independence and originative power'.[108] For the college tutor, the effects of the system were wholly pernicious. 'The man who gives all his days in personal attention to pupils has no leisure for work of research himself', Gardner complained. 'If there is one thing certain as regards university education, it is that he who would teach freshly and effectively must carry on advanced studies of his own in the subject on which he lectures.'[109] It was indicative of the degree of

---

[105] 'New Lamps for Old Ones', *Macmillan's Mag.* lv, no. 325 (1886), 51.
[106] See above, pp. 225-9.
[107] *Oxford at the Crossroads* (London, 1903), 17.
[108] Ibid. 34.   [109] Loc. cit.

polarization in university politics that despite differences in goals and in modes of expression, both Gardner and the scientists saw the colleges and the tutorial. system as their most important enemies.

It was well understood in Oxford that the causes of 'specialism' and research were inextricably connected. George Brodrick explained that the growth in the desire for increased opportunities for specialization in the university examinations, especially in the dominant school of *Literae Humaniores* was 'an off-spring of the demand for "Endowment of Research"'.[110] He complained, citing Goethe's account of the younger German professors of his own day, that 'these Professors teach only that they may learn, . . . they acquire their own cultivation altogether at the cost of their hearers, since these are not instructed in what they really need, but in that which the Professor finds it necessary to elaborate for himself'.[111] Brodrick concluded that from the viewpoint of education this new ideal 'seems to me a grievous error, and one calculated to undermine the best characteristics of Oxford culture'.[112] W. L. Courtney also complained bitterly that the product of this new system of 'specialism' would be 'a narrow, abstract, one-sided pendant'.[113] He drew a vivid contrast between this result and the student who completed the traditional *Literae Humaniores* course of 'liberal education'. 'He has been given the inestimable benefit of an open mind, not destitute of such graces of culture as the study of ancient civilization can impart', Courtney argued. 'Concentration, no doubt, he now finds to his advantage; but it is because he has had a sort of general training.'[114]

The most substantial argument in favour of 'specialism' was provided by Percy Gardner's *Oxford at the Crossroads*, a closely-reasoned volume of 132 pages published in 1903. A large part of this work was devoted to arguing for increased opportunities for specialization in the *Literae Humaniores* course, especially in Gardner's field of classical archeology.

[110] *Memories and Impressions 1831–1900* (London, 1900), 353.
[111] Ibid. 353–4.   [112] Ibid. 355.
[113] 'New Lamps for Old Ones', *Macmillan's Mag.* lv, no. 325 (1886), 53.
[114] Ibid. 52. See also Courtney's earlier article, 'Recasting the Oxford Schools', *Fortnightly Rev.* xl (1884), 675–82.

For Gardner, the connection of 'specialism' and research was as close as it was for Brodrick. He noted bitterly that at Oxford, 'research is branded as specialism or despised as valueless'.[115] He argued that the existing Oxford system excluded many important areas of knowledge, like classical archaeology, from the curriculum and placed more emphasis on facile writing than on the acquisition of real knowledge. Gardner concluded, 'But the worst side of the course of *Literae Humaniores* is, perhaps, neither its encouragement of superficiality nor its one-sidedness, but its exclusion of personal research and contact with fact, its discouragement of all advanced study.'[116] He painted a vivid picture of the inadequacy of the Oxford graduate who won a senior scholarship or fellowship for study abroad, especially his deficiencies in relation to students trained in Germany or France. 'The Oxford men who do go abroad on these foundations are seldom in a condition duly to profit by their opportunities', Gardner complained.

Having passed the final examination at Oxford, they think themselves above going to the lectures of specialists or doing the drudgery with which all real investigation must begin. And never having been trained in the methods of research, they do not know how to set about their work. The German and French students, armed with all modern appliances, filling their notebooks with systematic knowledge, always on the alert to find what is new or unpublished, are a marvel to them. A few, who have an inborn talent for research, triumph in spite of all obstacles, make their own methods, and do admirable work. But the system, or want of system, is very wasteful. The best men waste years in learning abroad the methods they might very well have learned at home, and in following blind alleys against which they had never been warned.[117]

For Gardner, the only remedy was to incorporate elementary training in the methods and ideals of research into the BA curriculum by allowing more latitude for 'specialism'.

The advocates and the opponents of 'specialism' both wrote as though their cause was doomed, despite its intrinsic merits, because of the superior force of their enemies. George

---

[115] *Oxford at the Crossroads* (London, 1903), 31.
[116] Ibid. 47.   [117] Ibid. 56.

Brodrick complained that, by 1900, the university examinations were dominated by specialist ideals. 'Not only is the
student encouraged at every turn by Professors, tutors and
examiners, to specialize his studies,' Broderick complained,
'but he is allowed — nay, tempted — to concentrate himself
on a few questions in each examination paper, so as to produce
on the examiner's mind the impression of having devoted
himself to special "research."'[118] This view was not shared,
however, by the proponents of 'specialism'. Percy Gardner
noted bitterly how often his plans for the incorporation of
classical archaeology into the *Literae Humaniores* course had
been foiled by the concerted opposition of the younger
members of the Board of Faculties.[119] He argued that it was
the supporters of research and specialism who were helpless
before the obstructionism of the young dons. Some justification existed for both these views. The inability of Young
Oxford to prevent the alliance of 'literary and scientific
radicals' from controlling the university legislatures on most
routine issues involving new appropriations for appointments
or equipment[120] lent substance to Brodrick's pessimism.
Ample grounds for Gardner's complaints were provided by
both the powerlessness of the academic residents in Congregation when an issue was sufficiently important to call out
the increasing numbers of non-academic voters[121] and the
unexpected domination of the Boards of Faculties by the
young dons.

Young Oxford's seizure of the Boards of Faculties was the
result of the distribution of power, established by both statute
and customary practice, between university and collegiate
representatives. It was soon apparent that the university
professors and readers could not be expected either to attend
board meetings regularly or always to vote together. In
contrast, the representatives of the college tutors formed
well-organized blocs which were assiduous in attendance and
disposed to act in concert. Lord Curzon in 1909 lectured the

---

[118] *Memories and Impressions 1831–1900* (London, 1900), 355.
[119] See above, p. 215, n. 43.   [120] See above, pp. 229–30.
[121] See above, pp. 212–14 for a more extensive treatment of the distribution
of power in Congregation in the late nineteenth century.

professoriate for this failure to fulfil their faculty responsibilities. '[I] t appears probable that if the Professors made
a regular point of attending the ordinary meetings of the
Boards, of which they are *ex officio* members', he petu-
lantly complained, 'they would be able to exercise at least
an equivalent, if not a superior influence to the College
Tutors'.[122] An explanation for the professors' lack of interest
in the affairs of the Boards of Faculties was supplied by an
anonymous reviewer in 1911. He explained cooly,

> The Board of Faculty of Modern History, for example, consists at the
> present time, apart from co-opted members, of fourteen official and
> fourteen elected members; but of the fourteen professors and readers,
> there are six whose subjects of teaching would not qualify them as
> college tutors for membership of the History Faculty, and who, there-
> fore, cannot be expected to attend with any regularity. The elected
> members, all college tutors, do attend regularly, and are generally in a
> large majority.[123]

The effect of this statutory arrangement was compounded by
the custom of allowing the number of college tutors elected
to each of the boards always to equal the number of professors
and readers. This became the accepted practice despite the
fact that, as Lord Curzon noted irately, the statute 'only
provides that the number of elected members or College
representatives *shall in no case exceed* that of the *ex officio*
members; it does not say that it shall in every case, or in the
majority of cases, equal it'.[124] Curzon concluded dryly that
'if the University has so chosen to apply the Act, it has only
itself to thank for the consequences'.[125]

The consequences of this distribution of power on the
Boards of Faculties was that plans for the control of university
lectures by the boards quickly became dead-letters. The
commissioners had expected that combination lecturers and
professors would submit to their boards the topics on which

---

[122] *Principles and Methods of University Reform* (Oxford, 1909), 129.
[123] 'Oxford University Reform', *Quart. Rev.* ccxiv, no. 427 (1911), 439–40.
[124] Op. cit. 129.
[125] Ibid. 129. In 1909 C. H. Firth, the Regius Professor of Modern History,
proposed that the elective element be confined to two-thirds or three-fifths the
ex officio members. See his *The Faculties and their Powers* (Oxford and London,
1909), 28–41.

they proposed to lecture and the hours which were most convenient for them. The boards would then form a harmonious syllabus, eliminating unnecessary duplications and clumsy scheduling, by altering these individual proposals to suit university needs. In practice, however, the old combinations continued to meet socially each term to compile their lecture lists. These lists were then presented to the Boards of Faculties as accomplished facts. The boards soon degenerated into mere rubber-stamps for the decisions of the combinations of college lecturers. Ernest Barker, who taught modern history in Oxford from 1899 to 1920 before becoming a Cambridge professor, described in his autobiography the operation of this system. He admitted that it led to 'wide, and necessarily shallow, diffusion' in university lectures.[126] Lord Curzon noted that in classical studies as well the same appropriation of the power of the Board of Faculty by the old combinations had been allowed to occur.[127] Even in the Theology faculty, weighted as it was with professors, the same pattern appeared.[128]

This situation dashed any hopes that the Boards of Faculties would be used to promote the interests of research by drawing a closer connection between college teaching and scholarly work. Edward A. Freeman complained that 'in the present system neither the college tutor prevails nor the University professor, but the combined lecturer. He has shoved the college tutor aside, and he tramples the University professor under foot.'[129] He concluded bitterly, 'There never was a more singular case of a movement being turned about to a result the exact opposite of that for which it was intended than the fact that the last Commission arose out of a movement for the advancement of research.'[130] Ernest Barker also made the connection between the tutors' seizure of the Boards of Faculties, the rejection of 'specialism', and the lack of encouragement for research. Barker contrasted

---

[126] *Age and Youth* (London, 1953), 24.
[127] *Principles and Methods of University Reform* (Oxford, 1909), 128.
[128] See above. Ch. IV, p. 172, n. 51. Canon Liddon had similar problems as Professor of Exegesis. See Pusey House MS letters, EBP to HPL, iii, nos. 58-9 and HPL to EBP, ii, no. 111.
[129] 'Oxford After Forty Years', *Contemp. Rev.* li (May 1887), 618.
[130] Ibid. 620-1.

Oxford with Cambridge where the lecture lists actually were arranged by the official faculty boards and not by unofficial combinations of college tutors. 'The Cambridge method specializes the lecturer and encourages him to connect his writing of books with his delivering of lectures;' he explained, 'bidding him delve deep in the lectures he gives, it leads him on naturally to delve deeper still in the same field of inquiry and to turn his lectures into a book. The Oxford method, for me at any rate, had the result of creating a distinction between the art and practice of lecturing and the art and practice of writing a book and adding to the sum of knowledge.'[131]

The financial crisis exacerbated these tendencies toward the separation of lecturing and research work. The weakened condition of the colleges' property made it impossible to raise from endowment sources the incomes of the older married fellows enough to keep pace with their growing family responsibilities. Although tuition funds were often apportioned to some degree according to seniority, there was a limit to how much the young tutors could be squeezed in the interests of their seniors.[132] It became a matter of financial necessity for many married college tutors, especially those with large families, to seek extra income through private pupils and outside examination work. The feverish energy which A. L. Smith devoted to these activities was clearly dictated to some degree by these practical considerations.[133] His wife admitted that A. L.'s ready acceptance of the 'important Examinerships' which were offered to him was, in part, 'necessitated by the need of adding to our income in proportion as the family grew'.[134] In the absence of official insistence on specialized lectures, it was not economically advantageous for college tutors to give them since the broader the area they were willing to teach, the more opportunity they would have to obtain extra income through private pupils and examining work. Barker noted frankly that 'to

[131] *Age and Youth* (London, 1953), 25.
[132] See above, Ch. IV, p. 180, nn. 76–7 for a discussion of Balliol's attempt to provide graduated incomes for college tutors through this method. See also below, pp. 249–50.
[133] See above, Ch. III, p. 110 for Smith's acceptance of private pupils in his house while he was a fellow and tutor of Balliol.
[134] *A. L. Smith, Master of Balliol,* 111.

bring more grist to the mill — it was necessary to add to the core and to widen the range of my teaching'.[135]

In contrast to the controversy over 'specialism' in the *Literae Humaniores* course and the closely related issue of the distribution of power on the Boards of Faculties, the struggles concerning the content of the new Honour School of English Language and Literature and the appropriate qualifications for the new professorship in that subject showed the supporters of research in a much more powerful position. The researchers wanted the primary emphasis in this new university study to be placed on philology and the development of the English language. Their opponents hoped that greater weight would be given to the appreciation of English literary traditions. In these battles, the advocates of research were able to mould this new chair and the new examination school to their own ideals. One reason for this victory was that, unlike the issues of 'specialism' in the *Literae Humaniores* course and the distribution of power in the Boards of Faculties, this confrontation occurred in the university legislatures where the alliance of 'literary and scientific radicals' could be mobilized to support a philological school of English. Another reason for the success of the advocates of research was that they did not have to fight against the combined forces of Young Oxford and their allies on this issue. There were good tactical reasons why many conservative young dons were willing to leave this new subject of university study to the researchers exclusively.

Provision for the first Oxford professorial chair in English was made by the 1877 commissioners. Merton had agreed to endow a chair in this field with the generous sum of £900 p.a. including a fellowship.[136] The statute establishing the chair did not decide conclusively the issue of whether the primary qualification would be philological training or experience in writing literary criticism. It was to be called the Merton Professorship of English Language and Literature and the professor's duties were to 'lecture and give instruction on the history and criticism of the English Language and Literature,

---

[135] *Age and Youth*, 52.
[136] III, 11(a)(ii) and III, 14; both on p. 124 (PP 1882, li).

and on the works of approved English authors'.[137] The only indication that language was to be emphasized more than literature was a clause which allowed for the possibility that this new chair would be merged eventually with the Rawlinson Professorship of Anglo-Saxon.[138] None the less, there was nothing in the statute which would have prevented the election of a literary critic rather than a philologist. However, the researchers scored a clear victory in the first election in 1885. The successful candidate was A. S. Napier, a young Anglo-Saxon philologist, who had studied and taught in Germany after completing his undergraduate studies at Oxford.[139]

This victory for the proponents of philology could not have been taken, however, as indicative of the direction of Oxford opinion on the general question of the proper relation of language to literature in the university study of English. The election of Napier was only the decision of the few individuals who comprised the electorial board.[140] Furthermore, it could have been argued with some justice that research qualifications generally were emphasized in professorial appointments regardless of the nature of the examination school in the professor's subject. One angry critic blamed Napier's election on the professoriate 'to whose influence must be attributed the conversion of the chair of English Language and Literature into a second chair for the promotion of the educationally valueless study of the archaic dialects of Northern Europe'.[141] For these reasons, it soon became apparent that the crucial struggle between the advocates of philology and literature would concern the syllabus for the proposed honour school. This topic was

---

[137] 'Forty-one Statutes made by the University of Oxford Commissioners on the 16th June 1881, concerning certain professorships . . .', See clause 1, of the statute for the Merton chair, p. 3 (PP 1882, li).

[138] Ibid., clause 5, p. 4 (PP 1882, li).

[139] The best source on Napier's work at Oxford is the thorough essay by Neil Ker, 'A. S. Napier, 1853–1916', in J. L. Rosier (ed.), *Philological Essays* (The Hague, 1970), 152–81. I owe this reference to Dr A. C. Kimmens.

[140] For a detailed account of the politics of the election, see the correspondence on this issue of E. B. Nicolson, Bodley's Librarian and one of the electors. Bodl. MS Top. Oxon. d. 166, esp. f. 35.

[141] [J. E. Thorold Rogers,] 'Oxford and its professors', *Edin. Rev.* clxx, no. 348 (1889), 321.

discussed seriously in Congregation beginning in 1887. The proponents of a more literary examination hoped that they could achieve in this large body representing the views of all resident MAs the victory which had been denied to them by a small electoral board.

The leader of the fight for an examination school dealing primarily with English literature was J. Churton Collins, a Balliol graduate who was a lecturer for the London Society for the Extension of University Teaching, a Civil Service coach, and a literary journalist.[142] Collins had been one of the unsuccessful candidates for the Merton chair.[143] He had denounced bitterly the election of Napier as a 'perversion of the Merton Chair' from 'literary culture' to 'philological learning'.[144] Collins argued that the establishment of an examination school on the same basis would minister only to the interests 'of a sect of technical scholars'.[145] He advocated, instead, the creation of an Honour School of English Literature modelled on the *Literae Humaniores* course in which classical philosophy was used as a point of departure for considering modern philosophical writings. The theme of this new school would be the tracing of the connections between classical literature and English literature. Collins conceived his scheme as a modern 'Greats' course to be taken after classical Moderations.

It was indicative of the polarization of Oxford opinion that Collins's strategy was to mobilize sentiment against his opponents by arguing that their plan for a philological school of English was merely another plot of the 'specialists'. Of Oxford philologists, he indignantly remarked, 'In their eyes the Universities are simply nurseries for esoteric specialists, and to talk of bringing them into touch with national life is, in their estimation, mere cant.'[146] He asserted that the

---

[142] For a fuller account of this controversy, see D. J. Palmer, *The Rise of English Studies* (Oxford, 1965), esp. Ch. VI and VII, 78–117.

[143] A satire of Collins's views on this issue addressed him as 'Would-be Professor of Would-be'. See 'Unity Put Quarterly' by 'Q' [A. T. Quiller-Couch, Trinity College], in the *Oxford Magazine* for 2 Mar. 1887, reprinted in *Echoes from the Oxford Magazine* (Oxford, 1890), 85.

[144] [J. Churton Collins,] 'A School of English Literature', *Quart. Rev.* clxiv, no. 327 (1887), 244.   [145] Ibid. 245.

[146] J. Churton Collins, 'Language versus Literature at Oxford', *Nineteenth Century* xxxvii, no. 216 (1895), 292.

researchers wanted an honour school only as an effective means of inducing the university to create more academic offices for philologists and other specialists than it was willing to establish for research alone.[147]

Collins also tried to utilize the resentment felt by many younger dons toward the attempts of the specialists to alter the *Literae Humaniories* course. He argued that his plan would better embody the traditional ideals of 'Oxford culture' than the plans of the philologists. 'Up to the present time it [philology] has . . . been allowed to fill a place in education altogether disproportionate to its significance as an instrument of culture', Collins insisted. 'As an instrument of culture it ranks, in our opinion, very low indeed. It certainly contributes nothing to the cultivation of the taste. It as certainly contributes nothing to the education of the emotions. The mind is neither enlarged nor refined.'[148] This was precisely the criticism W. L. Courtney had made of the attempts of the specialists to alter the *Literae Humaniores* course.[149] Similarly, when Collins described the educational benefits of his new school of English literature, his description was remarkably close to the account of the benefits which a host of Oxford proponents of 'liberal education' from Bishop Copleston to W. L. Courtney had ascribed to the traditional Greats course.[150] Collins noted confidently, 'whatever may be the future calling of these students, the positive knowledge they will have attained will, unlike a knowledge of Philology, be of immense and immediate service to them; the liberal training to which, in the course of acquiring that knowledge, they have been submitted, will, unlike the narrow and narrowing discipline of mere philological culture, send them forth with enlarged minds and with cultivated tastes.'[151]

Despite these appeals to the animosities and loyalties of Young Oxford, Collins was not wholly successful in mobilizing their support for his scheme.[152] Unlike the controversies

---

[147] Ibid. 292–3.

[148] 'A School of English Literature', *Quart. Rev.* clxiv, no. 327 (1887), 265.

[149] See above, p. 233, n. 113.

[150] For Copleston's views, see above Ch. I, p. 16, n. 6. For Courtney's views, see above, p. 233, n. 114.

[151] 'A School of English Literature', *Quart Rev.* clxiv, no. 327 (1887), 266.

[152] Despite this failure, Collins continued to write on this topic. See the series

involving science and professors, the creation of a new examination school did not infringe as heavily on the financial resources of the colleges. Neither could a new school, unlike Percy Gardner's plan, undermine the classical curriculum to whose preservation Young Oxford was committed. Furthermore, a popular school of English literature, such as Collins envisaged, might have proved a threat to the ascendency of *Literae Humaniores.* This prospect certainly would have had little appeal for Young Oxford. No doubt many conservative young dons responded gleefully to the savage characterization of Collins's scheme which appeared in the *Oxford Magazine* in 1887:

> Come chasten the cheap with the classic
> Choose Churton, thy chair and thy class
> Mix, melt in the must that is Massic
>   The beer that is Bass.[153]

Young Oxford had no wish to ruin the 'classic' wine of its traditional studies by mixing it with the 'cheap' beer of modern English literature. The plans of the advocates of research had at least the negative value of preserving the *Literae Humaniores* curriculum uncontaminated.

When the new Honour School of English Language and Literature was finally approved in 1895 by Congregation and Convocation, it was clear that the philologists had been victorious. The subject-matter of the new examination school was to include both literature and the study of the language, but the philological aspect was given greater weight. Lewis Farnell boasted proudly that this victory was the greatest 'triumph' of his 'militant dining club' and its scientific allies. 'The longest and hardest conflict, in which we were

---

of articles he wrote for the *Nineteenth Century*: 'Can English Literature be taught', xii (Nov. 1887), 642–58; 'The Universities in contact with the people', xxvi (Oct. 1889), 561–83; 'The "ideal" University', xxxi (Feb. 1892), 243–54; 'A University for the People', xlv (Mar. 1899), 465–76. Collins also attempted to mobilize support privately by holding out the lure of endowments. See his letter to Sir William Anson of All Souls on this subject, Bodl. MS Top. Oxon. d. 310, ff. 48–9.

[153] 'Q' [A. T. Quiller-Couch, Trinity College,] 'Unity Put Quarterly', reprinted in *Echoes from the Oxford Magazine* (Oxford, 1890), 84. It first appeared on 2 Mar. 1887.

ultimately successful, was to carry through the statute founding the English School', he asserted. 'We worked hard together, and guided by Napier we succeeded in giving it at its outset a firm basis in philological science.'[154] No systematic attempt was made to organize this new course around the classical background of modern English literary traditions. Collins asserted contemptuously of the first syllabus for the new school, 'I can assure these legislators, and I speak from knowledge, that setting aside the philological portion of this curriculum, which is, so far as it goes, solid enough, an experienced crammer would in about three months furnish an astute youth with all that is requisite for graduating in this school.'[155] This victory for 'specialism' was attributable in part to the refusal of many conservative young dons to view Collins's plan as their own. Furthermore, the initial educational content of the English school was decided in the university legislatures. Since this issue did not arouse the party-spirit of the non-academic voters, the alliance of 'scientific and literary radicals', which had done so much to aid the cause of science, finally was able to operate as well for the benefit of the advocates of literary research. The course of study established for the new Honour School of English Language and Literature was a substantial victory for their cause.

Despite Young Oxford's repeated protests of helplessness before the ogre of 'Science and Specialism', it seems clear that they were more successful in foiling the plans of the specialists than they were in halting the advance of science. Although the advocates of research were able to rely on the powerful support of the scientists on issues fought in the university legislatures, they were unfortunate in that many crucial decisions involving their interests were made in the Boards of Faculties where they were weak. None the less, Young Oxford was not able either to halt totally the progress of 'specialism' or to deny completely the role of the university in the encouragement of research. The 1877 Commission had

---

[154] *An Oxonian Looks Back* (London, 1934), 271.
[155] 'Language versus Literature at Oxford', *Nineteenth Century* xxxvii, no. 216 (1895), 296.

built a certain degree of recognition for these ideals into their new statutes. Furthermore, with the increasing number of older married tutors and the growth in the professoriate, the values of Young Oxford no longer represented university opinion.

E. The Agricultural Depression and the Problem of 'Progressive Careers'

The financial crisis caused by the agricultural depression wrecked the 1877 Commission's plan to use university readerships to provide 'progressive careers' for college tutors. The Common University Fund from which these readerships were to be financed did not grow at the rate which had been anticipated by the commissioners. Although this failure was partially the result of defects in the original statute, the major cause was declining collegiate external income in the 1880s and 1890s. The university could not afford to expand the number of readerships significantly beyond the seven which had been created initially. Therefore, the college tutor was never able to consider these offices as a regular mid-career promotion. The weakened financial condition of most colleges was also largely responsible for their inability to supply this need internally. The 1877 Commission had freed tutorial fellows to view their collegiate positions as professional careers, but the agricultural depression had robbed them of the opportunities for advancement which they had expected as a concomitant of this new status.

The sluggish expansion of the Common University fund in the twenty-five years after the 1877 Commission was the most important factor accounting for the collapse of the university readership scheme. The fund collected £2,960 in 1885[156] when the colleges were only contributing one-fourth of the amount they would be called upon eventually to pay. Although by 1893 the colleges were assuming one-half of their ultimate burden of taxation for university purposes, the fund only rose to £4,334.[157] By 1903, when the colleges

[156] J. E. Thorold Rogers, 'Return Relating to the Universities of Oxford and Cambridge', Part E(I), p. 73 (PP 1886, li).
[157] *Jour. of the Royal Stat. Soc.* lviii (1895), Table IX, 64.

were contributing the entire amount the statutes demanded, their payments had fallen to £3,513.[158] This sum was over £8,000 less than a minimum calculation based on the statistics of 1885 would have justified. Of course if the Cleveland Commission's anticipation of a one-third rise in collegiate external income by 1895 also had been included in determining reasonable expectations, the gap between hopeful projections and dismal realities would have been greater still.

Although the failure of the Common University Fund to fulfil the expectations of the 1877 Commission was largely due to the decline in the external income of the colleges, a loophole in the original statutes exacerbated this problem to a considerable extent. By the statute 'concerning college contributions to university purposes' the colleges were permitted to deduct from the total amount which they would have to pay into the fund any sums which they voluntarily disbursed for university purposes.[159] Included in this category were payments to the Bodleian Library or to any of its staff and fellowships or other sums given to university readers, to scholars engaged on research projects, or to professors who were not attached to the college by statute. As the rate of taxation on collegiate external income rose at five-year intervals through the 1880s and 1890s, the colleges availed themselves of this clause with increasing frequency. In 1893 the colleges contributed £1,206 for university purposes of their own choosing;[160] by 1903, this sum had risen to £3,498.[161] The absence of these monies from the Common University Fund contributed to its failure to grow at the rate anticipated by the 1877 Commission.

By the turn of the century, there were those who considered this clause a serious defect in the original statute. In 1909 Lord Curzon criticized the operation of this loophole. '[G]enerous as is the manner in which the Colleges have hitherto voluntarily recognized the call upon them, there has been a lack of system and co-ordination in the manner in which the payments have been made', he suggested diplomatically.

---

[158] Ibid. lxvi (1904), Table XV, 638.   [159] No. 7, p. 2 (PP 1882, li).
[160] *Jour. of the Royal Stat. Soc.* lviii (1895), Table IX, 64.
[161] Ibid. lxvi (1904), Table XV, 638.

'Nobody places before a College Meeting a reasoned statement of the University's needs. Neither Council nor the Board of Faculties has ever been known to undertake such a task. No representatives or spokesmen of the University is there to plead its cause. The College contributes from a sincere sense of its obligation, but necessarily in a haphazard fashion . . .'[162] Curzon also complained more severely that the clause which insured that the colleges deducted only such sums as the university considered to be for 'university purposes' had been allowed to become 'a dead letter'.[163] In practice, the Hebdomadal Council and the curators of the University Chest permitted each college to decide this matter for itself.

None the less, the Common University Fund still would have grown at a disappointing rate, especially in the late 1890s, even if this defect in the original statute had never existed. Assuming that this loophole had been eliminated, the fund would have contained £5,540 in 1893, only £400 less than the minimum expectations based on the 1885 figures. However, by 1903 the income of the fund would have risen to only £7,011, more than £4,800 less than could have been expected on the basis of 1885 calculations. Although the existence of this method by which the colleges could legally evade their statutory obligations undoubtedly contributed to the sluggish growth of the Common University Fund, the financial crisis clearly created the problem in the first place.

The combined effect of the agricultural depression and this defect in the original statute was that the number of readerships never grew to any great extent. The 1877 Commission had created seven of them and by 1893 the university had only been able to raise this figure to nine.[164] Although this number of readerships was maintained in 1903[165] despite

---

[162] *Principles and Methods of University Reform* (Oxford, 1909), 151.

[163] Ibid. 153.

[164] There were actually twelve university readerships in 1893, but three of them were wholly financed by the colleges. All Souls was responsible for those in Roman and Indian law and Christ Church paid the entire stipend of the Reader in Indian History.

[165] There were actually only six readerships in 1903, but three more had simply been given the title of professor. The biographer of one of these three, E. B. Tylor, Professor of Anthropology, noted that his readership 'only became a Professorship by way of personal compliment'. See R. R. Marett, *Tylor* (London, 1936), 15.

the fall in the income of the fund, it was apparent that any increase would be impossible. No prospect existed for the foreseeable future of the fund being able to finance reader-ships on a scale sufficient to allow college tutors to view them realistically as regular mid-career promotions. The university readerships which remained gradually assumed their modern character as merely lesser professorial chairs with similar duties but lower pay. These vestigial offices could serve only as exceptional promotions for the few college tutors who were fortunate enough to be serious candidates at the infrequent intervals when they became vacant.[166]

With the collapse of the 1877 Commission's readership plan, most college tutors lost the realistic possibility for a 'progressive career'. About 70 per cent of the dons first appointed to teaching posts between 1881 and 1900 were able to obtain permanent academic positions in Oxford[167] but only about one-quarter ever advanced in Oxford beyond the rank of official college fellow.[168] Although this figure could be viewed as a reasonable percentage of promotions as rewards for exceptional merit, it could not be considered adequate to supply the need for regular mid-career advance-ment. Even including those college tutors who left Oxford to obtain academic promotions, only 40 per cent attained 'progressive careers' in university work.[169] About 60 per cent of those college tutors who decided in the late nineteenth century to make academic life their profession received no significant advancement in status or duties between the age of twenty-five and retirement, and only such increases in income as could be obtained at the expense of the younger tutors through unequal dividing of tuition funds.

[166] See below, Ch. VI, pp. 276–7 for the attempt of the university to remedy this defect again by creating university lectureships as rewards for college tutors.

[167] See below, Appendix 1, p. 286. This figure includes those who had 'mixed careers' as well as those who had exclusively 'university careers'.

[168] Of the fifty-four who attained permanent academic positions, fourteen of them obtained promotion in Oxford; six to professorships, seven to college head-ships, one to the Oxford Secretaryship of the Rhodes Trustees.

[169] Seven more obtained academic promotion outside Oxford: three to pro-fessorships and four to college or university headships. Therefore, a total of twenty-one of the fifty-four dons who attained permanent academic positions in Oxford were successful in obtaining 'progressive careers' in university work.

The colleges were also powerless to provide the majority of their teachers with improved opportunities for advancement. This goal could have been fulfilled only by augmenting tuition funds considerably, either by diverting endowment income or by raising fees. Neither of these methods was practicable. No college was permitted by its statutes to supplement their tuition fund from external income by more than £5 p.a. per student.[170] Furthermore, financial conditions insured that few colleges would be able to avail themselves of even this limited option. Raising tuition fees sharply also was not feasible, despite the convincing case which could be made in principle for this change. Since approximately one-third of most college tutors' incomes was derived from their fellowships, one logical critic suggested that fees ought to be raised by one-third to eliminate this indiscriminate subsidy to students who in most cases neither required charity nor deserved prizes.[171] Tradition as well as unwillingness to court public indignation, however, made this suggestion unrealistic. The result was that the colleges were unable to supply the deficiency caused by the failure of the Common University Fund to finance a sufficient number of readerships to fulfil the intentions of the 1877 Commission.

One perceptive critic foresaw this problem of the inadequate opportunities for the promotion of college tutors as early as 1887. '[T]he married tutor is undoubtedly living in a sort of fool's paradise. What is eventually to become of him, no one knows or thinks it worth while to reflect', he complained. 'As he surveys his increasing progeny, does he never count the grey hairs which are showing themselves on his temples, and wonder what will be done with him when he is past his work? Or does he console himself with the chance of getting a professorship, or even the headship of a house, *spectatus satis et donatus jam rude?*[172] Merely allowing tutors to marry, as the 1877 Commission had done, did not make their position in Oxford a satisfactory career according to this critic. He bluntly stated the problem while alluding as well to the exacerbating

---

[170] See, for a typical example, the Christ Church statute, X, 1(b), p. 44 (PP 1882, li).
[171] 'Oxford University Reform', *Quart. Rev.* ccxiv, no. 427 (1911), 446–7.
[172] 'Social Oxford', *Macmillan's Mag.* lvii (Dec. 1887), 107.

effects of the agricultural depression. '[I] t is no use encouraging a man to marry unless the hope is held out to him of a steady increase of income', he insisted. 'But the married Fellow will earn no more at fifty years of age than he does at twenty-five; while the chances are that the expenses of his household will be exactly doubled during the interval, and his Fellowship, owing to agricultural depression, be probably represented by a steadily diminishing quantity.'[173] Despite the anonymous critic's attempt to disguise his identity by describing himself as 'one who . . . has returned after some years absence to the Oxford which once was so familiar',[174] the *Wellesley Guide to Victorian Periodicals* has identified him as W. L. Courtney, who had been resident as an official fellow of New College for ten years when he wrote this article.

Courtney's own career presents a vivid illustration of the problem which he expressed so clearly.[175] His desire to marry forced him to leave Oxford as a young graduate in the 1870s while his ambition impelled him in mid-career to leave for the second and last time. Courtney's first brief Oxford career began with his election to a fellowship at Merton after he had taken a First in *Literae Humaniores* in 1872. It ended, however, only one year later since he wished to marry and all four tutorial fellowships which Merton allowed married men to hold were already filled.[176] The headmastership of Courtney's old school, Somersetshire College, Bath, fell vacant in 1873 and his academic successes induced the governors to offer him the position despite his youth. He accepted enthusiastically, married, resigned his fellowship and left Oxford. Unfortunately, Courtney was not successful as the headmaster of a private school. His youth was resented by the older staff who could easily have remembered him as a boy. To his youthfulness also could be ascribed his poor judgement in supposing that the governors and 'gentry' parents would accept his plan to raise numbers at the school by accepting

---

[173] Ibid. 108.   [174] Ibid. 105.

[175] The basic sources for Courtney's life are his autobiography, *The Passing Hour* (London, [1925]) and the biography by his wife, *The Making of an Editor: W. L. Courtney 1850–1928* (London, 1928).

[176] See above, Ch. III, pp. 111–13 for a discussion of Merton's early statute permitting four married tutorial fellows.

[177] *The Passing Hour* (London [1925]), 97–102.

the sons of local tradesmen. After a few years, Courtney was desperate to leave this uncongenial occupation.[177] Deliverance came in the form of an offer in 1877 from New College of one of its tutorial fellowships which could be held by a married man. Courtney accepted and returned to Oxford at the age of twenty-seven to teach moral philosophy for the *Literae Humaniores* course.

Although this tutorial fellowship at New College was a career position tenable for life, Courtney only remained in Oxford for thirteen years, leaving in 1890 at the age of forty to become a London journalist. In his autobiography, written thirty-five years later, Courtney described his reason for leaving the university with a mellow air of good sportsmanship which he had not felt it necessary to muster for an anonymous article in 1887. 'I had been disappointed in an election to a professorship', he stated simply. 'I certainly thought I was worthy to be Whyte's Professor of Moral Philosophy. No doubt I was wrong, and my assumption of eligibility was a piece of vanity of which I ought to be ashamed. But, whether I understood the matter rightly or not, it was a bitter blow to me, and one which suggested by its very nature, reasons for some thorough-going decision.'[178] Although this explanation had the literary advantages of simplicity and directness, it was factually incorrect to the extent that it telescoped a series of disappointments into one event.

Courtney's first Oxford defeat came when the Whyte's chair fell vacant in 1882 with the premature death of T. H. Green. Green had been Courtney's mentor in philosophy. The major candidates were Courtney and William Wallace of Merton, who was also a follower of Green's neo-Hegelianism. Wallace's main advantage over Courtney was that he was somewhat older and had served his college for much longer. In 1882 Wallace was thirty-eight years old and had been a successful college tutor for fifteen years. Although Courtney was thirty-two at this time, he had taught at Oxford for only four years. In terms of scholarly writing, however, Courtney and Wallace were more evenly matched. Wallace's most important work before the election was his translation of

[178] Ibid. 176-7.

Hegel's *Logic*, which had appeared with an introductory essay in 1873. Since then he had only published slight works on Epicureanism under the auspices of the Society for Promoting Christian Knowledge and on Kant for Blackwood's Philosophical Classics.[179] Although Courtney's academic career had only begun in 1877, he had already published two books by 1882; a volume of philosophical essays[180] and a study of the ideas of John Stuart Mill.[181] When Wallace was elected to the professorship, Courtney expressed his disappointment by becoming a candidate for the headmastership of Dulwich College, despite his previous unpleasant experience of schoolmastering.[182] He did not obtain the post, however, and decided to remain at Oxford.

The really crucial events which impelled Courtney to leave Oxford were the professorial elections of 1889 to the two remaining chairs in his field, the Wykeham Professorship of Logic and the Waynflete Professorship of Moral and Metaphysical Philosophy. Courtney was probably reluctant to give up all hope of a 'progressive career' in Oxford until he had a chance for these two positions. The strength of his candidacy had been improved by seven more years of collegiate teaching and one more book, a historical and critical treatise on ethics which had attained considerable popularity among students reading *Literae Humaniores*.[183] The Wykeham chair fell vacant first and the most important candidates were Courtney, J. Cook Wilson of Oriel, and Thomas Case of Corpus Christi. Cook Wilson was elected. When the Waynflete chair became available later in the same year, Case and Courtney were both candidates but Case was elected. Courtney's wife explained that it was these disappointments which caused her husband to leave the university.[184]

Courtney was forty years old at the time of these final

[179] *Epicureansim* was published in 1880 and *Kant* in 1882.

[180] *Studies in Philosophy, Ancient and Modern* (London, 1882).

[181] *The Metaphysics of John Stuart Mill* (London, 1879).

[182] [Mrs J. E. Courtney,] *The Making of an Editor: W. L. Courtney 1850–1928* (London, 1930), 18-20.

[183] *Constructive Ethics* (London, 1886). Courtney noted its popularity in his autobiography, *The Passing Hour* (London, [1925]), 154-5. A second, revised edition was called for in 1895.

[184] [Mrs J. E. Courtney,] *The Making of an Editor: W. L. Courtney 1850–1928* (London, 1930), 17-18, 33-4, 36-7.

disappointments. He had been passed over for all the professorial chairs in his field and the state of college finances in 1890 precluded his entertaining any further expectations from New College. Mrs Courtney suggested that her husband's theatre journalism and especially his acting in Oxford plays were responsible for his not being elected to a professorship. 'Over Courtney, serious Oxford shook its head', she complained.[185] 'All this versatility had its dangers from the point of view of academic advancement. Some of his seniors were shocked by it, or at the very least made uneasy.'[186] The last professorial elections also indicated that the philosophical school to which Courtney belonged had been superseded in Oxford. Both Case and Cook Wilson were proponents of the Realism[187] which was a reaction against the previously ascendant Idealism of Green, Wallace, and Courtney. In any case, whether Courtney was the victim of Oxford priggishness or of changes in philosophical fashions, the result was the same. The university could no longer offer him a 'progressive career'. Courtney left Oxford in 1890 for a second career as a journalist and man of letters in London. He became the drama critic and book reviewer for the *Daily Telegraph* and eventually rose to the editorship of the *Fortnightly Review*.

Although Courtney made a point of not regretting his decision to leave Oxford, the breezy tone of his autobiography in describing his academic defeats was probably only a polite mask. Courtney insisted that his disappointments were fortunate since he was not tempermentally suited for a university career. '[M]ine was not an academic character', he concluded with satisfaction. 'I was beginning to get a little tired of the academic life.'[188] None the less, when the Warden of New College died in 1903, Courtney discussed with his wife the possibility that he might have been elected to the headship if he had stayed on as a college tutor.[189] 'Oxford takes a lot of forgetting', Mrs Courtney concluded wistfully.[190] If the university had been able to offer Courtney a readership in the

---

[185] Ibid. 33–4. [186] Ibid. 17–18.
[187] R. G. Collingwood discussed them in these terms in his *Autobiography* (Oxford, 1939). [188] *The Passing Hour*, 177.
[189] *The Making of an Editor: W. L. Courtney 1850–1928*, 60–1.
[190] Ibid. 46.

late 1880s when he experienced his mid-career crisis, he might have been willing to wait longer for further promotions. With the collapse of the 1877 Commission's readership plan under the strain of financial hardship, this alternative to either accepting a static career in Oxford or seeking promotion elsewhere was eliminated.

The careers of the other members of the Non-Placet Society who protested publicly against 'modern innovations' showed the range of possibilities which faced the young don in the 1880s. Like Courtney, both Charles Oman and A. T. S. Goodrick were able to obtain permanent career positions in Oxford. Oman received a 'permanent lectureship' at New College in 1885 to hold in conjunction with his All Souls fellowship,[191] while Goodrick's fellowship at St. John's was converted to an official one in 1883 as soon as the new statutes came into effect. In contrast, H. H. Henson never obtained a permanent post in Oxford. The prize fellowship at All Souls which he won in 1884 was only tenable for seven years and in 1889 he accepted the college living of Barking, Essex. Henson had a long, active, and successful career in the Church which culminated in his elevation to the bishopric of Durham.[192] He also continued to pursue the historical studies he had begun at Oxford, writing extensively on the history of the English Church.[193] A. T. S. Goodrick also chose to leave Oxford despite his obtaining an official fellowship. In 1890 he took the college living of Winterbourne,

[191] This eccentric arrangement was the result of a combination of loyalty to All Souls and bitterness toward New College. Oman had been an undergraduate at New College but had been rejected for a fellowship in favour of a 'Cambridge mathematician'. He won an All Souls fellowship instead. Although New College later offered to make Oman an official fellow when his prize fellowship expired in 1890, he refused. He was willing to teach for the college but he did not wish to be a member of the senior common room which had rejected him. Oman was able to make this stand since All Souls had signified its willingness to retain him under the clause which permitted the college to keep prize fellows beyond the initial seven years so long as they only received £50 p.a. from their fellowships. See Oman's autobiography, *Memories of Victorian Oxford* (London, 1941), 135-6.
[192] See Henson's autobiography, *Retrospect of an Unimportant Life* (3 vols., London, 1944-50).
[193] Henson had taken a First in Modern History in 1884 and had been the first Non-Collegiate student to win a fellowship at All Souls. His later writings included *Studies in English Religion in the 17th Century* (London, 1903), *Puritanism in England* (London, 1912), and *The Church of England* (Cambridge, 1939).

Gloucestershire, which he held until his death in 1914.[194] During this period Goodrick maintained his learned avocations by editing several seventeenth-century documents.[195] Charles Oman was the only one of these four members of the Non-Placet Society to remain in Oxford for his entire career. After twenty-two years as a college lecturer, he was elected Chichele Professor of Modern History in 1907, a post he retained until his death in 1946. Of these four young dons of the 1880s, three achieved 'progressive careers', but only one was able to find this opportunity in academic life.

Most college tutors who remained at Oxford had to accept the fact that university work would offer them few opportunities for advancement. The 1877 commissioners' plan to use university readerships as mid-career promotions miscarried and the colleges were powerless to compensate their teachers for this disappointment. In the late nineteenth century, for the first time, the majority of Oxford dons were able to view academic work as a life career, but the agricultural depression destroyed the possibility that this new profession would offer opportunities for promotion analogous to those offered by the traditional learned professions.

The agricultural depression exercised a pervasive influence over virtually all aspects of the 1877 Commission's plan for the establishment of a 'tutorial profession' in Oxford. The balance between this new profession and the claims of research and science was completely overthrown and the conflicts of prize fellows versus college tutors, clergymen versus lay fellows, scientists versus classicists, young married tutors versus older married ones, academic versus non-academic resident MAs, and the professoriate versus the colleges were all greatly exacerbated. The commissioners had dealt generously with each rival conception of the proper functions of the university

[194] The only source for Goodrick's life is the brief entry in J. A. Venn, *Alumni Cantabrigiensis* (Cambridge, 1947), Part II, Vol. iii, p. 85. Goodrick was admitted as a sizar at St. John's College, Cambridge in 1874 but migrated to a demyship at Magdalen College, Oxford in 1875.

[195] He edited the sixth and seventh volumnes of *The Memorials of Edward Randolph* (London, 1898-1909) for the Prince Society. He also edited *The Relation of Sydnam Poyntz 1624-1636* (London, 1908) for the Royal Historical Society (Camden 3rd Series, vol. xiv).

in the mistaken belief that the economic problems of agriculture were only temporary. With the collapse of these sanguine expectations in the 1880s and 1890s, the proponents of each claim had to struggle fiercely simply to retain a portion of what the commissioners had granted.

Although all interests suffered to some degree, the greatest disappointments were sustained by the advocates of research and by those college tutors who had hoped that the new 'tutorial profession' would be a 'progressive career' for most of its practitioners. The claims of science were better protected because of the statutory and institutional safeguards built into the 1877 settlement. New alliances were formed and old ones were refurbished to protect each faction. Lasting animosities were also created and intensified. The Non-Placet Society rallied the supporters of the Church, the colleges, and traditional 'Oxford culture' against the combination of 'literary and scientific radicals'. A stark dichotomy was drawn between the advancement of science and the well-being of the collegiate and tutorial systems. The university as a place of education was placed in rigid opposition to its role as a centre of learned research. The new academic profession which emerged from these conflicts was largely the result of the distribution of power established by the 1877 Commission, counterbalanced by the rise in the number of non-academic voters in Congregation, and forced to operate in a period of unforeseen financial stringency.

Chapter VI

THE OXFORD DON AS A
PROFESSIONAL MAN 1882–1914

The enduring structure of the academic profession in Oxford emerged through the gradual modification to suit the altered conditions of the late nineteenth and early twentieth centuries of the statutes originally written under the auspices of the 1877 Commission. Every year between 1882 and the advent of World War I, the governing bodies of several colleges availed themselves of the privilege accorded them by the Act of 1877 to alter any part of their statutes by a two-thirds majority of a college meeting summoned especially for this purpose.[1] If these alterations affected the interests of the university, they had to be approved by the Hebdomadal Council. All collegiate statute revisions also had to receive the final acceptance of the Education Committee of the Privy Council. Neither the university nor the Privy Council, however, chose to use their power to overrule the internal decisions of the colleges and, in practice, each governing body was left completely free to make any revisions it wished. The university also had been granted by the Act of 1877 the same privilege as the colleges[2] and, subject to similar restrictions, the university also used these powers to alter its statutes.

A. The Declining Influence of the
Non-Academic Professions:

i. The Prize Fellowship System

The growing demands of the academic profession during a period of unforeseen financial stringency left little scope for the traditional learned professions which previously had exercised substantial claims on university endowments. This trend was the result of both economics and ideology: the

---

[1] 40 and 41 Vict. ch. 48, cl. 54–5, in Shadwell iv. 88–9.
[2] Ibid., cl. 53, p. 88.

agricultural depression substantially reduced available resources, making essential the choosing of priorities; but the choices made were determined largely by changed conceptions of the university's duties toward society. The 1877 Commission had greatly reduced the extent of the prize fellowship system, but had shown no intention of totally abolishing it. The commissioners had hoped that restricting the tenure of 'ordinary fellowships' to seven years would increase their turnover rate[3] and counterbalance to a large degree the inevitable effects of using 'official' and 'professorial' fellowships as career positions. The new system, however, did not remain undisturbed long enough to verify their hypothesis.

The financial inability of the colleges to support the full plans of the 1877 Commission was one factor contributing to the demise of the remaining prize fellowships. For example, when Queen's realized in 1896 that its pension fund would not be sufficient in the near future to meet all claims, a new statute was sanctioned allowing the college to relieve the fund by electing three retired officials to ordinary fellowships without examination.[4] In effect, three prize fellowships were suspended until the pension fund was able to meet all its obligations without this aid. In a few colleges, financial pressures also forced a reduction in the total number of fellowships.[5] Since the governing bodies of these colleges always decided against eliminating official fellowships, the entire burden of this policy fell on the ordinary fellowships. The programme of retrenchment dictated by the fall in endowment income resulted in a reduction in prize fellowships because of the low priority the colleges accorded this traditional obligation.

Another factor leading to the virtual elimination of prize fellowships was the gradual increase in the number of official fellows. Several colleges raised their statutory maximum, reducing the margin for ordinary fellowships of all kinds.[6]

---

[3] This view had some credibility since the average tenure of a fellowship under the old system had been about thirteen years. J. E. Thorold Rogers made this calculation for the period 1840–60 in *Education at Oxford* (London, 1861), 213.

[4] See PP 1897, lxx.

[5] See, for example, Jesus in 1895 (PP 1895, lxxvii), Worcester in 1904 (PP 1904, lxxv), and Oriel in 1909 (PP 1910, lxii).

[6] See, for example, Trinity in 1893 (PP 1893–4, lxviii), Magdalen in 1898

The increase of less than 10 per cent in matriculations between the Commission and 1900 could account for only a part of the expansion of over 25 per cent in tutorial fellows. The primary causes of this trend were instead the growth in the number of examination schools and the greater degree of specialization within each subject.[7]

The expansion in alternate uses for ordinary fellowships also had the effect of reducing the availability of prize fellowships. Virtually all the collegiate statutes written in 1881-2 provided that a small and strictly limited number of ordinary fellowships could be awarded by nomination rather than competitive examination to professors, other university officials, or independent researchers. The tendency, especially after the turn of the century, was for colleges to increase their ability to make awards of this type in place of prize fellowships.[8]

The establishment of 'senior scholarships' as a new category of graduate award also infringed on the prize fellowship system since these new awards were usually created through the suppression of ordinary fellowships.[9] The fact that their purpose was to enable the young graduate 'to pursue some course of special study, or to undertake some definite work of research, or to enter upon a course of higher professional training, with a view to their future career'[10] represented an even more serious threat to the prize fellowship system. Senior scholarships clearly were intended to fulfil the proper functions of prize fellowships more efficiently than the existing system. These new awards were of less value than the old ones, £100 to £150 p.a. instead of £200 p.a.; they were

---

(PP 1898, lxx), St. John's in 1899 (PP 1900, lxvi), Worcester in 1904 (PP 1904, lxxv), Merton in 1904 (PP 1906, xc), and University College in 1906 (PP 1907, lxiv).

[7] Matriculations grew from 758 in 1881 to 814 in 1900. These figures are very close to the decennial averages for the 1880s and 1890s compiled by Professor Lawrence Stone. See Stone, Table IA, p. 91 (1880-9: 766, 1890-9: 821). During this same period, the number of tutorial fellows expanded from 110 to 137. For tutorial fellows in 1881 and 1900, see below Appendix 4, pp. 289-90, nn. 8, 11.

[8] See, for example, New College in 1903 (PP 1904, lxxv), Merton in 1904 (PP 1906, lxx), and Corpus Christi in 1909 (PP 1910, lxxii).

[9] See, for example Corpus Christi in 1909 (PP 1910, lxxii), St. John's in 1911 (PP 1912-13, lxv), and Trinity in 1913 (PP 1914, lxiv).

[10] Quoted from the statute revision of Trinity in 1913 (PP 1914, lxiv).

tenable for only three or four years instead of seven; and they did not give their recipients a position on the governing bodies of the colleges. These three changes reflected the desire of many dons both to limit and control more carefully the use of collegiate income to support professional studies and to exclude non-academic persons from power in the colleges.

Even in those colleges which continued to offer a significant number of prize fellowships, academic dissatisfactions with the existing system were often expressed through the imposition of concrete duties where previously none had been required. All Souls, the largest source of prize fellowships, altered its statutes in 1911 to insist that the prize fellow 'pursue during the tenure of his Fellowship some course of study or investigation to be specified by him to the Warden and Fellows and approved by them'.[11] In virtually the same terms, St. John's amended its statutes in 1911[12] and New College followed suit in 1914, adding, to make the obligation somewhat stronger, the explicit warning that '[a]ny Fellow who fails to give, or, having given, fails, in the judgement of the Warden and Fellows, to perform such undertaking shall vacate his Fellowship'.[13] At Christ Church, also in 1914, a firm distinction was drawn between 'students by examination', i.e. prize fellows, who were to continue to be elected under the traditional clause contained in the 1882 statutes that they be 'of the greatest merit and most fit to be a Student of the House as a place of religion, learning and education', and a new category of 'research students' with formal obligations to pursue literary or scientific investigations.[14]

Although only one college explicitly abolished prize fellowships before World War I,[15] many others in effect eliminated them by abolishing the maximum figures for official fellowships,[16] for ordinary fellowships by nomination,[17] or

[11] p. 2 (PP 1911, lix).   [12] PP 1912–13, lxv.
[13] III, 19, p. 3 (PP 1914–6, li).   [14] XIII, 5, p. 3 (ibid.).
[15] Brasenose in 1903 (PP 1904, lxxv).
[16] See, for examples, Worcester in 1910 (PP 1911, lix) and Pembroke in 1912 (PP 1912–13, lxv).
[17] See for example, New College in 1914 (PP 1914–16, li). University College in 1904 abolished all limitations on researchers but retained its restrictions on professors or readers elected to ordinary fellowships by nomination. See PP 1905, lx.

for both of these categories.[18] By expanding the number of fellowships for college tutors, university professors and readers, or independent researchers, prize fellowships might in practice be totally eliminated. The nascent academic profession had begun to insist that in a period of financial retrenchment university endowments ought to be confined to a narrower range of purposes than had been accepted previously as legitimate. For example, when University College decided to abolish its limitation on the number of ordinary fellowships which could be awarded to researchers, the governing body expressed their dissatisfaction with the prize system. 'Fellowships given as prizes tenable only for a short term, and entailing no duties, have not in practice tended to advance the pursuit of learning', they argued. '[S]uch advance seems to the College more certainly secured by the election to Fellowships of Students undertaking to pursue some definite branch of learning '.[19] This explanation was somewhat disingenuous, of course, since the 1877 Commission had retained prize fellowships not 'to advance the pursuit of learning' but to maintain the connection between the colleges and the non-academic learned professions. University College clearly announced by this statute revision its rejection of the traditional mode of maintaining that connection.

The period from the 1877 Commission to World War I thus witnessed the gradual elimination of the remaining prize fellowships. One astute critic in 1911 gave a clear and succinct account of the existing situation. 'The Statutes of the last Commission contemplated an annual expenditure of about £35,000 in prize fellowships . . . The actual expenditure on prize fellowships in recent years has been about £7,000 annually; and a large proportion of that sum is expended by a single college [All Souls]. The decrease in college revenues partly explains the suspension of so many prize fellowships; but nothing like the amount of money actually available for the purpose has been spent in this way. The increased demands upon University and college teaching, and the claims of

[18] See, for examples, St. John's in 1908 (PP 1909, lxix), and Queen's in 1907 (PP 1908, lxxxvi). [19] III, 1 (PP 1905, lx).

research, have led colleges to obtain powers to expend their revenues in other ways than rewarding ability by gifts of £1,400.'[20] Prize fellowships virtually disappeared from Oxford because, in a period of financial crisis, the claims for the expansion of academic careers and the endowment of research could best be satisfied at their expense. There was a growing feeling within the colleges that prize fellowships were an illegitimate use of academic endowments and, furthermore, that their legitimate function as aids for professional education could be fulfilled more appropriately through the creation of awards of lesser value with more explicit duties.

ii. The Church

The influence of the Church as well as the other non-academic learned professions continued to decline in Oxford even after the severe depredations of the 1877 Commission. This trend was similar to that concerning the prize fellowship system, but its impact was less since the 1877 commissioners had left the Church fewer privileges which could be revoked. Although financial pressures certainly exacerbated this tendency, the desire of the new academic profession for complete hegemony fundamentally dictated this policy of hostility to the few vestigial preserves of the Church.

The attack on the requirements of the 1881–2 statutes concerning the number, income, and other privileges of the few remaining obligatory clerical fellows expressed directly collegiate hostility to Church interests. Several colleges whose statutes had demanded more than the one fellow in holy orders needed to act as chaplain, later reduced their minimum requirement.[21] One college even managed to eliminate their one obligatory clerical fellow if the headship was held by a clergyman willing to undertake religious services and instruction.[22] There was also a tendency to downgrade the position of chaplains. Wadham reduced the

---

[20] 'Oxford University Reform', *Quart. Rev.* ccxiv, no. 427 (1911), 447. Lord Curzon made precisely this same argument in *Principles and Methods of University Reform* (Oxford, 1909), 97.

[21] See, for example, Christ Church in 1908 reduced from three to two (PP 1908, lxxxvi). Pembroke in 1912 reduced from two to one (PP 1912-13, lxv), and Magdalen in 1913 reduced from two to one (PP 1913, 1).

[22] University College in 1882 (PP 1882, li).

stipends of its chaplain and divinity lecturer in 1890, largely no doubt in response to extreme financial hardship.[23] This justification, however, would not serve to explain Magdalen's revoking in 1909 of its chaplains' rights to free rooms in college,[24] or St. John's conversion in 1903 of its fund for the purchase of advowsons into capital for the pension fund.[25]

The interests of the Church had come to be viewed as a matter of very low priority in Oxford. Although a majority of college tutors even at the end of the nineteenth century were still in holy orders,[26] they had come to view themselves more as academics than as clergymen. When forced to make hard choices between the various functions which the colleges had been expected traditionally to fulfil, governing bodies tended to choose the duties of the college 'as a place of . . . learning and education' over its obligations 'as a place of religion'.

The pastoral vocation of the average don also came to be questioned seriously in the late nineteenth century. One intemperate critic decried 'the modern young Don' as 'an open derider of religion' and 'an agnostic in the majority of cases'.[27] The most damning testimony was, however, provided by an ostensible defender of the universities' religious influence. While abjuring this critic's lurid account, he admitted none the less, 'It is only too true that there are many priests holding fellowships at Oxford who never seem to do a stroke of work for the Church amongst the undergraduates.'[28] He angrily concluded that 'they did not have the words of the office for the ordination of priests thundered over their heads that they might sit in their comfortable rooms and do nothing except cram men in Latin and Greek for examinations'.[29] Many clerical dons certainly would have dismissed these references to their pastoral duties as mere cant; academic work had become their vocation. Archibald Sayce, for example, complained that the preacher at his ordination by the Bishop of Oxford 'harped upon the mode in which we

---

[23] PP 1980–1, lxi. Also see above Ch. V, p. 205, n. 9–10 for Wadham's extreme economic plight during this period.   [24] PP 1910, lxxii.
[25] PP 1904, lxxv.   [26] See below, Appendix 1, p. 286.
[27] Anthony C. Deane, 'The Religion of the Undergraduate', *Nineteenth Century* xxxviii, no. 224 (1895), 677.
[28] H. Legge, 'The Religion of the Undergraduate', *Nineteenth Century* xxxviii, no. 225 (1895), 866.   [29] Ibid. 868.

should "catch souls." Whenever the expression recurred, as it did pretty frequently, my next-door neighbor had an increasing difficulty in restraining convulsive fits of laughter, much to the discomfort of his neighbors.'[30] Sayce himself considered that the ordination preacher 'was sadly deficient in humour'.[31] The fact that this young clerical don experienced only 'discomfort' in this situation was eloquent testimony to his own lack of pastoral ideals.

iii. Conclusion

In the period between 1882 and 1914 both the Church and the other non-academic learned professions suffered a gradual decline in influence at Oxford. The 1877 commissioners had considered that the new academic profession could coexist amicably with these representatives of earlier university traditions. This calculation proved incorrect, however, since the needs and aspirations of this nascent profession for increased power required the curtailment of all other substantial claims while the decline in the external income of the colleges accelerated this trend. So long as money was available, a few fellowships awarded as prizes or restricted to clergymen could be tolerated as mere insignificant anomalies but the right of the non-academic learned professions to an important share in the distribution of collegiate endowments or power had to be firmly rejected. This process was successfuly completed before World War I.

B. The Diffusion of Research Ideals

The late nineteenth century was characterized by little advancement for the cause of research beyond the expansion of the professoriate demanded by the 1877 Commission.[32] Although the effect of the agricultural depression on college revenues contributed to this period of stagnation, a full explanation must include collegiate hostility as well. The antipathy of the colleges toward research ideals was revealed by their statute revisions eliminating some of the supports for advanced study imposed by the 1877 Commission. A fund

---

[30] *Reminiscences* (London, 1923), 56.   [31] Loc. cit.
[32] The professoriate grew by about 40 per cent between 1881 and 1900. See Appendix 4, below p. 289.

which had been established at Oriel by its 1882 statutes to provide two post-graduate awards of at least £100 p.a. 'to encourage mature study and research'[33] were eliminated in 1886 to create more undergraduate scholarships.[34] Jesus in 1895 also altered its statutes to reduce the position of independent researchers elected to ordinary fellowships. Their stipends were reduced by £100 p.a., their right to free rooms in college was revoked, and they were removed from the governing body.[35] Although the financial aspects of these alterations were probably dictated to some degree by economic pressures, since two fellowships were suppressed at the same time, the purpose of removing researchers from the governing body could only have been to eliminate the influence which the 1877 commissioners had wished them to exercise in the counsels of the college. The only counterpoise to this trend was the decision of Christ Church in 1892 to revise its statutes to permit the election to ordinary fellowships by nomination of independent researchers as well as university professors and readers.[36] This was only a very minor victory for the advocates of research ideals though, since it merely brought Christ Church into conformity with the other colleges.

After about 1895, however, a more favourable attitude toward research was discernible. In that year, new degrees were created for research in the humanities and sciences (a B.Litt. and a B.Sc.).[37] College statute revisions after the turn of the century also revealed a greater acceptance of the importance of research. In 1903 Brasenose became the first college to establish a separate category of 'research fellowships'.[38] The regulations governing appointment to these new

---

[33] IV, 11, p. 154 (PP 1882, li).　　　　　　　　　　　　[34] PP 1887, lxv.

[35] PP 1895, lxxvii.　　　　　　　　　　　　　　　　　　[36] PP 1893-4, lxviii.

[37] These were not graduate degrees for supervised research but, instead, honours awarded on the basis of writings presented for judgement to a faculty board. In 1900 provisions were made for a D.Litt. and a D.Sc. on the same basis. It was the Rhodes bequest of 1902 and the three hundred post-graduate students it brought which would eventually lead to the development of formal graduate education in Oxford after World War I. On the impact of the Rhodes scholarships, see the prophetic article by H. P. Biggar, 'A Graduate School at Oxford', *The University Review*, iii, no. 13 (1906), 111-32.

[38] PP 1904, lxxiv. See esp. III, Part III, 10-11, p. 5. The college had prepared for this action in 1900 by altering its statutes to permit the creation of new fellowships other than ordinary ones. The 1882 statutes had insisted that only new ordinary fellowships could be established. See PP 1901, lvi.

positions were better suited to the needs of advanced study than the 1882 statute, whose provisions Brasenose shared with virtually all other colleges. Under the old system, awards could be made only by nomination while the new statutes permitted open competition in particular fields of study. Other colleges followed Brasenose's lead in establishing new research awards.[39] The stipends of independent researchers elected to ordinary fellowships were raised in a few colleges.[40] Several colleges allowed themselves greater flexibility in the number of awards,[41] and in their length of tenure and requirements for eligibility.[42] The increasing diffusion of research ideals was also revealed during the Edwardian period in the attempts of some colleges to offer sabbatical leaves for tutorial fellows and the efforts of the university to establish lectureships to relieve tutors of 'teaching drudgery'.[43]

Although the improved financial prospects of the colleges after 1900 and the increased urgency of their desires to evade statutory obligations to the Common University Fund both contributed to the growing collegiate support for research, these factors cannot fully explain this trend. Rising external income certainly allowed the colleges for the first time in twenty years to contemplate new forms of expenditure, but this financial change alone would not explain which new projects were emphasized. It also would not account for the modifications introduced into college statutes to improve the effectiveness of research awards, to enhance the position of independent researchers among the senior members of the university, and to encourage research by the tutorial fellows.

[39] See, for example, the creation of 'research studentships' at Christ Church in 1914 (above, p. 260, n. 14). The 'research studentships' established at Queen's in 1911 were also similar except that they did not make their recipients members of the governing body. See PP 1911, lix. See also the discussion of 'senior scholarships' above, pp. 259-60.

[40] Maximum stipends were raised by £100 p.a. at Queen's in 1906 (PP 1906, xc) and at St. John's in 1912 (PP 1912-13, lxv). Magdalen raised its maximum stipend for research awards by £200 p.a. in 1912 (PP 1913, 1).

[41] See above, pp. 260-1, nn. 17-18.

[42] Ordinary fellowships could be awarded to researchers for periods of three to seven years, rather than for an inflexible period of seven years at Merton in 1904 (PP 1906, xc) and St. John's in 1908 (PP 1909, lxix). In 1904, All Souls abolished the requirement that candidates for its research awards must be Oxford graduates (PP 1906, xc).

[43] See below, pp. 277-80 for the collapse of these plans.

The growing fear of German economic and military power which characterized English public opinion in the early twentieth century also contributed to the increasing acceptance for research ideals in Oxford.[44] German achievements were linked to the success of their universities in applying academic research to problems of industrial and military technology. The predominantly literary culture of the best-endowed English universities and their emphasis on ideals of 'liberal education' were seen as crucial for explaining Britain's failure to keep pace with Germany. The importance of this issue increased proportionally as war came to be viewed as inevitable. The failure of the English universities to accept their responsibilities toward research was considered to jeopardize the very existence of the nation.

The advocates of science clearly were able to make the most effective use of these public fears of prospective military and commercial defeats. Professor Perry's denunciation of Oxford for sabotaging the plans for scientific educaton was suffused with war imagery. He stridently warned his audience that 'in future the nation that has not prepared during peace for possible war, by the exercise of the highest scientific faculty, will certainly be destroyed'.[45] '[I]f our rulers set a fashion of jibing at scientific things, at technical education, for example, through ignorance', Perry threatened, 'it is not unimportant to know that the complete loss of trades like the coal tar industries may be more serious evils than the loss of several campaigns in war used to be'.[46] Perry concluded that Oxford was no longer merely wasteful and inefficient; since the nation was faced with these grim realities, the university had become 'dangerous . . . through her influence on the ruling families of England'.[47]

Although fears of German military and industrial dominance could be used most effectively by the scientists, they also served with minor modifications to advance the cause of

---

[44] See, for a discussion of this crisis mentality, Samuel Hynes, *The Edwardian Turn of Mind* (Princeton, 1968), ch. ii, esp. pp. 34–53. See also G. R. Searle, *The Quest for National Efficiency* (Oxford, 1971).

[45] 'Oxford and Science', *Nature*, lxix, no. 1783 (1903), 209.

[46] Ibid. 210.

[47] Loc. cit.

'specialism' and research in general. Percy Gardner's argument
for a more learned ideal of university education often displayed
ominous notes of military imagery. He noted that education
'has made Germany prominent in science, in applied knowledge, in arms'.[48] Gardner likened the difference between
Oxford and German educational ideals to 'the bow and arrow
in the hands of a giant pitted against the repeating rifle in the
hands of drilled soldiers'.[49] He even managed to defend the
most elevated ideal of pure research on the basis of its relevance
to applied industrial technology. 'Students and workers who
merely receive practical instruction in technical schools learn
the routine of a trade . . . But they learn unintelligently: their
minds are not exercised and trained', Gardner argued.

[B]efore a man can plan a steamship, or build a bridge, or even invent a
new soap, he must commonly have a broad and deep education in the
sciences of nature from mathematics upward. And we may go further
still and say that for full efficiency the most practical man requires a
thorough drilling in the use of words, some acquaintance with literature
and history and especially some systematic knowledge of mankind, of
men as individuals and of men in society. And above all, he needs to be
inspired with a pure love of knowledge for its own sake. Science is a
fastidious mistress, and seldom reveals her secrets to those who only
desire to make profit of them; her choicest favours she reserves for those
who love her for her own sake, and without thought of reward.[50]

After propounding the familiar Germanic unity of the
Wissenshaften,[51] Gardner concluded that research in 'human
science' would provide solutions to the nation's economic,
social, political, military, and spiritual problems.

I believe that in our days the way of human science is the only sure
refuge from scepticism, rationalism and nihilism in religion, in art, in
politics, and in social studies. And I believe that the nation which is
most devoted to human science must needs, among the new conditions
of the new age, most prosper and flourish; the future of the world
belongs to the people who have most knowledge of fact, most reverence
for fact, most determination to make their conduct conform to the
realities of the visible and the spiritual world.[52]

[48] *Oxford at the Crossroads* (London, 1903), 5.   [49] Ibid. 6.   [50] Ibid. 64–5.
[51] Gardner insisted that 'science can be nothing but ordered knowledge, and
whenever truth is sought by the method appropriate to the case, a scientific
investigation is in progress'. Ibid. 81.   [52] Ibid. 84.

Gardner implied strongly that through the acceptance of research ideals England could both solve its internal problems and maintain its position of world hegemony.

This type of portentous rhetoric aroused the ire of Max Beerbohm, the theatre critic for the *Saturday Review*. Beerbohm ridiculed Gardner's notion that Oxford was 'at the crossroads' and suggested that the university ought to be spared 'as a curiosity, a relic of our dark ages'.[53] He satirized the national hysteria, proposing facetiously that all other English universities could be devoted to receiving 'the finest flower of our youth, to be tended up to the finest pitch of commercial culture . . . To Oxford need be affiliated as scholars only the halt, the maim, and the blind, the congenitally incapable of hustling our empire upward.'[54]

The crisis which Beerbohm ridiculed, however, was considered by many people to be genuine and urgent. They were persuaded that the success of the German universities in utilizing scientific research for technological innovations had been largely responsible for that nation's recent economic and military achievements. The advocates of research were able to argue effectively in this situation that the acceptance of their ideals in Oxford was a matter of high national priority. The growing emphasis on research in the university after the turn of the century was, to some degree, a response to this change in public attitudes.[55]

Research ideals also gained increasing acceptance in Oxford because they were useful in the battle against 'teaching drudgery'. This tutorial grievance had been left unrevolved by the settlement of the 1850s[56] and the 1877 commissioners' plan to alleviate this problem had collapsed.[57] The fact that college tutors had been permitted to marry and view their collegiate work as a life-career made this problem of 'teaching drudgery' all the more urgent. The single-minded devotion to tutorial work, which previously had been expected of

---

[53] 'Drama at Oxford', *Saturday Rev.*, 23 May 1903, reprinted in *More Theatres* (London, 1969), 570.   [54] Loc. cit.

[55] The new civic universities profited from this change in attitudes. See Michael Sanderson, *The Universities and British Industry 1850–1970* (London, 1972), chs. 3–4.   [56] See above Ch. III, pp. 122–8.

[57] See above, Ch. V, pp. 245–8.

young unmarried college tutors who saw their ultimate careers as being in the Church, became increasingly unsatisfactory for older married college tutors who viewed academic work as their profession. Through the acceptance of research ideals, college tutors could argue effectively for both reducing the quantity of their tutorial work and diversifying its content.

Beginning in the late nineteenth century, protests began to appear against exclusively tutorial conceptions of academic work, coming from conservative and collegiate sources which previously had accepted this view of the don. A. D. Godley, a young fellow of Magdalen and a member of the Non-Placet Society, complained of the 'much-troubled and harassed' life of the college tutor; a life devoid of the 'learned leisure' which this position was popularly supposed to offer.[58] He defined the official fellow, with evident bitterness, as 'a schoolmaster, with a difference. He has rather longer holidays — if he can afford to enjoy them — and a considerably shorter purse than the instructors of youth at some great schools.'[59] Godley made an invidious comparison between this new-style don and the pre-1854 life-fellow who chose to remain unmarried. He imagined that before the first university commission 'even the don who meant to be a don all his days put study and learned leisure first and instruction second, the world not yet believing in the "spoon-feeding" of youth'.[60]

A similar alienation from exclusively tutorial ideals was revealed among the majority of the fellows of Balliol in 1893 when Benjamin Jowett died. They chose to reject Jowett's famous tradition of concentration on tutorial work and on driving their students toward university honours by electing Edward Caird, a distinguished Scottish philosopher, to the mastership rather than J. L. Strachan-Davidson, the Master's senior protégé. 'They wished more leisure for the pursuit of their own studies and researches, less concentration on preparing their pupils for the schools, a pursuit of knowledge more for its own sake and less for ulterior ends, however valuable', Strachan-Davidson's biographer concluded.[61] As

---

[58] *Aspects of Modern Oxford* (London, 1894), 128. See also Godley's vivid account of a typical day in the life of a don (ch. vii, 105–19).

[59] Ibid. 129–30.   [60] Ibid. 126.

[61] J. W. Mackail, *James Leigh Strachan-Davidson, Master of Balliol* (Oxford, 1925), 54.

the college tutors became professional academics, research ideals were necessary to differentiate their career from that of schoolmasters.

Research ideals also proved useful in surmounting some inherent difficulties in Oxford tutorial work as a secular profession. Collegiate teaching inevitably would become monotonous as a life-career if the content of the university examinations never changed, yet the traditional Oxford ideal of 'liberal education' provided no adequate rationale for a constantly evolving curriculum. W. L. Courtney, a firm adherent of the traditional conception of 'Oxford culture', provided a vivid description of the conflict between the educational needs of the student and the career needs of the don. 'The fatal drawback . . . in the tutorial work at Oxford, is that every few years the . . . don has to begin all over again with a fresh set of pupils', he argued. 'In order not to get humdrum, your pedagogue tells himself that he will try new methods — only to find that the old habitual methods are the best and most effective, so far as the pupils are concerned. So every few years the old weary round begins again, with fresh faces among the taught, but a tired and perhaps gloomy face for the teacher.'[62]

This aspect of 'teaching drudgery' had not been a serious problem so long as college tutors were virtually all young clergymen who saw their ultimate careers in the Church. They generally did not remain long enough for tutorial work to become unduly monotonous. Furthermore, their clerical vocation served to alleviate the monotony of tutorial work by allowing them to take a pastoral interest in the moral and spiritual development of the individual student rather than solely in his examination work.[63] The advent of the academic profession and the demise of pastoral ideals among the dons

---

[62] *The Passing Hour* (London, [1925]), 102.

[63] This ideal was expressed by John Hill, the fervently Evangelical Vice-Principal of St. Edmund Hall, in his diary entry for 10 Oct. 1821. 'Term commences, — I have been seeking divine guidance & assistance for the business of the term; and have been enabled to lay open before God in prayer . . . the cases of each of my pupils individually: — both as to their academical & other temporal concerns, & as to their conversion to G. or growth in grace. —' See Bodl. MS St. Edmund Hall 67/2, p. 27. After thirty years of tutorial work, it was only the pastoral aspect which still engaged his interest. See ibid. 67/19, p. 51 (18 Oct. 1851).

removed this traditional counterpoise to the repetitiveness of collegiate teaching. The college tutor who saw tutorial work as a life-career could easily become bored and disenchanted. The personal relationship between don and undergraduate, emptied of its traditional pastoral justification, also stood in danger of becoming tainted by implications of homosexuality. W. L. Courtney warned that if the tutor took an 'intense interest in the boys themselves', he might 'get too interested in them, and then the relationship is apt to grow morbid'.[64]

The acceptance of research ideals proved to be the only satisfactory rationale for overcoming the problem of 'teaching drudgery' for dons who viewed academic work as their profession. Greater diversity could be introduced into the content of the examination system by arguing for the necessity of incorporating new knowledge as it was discovered. This policy implied a recognition of the importance of research and required the don to maintain an active personal commitment to mature study and the advancement of learning in order to teach effectively. It was also possible to demand a reduction in the tutorial and other collegiate work which previously had been expected of the college tutor to provide the 'learned leisure' essential for research. Although research ideals were often suspect because of their earlier identification with anti-collegiate attitudes, their value to the nascent academic profession permitted their increasing acceptance after the turn of the century. The growing sympathy toward research in the university was, to some degree, an expression of this changing attitude among the dons.

Although the combination of agricultural depression and collegiate hostility insured the virtual stagnation of the 'endowment of research' in the 1880s and 1890s, the Edwardian period saw a subtle trend toward the encouragement of research ideals. The change was caused by a complex of new circumstances, both within the university and in British economic and political life as well. Their interaction resulted in the growing diffusion of sympathy for research which was evident in collegiate statute revisions after the turn of the century.

[64] Ibid. 236.

C. *The Shaping of the Academic Profession*

Virtually every aspect of the new academic profession established by the 1877 Commission was affected by the continuous process of collegiate statute-revisions which characterized the period until World War I. The general tendency of these changes was to enhance the position of the dons to the extent this goal was compatible with the limitations imposed by financial conditions and other collegiate needs. The decline in the use of ordinary fellowships for aiding the non-academic learned professions and the corresponding increase in official, professorial, and research fellows obviously served this function.[65] This change enabled the dons to continue to increase their power by reducing the influence of the Heads[66] and Visitors[67] in the colleges. The domination of Congregation by non-academic elements until 1913,[68] however, meant that university statute revisions could not be used to increase the power of the dons during this critical period. This had the effect of intensifying and fixing the loyalties of the new academic profession on the colleges rather than the university. None the less, the gradual removal from Congregation of resident MAs not engaged in official college or university work insured that the dons eventually would attain the dominance in the university legislatures which they had achieved already in the governing bodies of the colleges.

One of the most important uses which the dons made of their increasing power was the lessening of restrictions on the freedom of college officers to marry. Several colleges lowered the statutory minimum of unmarried official fellows required to be resident.[69] Others increased the maximum number of college officials permitted to marry[70] or allowed unmarried

---

[65] See above, pp. 257-64.

[66] For example, the power of the Principal to make tutorial appointments at Hertford was curtailed in 1893 (PP 1893-4, lxviii), and the traditional right of the Master of Pembroke to cast two votes at college meetings was eliminated in 1899 (PP 1899, lxxvi).

[67] For example, the right of the Visitor to represent Magdalen in elections to the Waynflete professorships was transfered in 1910 to an elected representative of the governing body. See PP 1910, lxxii.   [68] See above, Ch. V, pp. 213-14.

[69] See, for example, Corpus Christi in 1890 (PP 1890, lvi), Queen's in 1889 (PP 1890, lvi), Jesus in 1895 (PP 1895, lxxvii), and Christ Church in 1895 (PP 1896, lxv).

[70] For example, Queen's in 1893 revised its statutes to allow any four official

ordinary fellows as well as official ones to count toward the necessary minimum of residents.[71] Several colleges also revised their statutes to permit married college officers to be included among the necessary residents.[72] Although this clause could have been used to coerce married dons to live in college apart from their families during term,[73] its primary purpose was to harmonize more efficiently the needs of married officials with the requirements of collegiate discipline. Colleges were encouraged to incorporate suitable living arrangements for married dons into their building schemes or to purchase nearby houses for occupancy by married tutors.[74] During the late nineteenth century especially, this trend toward the gradual elimination of obstacles to the marriage of official fellows was one of the most important aspects of the collegiate statute revisions.

The increasing power of the dons was also used to make pension arrangements more desirable than those which the 1877 Commission had established and to protect collegiate pension funds during the hard times of the agricultural

---

fellows to marry. Previously, only the three senior official fellows had been given this privilege. See PP 1893-4, lxviii.

[71] See, for example, the statute revisions accomplished by Corpus Christi in 1906 (PP 1906, xc).

[72] See, for example, University College in 1882 (PP 1882, li), Corpus Christi in 1890 (PP 1890, lvi), Queen's in 1889 (PP 1890, lvi), Christ Church in 1895 (PP 1896, lxv), Worcester in 1900 (PP 1900, lxvi), Oriel in 1906 (PP 1907, lxiv), and Balliol in 1913 (PP 1914, lxiv) where one of the four residents was allowed to be married.

[73] The only case I have found of this use in Oxford was that one married official of Exeter in 1886 slept in his college rooms for three nights a week during term. See Thorold Rogers, 'Return Relating to the University of Oxford and Cambridge', Part B (I,4), Question no. 5, p. 53 (PP 1886, li). Evidently this practice was somewhat more common in Cambridge at this time since Peterhouse had one married tutor and Clare had two married tutors resident in college rooms without their wives or families during term. See ibid., Part B (II, 1,2), Question no. 5, p. 61.

[74] Merton acquired St. Alban's Hall in the 1880s as a residence for E. A. Knox so that he could continue to exercise disciplinary functions for the college despite his marriage. See *Reminiscences of an Octogenarian* (London, 1934), 64-118. G. B. Grundy, the dean of Corpus Christi, also lived in Beam Hall, a house on Merton Street opposite the front gates of the college. See *Fifty-five Years at Oxford* (London, 1945), 106. In 1887 New College had a house for a married tutor built within the college. The college also acquired property on Mansfield Road which it let on building leases to its married officials with the stipulation that the college might buy the house after the death of the present occupant. See H. B. George, *New College 1856-1906* (Oxford, 1906), 80-1.

depression. Several colleges whose 1882 statutes had only 'permitted' them to grant pensions, revised these statutes to give their career officials greater security by making them 'entitled as of right' to pensions after a certain number of years of service.[75] The desirability of the pensions was also enhanced by making obligatory the maximum which had been allowed in 1882,[76] by granting this maximum after fewer years of service,[77] and by allowing a larger outside income to be compatible with the holding of a college pension.[78] In the general financial retrenchment of the period, pension funds were protected either by eliminating other collegiate expenditures for this purpose[79] or by increasing contributions from general corporate revenues as soon as college finances permitted.[80] Although some colleges had desperate moments when it appeared that they would not be able to meet all calls on their pension funds,[81] the lean years were weathered without any college failing to fulfil its obligations toward retired dons.

The growth in the power of the dons was also manifested in other, less widespread, improvements in their position. A few colleges demonstrated their acceptance of a more professional conception of academic work by eliminating regulations which had tended to restrict their choice of college teachers to recent Oxford graduates.[82] Tutors also

[75] See, for example, Trinity in 1893 (PP 1893-4, lxviii), Exeter in 1895 (PP 1895, lxxvii), Queen's in 1896 (PP 1897, lxx), Christ Church in 1905 (PP 1906, xc). The quotation is from the Trinity statute.

[76] See, for example, Christ Church in 1907 (PP 1908, lxxxvi).

[77] See, for example, St. John's in 1913 (PP 1914, lxiv).

[78] See, for example, Exeter in 1914 (PP 1914-16, li).

[79] For example, Queen's suppressed three ordinary fellowships in 1896 to relieve their pension fund of some of its burden (PP 1897, lxx), Corpus Christi eliminated for this same reason in 1902 one ordinary fellowship previously reserved for the support of a university professor, reader, or independent researcher (PP 1903, lii), and St. John's incorporated into the pension fund in 1903 the capital of a fund previously used to purchase advowsons (PP 1904, lxxv).

[80] See, for example, Queen's in 1906 (PP 1906, xc), University College in 1914 (PP 1914-16, li), and Christ Church in 1914 (PP 1914-16, li).

[81] For example, Trinity decided in 1904 which pensions would be paid and which would not if the fund proved to be insufficient. They decided that obligations would be honoured in order of seniority. See PP 1904, lxxv.

[82] For example, University College decided in 1894 no longer to restrict eligibility for their official fellowships to Oxford graduates. See PP 1895, lxxvii. Wadham's decision in 1890 to permit lecturers as well as tutors to be elected by

gained in several instances greater influence on the collegiate boards which controlled their salaries and other terms of service.[83] The transfer of power over appointments to natural science professorships from outside dignitaries to representatives of the Boards of Faculties in Medicine and Natural Science[84] was one of the few victories in the university legislatures for professional autonomy before the removal of the non-academic plurality from Congregation.

Improving financial conditions during the Edwardian period enabled a few colleges to consider plans for increased expenditure to enhance the positions of their dons. Some colleges established schemes for sabbatical leaves to relieve the 'teaching drudgery' of the college tutors. The lead was taken by Brasenose which gave official fellows in 1899 the right to a paid leave of absence of one term every seven years.[85] In 1903 the college extended this policy by allowing a sabbatical of one full year every seven years.[86] This lead was followed by Trinity in 1914, who provided two terms leave every seven years for purposes of 'travel or study'.[87] The growing acceptance of research ideals at Oxford during this period undoubtedly contributed to the choosing of this particular method of increasing the desirability of academic careers.

Improved financial conditions and growing sympathy for research also influenced the decision of the university in 1912 to sanction the remodelling of the Common University Fund.[88] Their aim was to provide college tutors with the 'progressive careers' which the 1877 commissioners' readership plan had failed to achieve. Lord Curzon explicitly recognized this purpose in his introduction to the *Report of the Hebdomadal Council* on which this legislation was based. '[W]e are only reaffirming one of the objects contemplated by the

---

nomination rather than competitive examination struck at this same restriction indirectly since recent graduates would always have an advantage over more experienced college teachers in fellowship examinations. See PP 1890–1, lxvi.

[83] See, for example, the alterations in the membership of the 'Tutorial Board' at Magdalen in 1912; IV, 2, p. 10 (PP 1913, 1). See also, above, p. 273, n. 66, for increasing tutorial power at Hertford and Pembroke.

[84] PP 1911, lix.   [85] PP 1899, lxxvi.   [86] PP 1904, lxxv.

[87] PP 1914, lxiv. Trinity was less generous than Brasenose, however, since these sabbatical leaves had to be approved by a two-thirds vote of the governing body.   [88] PP 1912–13, lxv.

last University Commission under the powers given to the Delegates of the Common University Fund,' he insisted, 'although in practice the principle of creating Readerships in subjects not otherwise provided for in the University has taken precedence of the principle of recognizing the special services of College Tutors to learning and education'.[89] To accomplish this previously neglected goal, university lectureships were to be established with £3,000 p.a. from the Common University Fund. Their purpose was especially to free the successful college tutor from 'teaching drudgery', although his income might be raised as well. 'By these means,' Lord Curzon concluded, 'the University would secure the most efficient teaching that it can command, and the College Tutor would obtain the prospect of a position in which he might have greater leisure for his special work and study.'[90] The administration of the Common University Fund was also made more responsive to research needs by the abolition of the Delegacy, on which representatives of faculty boards had been in the minority, and the creation in its place of a General Board of the Faculties dominated by faculty representatives.[91]

All these attempts to improve the career prospects of the dons, however, were not successful. Changing conditions during the Edwardian period and the war years interfered in some cases with the implementation of goals previously considered feasible. The trend toward a loosening of restrictions on the marriage of official fellows was reversed, especially after the turn of the century, when it began to conflict with the disciplinary needs of the colleges. Renewed financial problems during and after the war, as well as loyalty to the college system, also interfered with the plans for the encouragement of research.

The major reason for the revived policy of retrenchment on the issue of marriage was that student numbers rose by approximately 10 per cent each decade between the 1877

---

[89] (Oxford, 1910), p. xv.   [90] Loc. cit.

[91] The Delegacy of the Common University Fund had contained only one representative of each faculty board with eleven other members. (See above, Ch. IV, p. 186, n. 98.) The new General Board of the Faculties consisted of the Vice-Chancellor, the proctors, and twenty members apportioned among the eight faculties.

Commission and World War I, with the largest increment occurring during the Edwardian period.[92] More resident dons were essential if college discipline and the traditional ideals of collegiate life were to be maintained. In several colleges, the minimum of residents was raised.[93] A few colleges also no longer allowed married fellows living in houses in or near the colleges to count as resident.[94] The length of time during which an official fellow, elected while unmarried, must remain unmarried or forfeit his fellowship without the possibility of re-election was also increased in many cases.[95] Many loyal college men must have agreed with J. L. Strachan-Davidson's wishful view that '[i] f tutors were crossed in love at any early age, they settled down and devoted themselves to the College.'[96] Faced with a direct conflict of interest, colleges chose to prefer the continued vitality of the collegiate system to the needs of the individual members of the academic profession.

The reform of the Common University Fund and the attempt to introduce regular sabbatical leaves also failed to produce the benefits which had been expected. Both changes had little chance to operate before the altered conditions of war destroyed their economic basis. The approximately 250 per cent inflation of the war years[97]   had a disastrous effect on collegiate finances. Many colleges, and the university as well, were pushed to the brink of bankruptcy during this period.[98] Despite the desirability of providing college tutors

[92] Average annual matriculations were 684 in 1870-9, 766 in 1880-9, 821 in 1890-9, and 905 in 1900-9. See Stone, Table IA, p. 91.

[93] See, for example, New College in 1902 (PP 1902, lxxx), University College in 1896 (PP 1897, lxx), and Trinity in 1913 (PP 1914, lxiv).

[94] See, for example, New College in 1896 (PP 1897, lxx), and University College in 1915 (PP 1916, xxii).

[95] Unmarried official fellows were required to remain unmarried for seven years at New College in 1902 (PP 1902, lxxx), and at St. John's in 1904 (PP 1905, lx). Magdalen insisted in 1912 that unmarried official fellows remain unmarried for three years (PP 1913, li), cl. 32, p. 6.

[96] Reported by A. J. Toynbee, in J. W. Mackail, *James Leigh Strachan-Davidson, Master of Balliol* (Oxford, 1925), 58.

[97] See P. Deane and W. A. Cole, *British Economic Growth 1688-1959* (Cambridge, 1967), endpaper graph, Figure 7.

[98] The 1922 University Commission was called as a direct result of this situation. The commissioners stated bluntly, 'Owing to the change in the value of money,

with 'learned leisure' for study and research, sabbatical leaves for these purposes became a financial impossibility.[99] The opportunity to use university lectureships to create 'progressive careers' for college tutors and alleviate their 'teaching drudgery' was also lost, since the Common University Fund was never prosperous enough to support these purposes.[100] The collegiate fear that, in a period of declining real income and increasing government aid to the university, this plan would lead eventually to the colleges' being forced to accept the dictates of the Boards of Faculties in fellowship elections also contributed to this result.[101] Although the category of

---

Oxford and Cambridge are no longer able to pay their way . . . [B]ut for the interim grant of £30,000 a year allowed by the State to each University for general purposes since 1920, it would have been impossible to continue their present work even provisionally'. *Royal Commission on Oxford and Cambridge Universities. Report* (1922), 48.

[99] The inflation of the war years made it impossible for most colleges to institute sabbatical leaves for their tutors. The 1922 commissioners failed to suggest a workable alternative plan despite their strong support for sabbaticals as a method of preventing the separation of teaching and research functions. Motives of 'public economy' and the fear that direct government grants to the colleges would lead to infringement on their autonomy induced the commissioners to place their major hopes on 'the creation of a central University Fund, assisted out of the general grants which we are recommending from public funds, to enable a specially qualified Professor, Reader or Lecturer to take a period of absence exceptionally for travel and research, without loss of income'. Beyond this suggestion, the commissioners could only add the vague hope that 'Colleges which can afford to do so will assist members of their teaching staffs in a similar way.' Ibid. 98, no. 108(c), also 233, no. 30(b–c). The new university statutes of 1926 failed to establish the central University Fund although they mentioned that such a fund might be created in the future. Furthermore, the usefulness to college tutors of even this hypothetical plan was virtually eliminated entirely by the confining of benefits to university professors and readers. See Titulus V, Section IX, 2, (1) (v), in *Statuta Universitatis Oxoniensis* (Oxford, 1930), 155. The ability of the colleges to provide tutors with sabbatical leaves for research purposes continued to be wholly dependent on the widely varying degrees of wealth of the individual collegiate foundations. For the wide differences in college wealth after World War I, see *The Government of Oxford* (Oxford, 1931), 2.

[100] Although the 1922 commissioners enthusiastically supported the goal of using university lectureships to free college tutors for research, they were only able to suggest weakly that the funds for this purpose ought to be derived from student lecture fees. This solution was a workable alternative to collegiate taxation in Cambridge where fees had become customary for university lectures. At Oxford, however, this alternative led inevitably to failure since fees had been eliminated for virtually all inter-collegiate lectures except for those in the natural sciences and the commissioners were unwilling to insist on the establishment of fees where previously they had not existed. Ibid. 79–94, esp. 91, no. 97.

[101] This fear was not entirely groundless. The 1922 commissioners had suggested

university lecturer remained, it degenerated into merely another title for the college tutor, signifying nothing more than faculty membership and carrying only an insignificant stipend.[102] For the second time, external financial conditions and collegiate loyalty had thwarted attempts to provide regular opportunities for mid-career promotions for Oxford dons. The encouragement of research through sabbatical leaves also fell victim to these same forces.

D. Conclusion

The transformation of the college tutor from a temporary academical clergyman to an Oxford don whose academic work was a career for life had been completed in its essential outlines by 1914. The institutions of the colleges and the university as well as traditional ideas of 'liberal education' had been modified to meet the needs of married men, while preserving the don's independence and high status as a member of a recognized profession. To compare the subsequent careers of dons first appointed to college offices at the beginning and at the end of the nineteenth century reveals the rough magnitude of the change. The number who attained permanent career positions in Oxford and who decided to make academic work their profession had expanded four times, from less than 15 per cent to almost 60 per cent of the total.[103] The percentage of college fellows engaged in educational work in Oxford rose from only 9 per cent in 1814 to 18 per cent in 1858 to 58 per cent in 1900.[104]

The rival concepts of the academic profession which had emerged during the first half of the nineteenth century had

---

that colleges ought to be penalized financially if they did not award a certain number of their fellowships to university officials. Ibid. 93, no. 101.

[102] L. R. Farnell angrily denounced this result. 'Though it was impossible altogether to evade the [1922] Commissioners' findings, it was not so difficult to nullify them by amendments or appended clauses', he asserted. 'This has happened most markedly in respect to their proposal concerning university lecturers and the allocation of fellowships to them. As originally intended, it was a far-reaching change which would have much increased the power of the university Boards of Faculties; as interpreted and manipulated, it has left matters very much as they were; and the college teachers, wholly appointed by the college, become almost automatically university lecturers.' *An Oxonian Looks Back* (London, 1934), 310.   [103] See below, Appendix 1, p. 286.
[104] See below, Appendix 8, p. 292.

been sifted and tested against both the material and social needs of the dons and the changing financial conditions of the colleges and university. The 'professorial system', in either its scholarly or its more practically orientated form, as well as private coaching, were rejected by academics. The value of the 'tutorial system' was vigorously affirmed since the alternative threatened the autonomy of the tutorial fellow. The 'Don of the Old School' had the independence of a property-owner, albeit an elected one who was not permitted to marry while retaining his interest in that property; he was neither subordinate to the university professors nor wholly dependent on student fees. As the 'Don of the New School' became a professional man, his career aspirations and loyalties were fixed on the colleges and the fellowship system in order to preserve a new version of the freedom his predecessors had enjoyed.

The growth in the power and importance of the tutors, especially in the colleges, through the reforms of 1854–8, tended to intensify their commitment to collegiate and tutorial ideals during the critical period between the two university commissions. The college system was found to be flexible enough to satisfy several tutorial aspirations left untouched by the Executive Commission. In the combination system, the means was introduced which led eventually to enhancing the tutors' opportunities for specialized teaching without abandoning the primacy of collegiate organization. The abolition of the religious tests which had interfered with the full operation of the merit system in fellowship elections was also accomplished without impairing the college system.

Although both educational methods and ideals in Oxford were modified in the nineteenth century, their basic collegiate orientation was preserved. The colleges were strengthened in the period between the two university commissions through the incorporation into the official 'tutorial system' of the method of individual instruction which had previously been used largely by private coaches. The examination system was also broadened without altering the traditional, college-orientated concept of 'liberal education'. The argument in favour of a new subject was simply altered from the view that it would make the system of university education more useful or practical, to the less threatening idea that it would be as beneficial as the traditional studies for inculcating mental discipline. The value of the personal supervision offered by the colleges was upheld despite this important change in the content of 'liberal education'.

Collegiate loyalties were also strengthened by the contrast between the relative influence of the tutors in their own colleges and in the university legislatures. While their power in the colleges was firmly established and growing during the critical period between the two commissions, their influence in Congregation actually declined. Although their position in university government had clearly improved over the pre-1854 system, the proliferation of non-academic voters in Congregation in the 1860s and 1870s meant that the tutors were more certain of their power in their own colleges than they could be of their influence in the university. The interests and values of these non-academic voters were only partially consistent with those of the tutors. The fact that this situation remained in effect until after World War I was a potent source of tutorial distrust of university power.

The college loyalties of academics were further strengthened after the second university commission. Large sums had been allocated from college endowment income for the support of science and the professoriate, based on the sanguine financial predictions of the Cleveland Commission. When the agricultural depression destroyed the basis for these financial calculations, the effect was to intensify the struggle for the remaining revenues. In these struggles, 'university purposes' were inexorably placed in opposition to the interests of the colleges. College tutors, especially the younger ones, were confirmed in their antipathy toward science and the university professoriate.

Loyalty to the collegiate system, however, also resulted in the failure of the dons to achieve the full and satisfactory professional career pattern for which they had struggled. The personal ideal of the tutorial relation between pupil and teacher was found to be not fully compatible with the tutor's position as a married man living outside the college. The emphasis on the paramount importance of tutorial work and the acceptance of an exclusively 'disciplinary' theory of 'liberal education' tended to make it difficult to accommodate the tutors' need for the recognition of advanced study and research as important parts of their academic work. Finally the modest size and organization of the colleges made it impossible for them to give the dons the progressive careers which they had sought. All these problems were further intensified by the effects on college income first of the agricultural depression and later of the inflation of the World War I period.

Permission to marry while remaining a college fellow was the most fundamental need of the members of the nascent academic profession. Beginning in the late 1860s, a few colleges had been able and willing to obtain alterations in their statutes allowing married fellows. These concessions, however, were often surrounded by severe restrictions which impaired the desirability of these positions. Although the 1877 Commission made provisions for married fellows in virtually all colleges and the trend in the late nineteenth century was generally to extend this privilege with fewer restrictions to larger numbers of tutors, the marked expansion of student numbers during the Edwardian period forced the colleges to reverse this trend. Since traditional collegiate ideals required a substantial number of resident fellows for maintaining both college discipline and the reality of a communal life, the colleges re-established restrictions on the marriage of dons to retain these ideals. Even today, the unoccupied bedrooms in married tutors' college rooms seem to reproach them for their refusal to reside.

The conflict between the collegiate system and research ideals was largely the product of the emphasis which the tutors had placed on their teaching function to justify their rise to power in the colleges. This emphasis was necessary to combat the interests of the Church and the other learned professions in the maintenance of the prize fellowship system, but it certainly contributed as well to the polarization of teaching and research. The emphasis which the proponents of 'liberal education' had placed on the form rather than the content of education in order to defend the colleges also contributed to this polarization. Throughout the nineteenth century, the advocacy of the importance of research in the definition of academic work was presented in sharp contrast to collegiate and tutorial ideals. The cause of the 'professorial system', as espoused by H. H. Vaughan and the royal commissioners of 1850, was conceived as a direct attack on the power of the colleges. The 'endowment of research' party which grew before the second University Commission of 1877 saw its enemies as the tutors and the examination system which was the basis for tutorial power. The 'specialists' of the late nineteenth and early twentieth centuries also saw the tutors, especially the younger ones, the rigidity of the examination system, and the colleges themselves as the chief obstacles to the acceptance of their views in Oxford.

Despite these anti-collegiate attitudes of the advocates of research, college tutors throughout the nineteenth century retained a commitment to learned ideals, at least to the extent they served to maintain the don's status. This commitment became increasingly important as rising student numbers and more intensive teaching methods threatened to transform the tutorial fellow into a 'teaching drudge'. Research ideals gained increasing acceptance as a valuable method of preventing the don from falling to the position of a mere schoolmaster. Although these ideals were recognized in the statutes written by the 1877 commissioners, the fortunes of research in Oxford fluctuated according to several opposing tendencies in the period between that Commission and World War I. Financial problems caused by the agricultural depression and the inflation of the war years prevented the full implementation of the Commission's plans, but public fears of German technological, economic, and military achievements and the influence of the growing number of older, professionally orientated college tutors tended to counterbalance these financial restraints. The result was the unresolved conflict between the values of teaching and the importance of research which has continued to serve as a perennial theme of academic debate.

Another problem was that the small size, democratic governing structure, and financial difficulties of the colleges all combined to make it impossible to establish the type of hierarchical organization on the collegiate level which could have provided academics with sufficient opportunities for promotion. Although several attempts were made to solve this problem on the university level, most notably through the readership plan established by the 1877 Commission and the university lectureship scheme adopted in 1912, the combination of financial exigencies and collegiate fears that these plans would infringe on their autonomy insured their failure. The result was a truncated professional hierarchy offering most dons full security at an early age but few possibilities for promotion in Oxford. There have always been too few university professorships and readerships for them to function as opportunities for regular promotion and no workable alternative method of attaining this goal has ever been accepted.

Collegiate loyalty emerged as the most distinctive characteristic of the majority of Oxford's academics. It survived the transformation of the college tutor from a temporary academical clergyman into a permanent college don and has proved to be the source of both the outstanding strengths and weaknesses of the academic profession in Oxford. On the one hand, the personal and intellectual independence of the don has been carefully protected from the encroachments of administrators or senior professors; a deficiency which has often marred other, non-collegiate university systems. On the other hand, college tutors never achieved a wholly satisfactory professional career pattern or a clear definition of their professional duties. The perennial suspicion of the colleges for the university and the effect of two successive economic crises combined to prevent Oxford dons from obtaining the full fruits of their long struggle. None the less, the compromise which they accepted has proved remarkably enduring. Although government commissions since World War I have altered the relation of the university to the state, to the colleges, and to the British system of higher education as a whole, the ideals and institutions of the academic profession which had taken shape in Oxford by 1914 became the firmly established traditions which all further reforms have been unable to do more than mildly modify.

Appendices

APPENDIX 1: Careers of Oxford Dons[1]

Dates	In Holy Orders	Future Career in Church[2]	Future Career in University[3]	Mixed Career[4]	Other Careers[5]	Total in Sample
1813–30	92%	53% (40)	13% (10)	13% (10)	21% (16)	76
1881–1900	69%	9% (7)	57% (44)	13% (44)	21% (16)	77

[1] Method of Sample: In each of these two time periods, a list of all men appointed to college offices was compiled, chronologically by college, using the *University Calenders*. The sample consists of every fifth name on each of these lists.

[2] Those who did not attain a professorship, headship, or 'official fellowship' in Oxford or an academic position in another university and who left Oxford for a career in the Church.

[3] Those who did attain a professorship, headship, or 'official fellowship' in Oxford or an academic position in another university and who spent their entire active careers within the university.

[4] Those who did attain a professorship, headship, or 'official fellowship' in Oxford or an academic position in another university but who did not spend their entire active careers within the university. In all cases but two in the 1881–1900 period (a law professor who became a judge and a colonial governor who became the head of a college), all men in this category held clerical as well as academic positions (e.g. a college fellow who became a country parson and later returned to Oxford as head of his college, or a professor or college head who became a bishop).

[5] Those who did not attain a professorship, headship, or 'official fellowship' in Oxford or an academic position at another university who spent their active careers outside the Church (e.g. barristers, schoolmasters, etc.).

APPENDIX 2: Social Background
(by Fathers' Occupation) of Oxford Dons[1]

		1813–30 (total: 76)		1881–1900 (total: 77)
I.	Gentleman-class	62 (82%)		61 (79%)
	a. clergymen[2]		34 (45%)	20 (26%)
	b. squires/private gentlemen		10 (13%)	7 (9%)
	c. merchants/ manufacturers		9 (12%)	14 (18%)
	d. professional men[3]		6 (8%)	16 (21%)
	e. 'armiger'[4]		3	1
	f. academics		-	2
	g. civil service		-	1
II.	Non-gentlemen-class	4 (5%)		11 (14%)
	a. clerks/shopkeepers		1	5
	b. farmers		1	2
	c. 'plebeian'[2]		2	-
	d. non-conformist minister		-	3
	e. parish schoolmaster (Scotland)		-	1
III.	Unknown	10 (13%)		5 (7%)
	a. 'gentleman'[2]		10	2
	b. other unknown[4]		-	3

[1] Method of Sample: See above, Appendix 1, p. 286, n. 1.

[2] These are the categories provided by the matriculation registers. Only 'clergyman' is unambiguous. I think, however, one is justified in assuming that no one would give 'plebeian' for his social background unless this designation was correct. Similarly, among those dons about whom I was able to find a concrete fathers' occupation from local directories, biographies, school registers, etc., there was no instance of a man giving 'armiger' whose father was not a 'gentleman'. The category of 'gentleman' itself, unfortunately, is too ambiguous to be of any use. I suspect that most of these, ironically, would not be 'gentlemen' by accepted nineteenth-century usage. Since matriculants were given no choice below 'gentleman' except 'plebeian', it is not surprising that most chose the higher designation.

[3] Virtually all of these were barristers, solicitors, physicians, or surgeons. I have included, however, one architect and one civil engineer.

[4] This category indicates those men who neglected to specify their social background in the matriculation register and about whom I could find no other social information.

APPENDIX 3: Oxford Teachers 1814–1900

		1814	1845	1858	1874	1888	1900
I.	College Teachers	41	61	89	122	165	170
	a. Fellows	41	54	80	96	. 123	138
	b. Non-Fellows[1]	0	7	9	26	42	32
II.	Other Official Teachers[2]	9	10	11	18	13	21
III.	Total Official Teachers	50	71	100	140	178	191
IV.	Total Undergraduates[3]	945	1368	1482	2407	2781	3091
V.	Teacher/ Pupil Ratio	1:19	1:19	1:15	1:17	1:15.5	1:16

[1] 'Non-Fellows' include former fellows, scholars, and chaplains who teach in their colleges. Also included are 'combined lecturers' and other lecturers not on the foundation of any college.

[2] 'Other Official Teachers' include those heads and lecturers of the halls and private halls, those tutors or lecturers to non-collegiate students, and those tutors or lecturers of Keble College who were not already counted as 'college teachers'. Keble was not counted among the colleges since, during this period, it more resembled a hall in that it had no fellowships. Hence the collegiate distinction between fellows and non-fellows would have been meaningless. No person has been counted more than once; college positions were given priority over other teaching posts.

[3] See below, Appendix 6, p. 291 for the changing distribution of scholars, exhibitioners, gentleman-commoners, and commoners.

Source: *Oxford University Calender* for 1814, 1845, 1858, 1874, 1888, and 1900. Unless otherwise noted, these are the sources for all remaining appendices.

APPENDIX 4: *Members of Congregation*
1858, 1874, 1881, and 1900

		1858 % (no.)	1874 % (no.)	1881· % (no.)	1900 % (no.)
I.	Heads of Colleges and Halls	8 (24)	8 (25)	7 (25)	4 (22)
II.	Professors[1]	9 (26)	12 (39)	12 (42)	14 (75)
III.	Fellows engaged as official tutors or lecturers[2]	27 (77)[6]	23 (76)[7]	28.5 (101)[11]	25 (131)[8]
IV.	Fellows holding other academic offices[3]	12 (34)	6 (20)	6 (20)	3 (16)
V.	Fellows not engaged in academic work	15 (44)	9 (28)	5 (18)	2 (12)
VI.	Resident MAs engaged as official tutors or lecturers	5 (14)	10 (39)[9]	11.5 (41)	9 (46)[10]
VII.	Resident MAs holding other academic offices[4]	5 (14)	3 (11)	6 (22)	9 (50)
VIII.	Resident MAs not engaged in official academic work	15 (45)	25 (83)	20 (71)	28 (151)
IX.	Miscellaneous[5]	4 (11)	4 (13)	4 (14)	6 (32)
X.	Total	100 (289)	100 (328)	100 (354)	100 (535)

[1] Includes demonstrators and readers, does not include those professors who were also heads of colleges.

[2] Includes fellows who taught for their own college or for any other college or hall in Oxford.

[3] In both 1881 and 1900 it includes two public examiners as well as college deans, bursars, etc.

[4] In 1858 all in this category were college chaplains. In 1874 there were eight chaplains, one bursar, one steward, and the schoolmaster of Magdalen College School. In 1881 it included nine chaplains, three bursars, one steward, one usher (at Magdalen College School), one member of the Council of Keble College, three public examiners, and four university officials (the Secretary to the Curators of the University Chest, the Registrar of the Vice-Chancellor's Court, a Clerk of the Markets [who was also an Auditor of Accounts], and Bodley's Librarian). In 1900 it included nine chaplains, nine public examiners, six members of Boards of Faculties, five secretaries of university delegacies (University

Chest, Lodgings, University Extension, University Press, and Non-collegiate Students), three members of university committees (Craven committee, Oxford school board, and Poor Law guardians), four administrative officers of private halls or affiliated colleges, three college organists, two college bursars, one college steward, one usher and one schoolmaster at Magdalen College School, and six other university officials (Bodley's Librarian, Radcliffe Librarian, Radcliffe Observer, a sub-librarian at the Bodleian, the University Coroner, and the Curator of the Pitt Rivers Museum).

[5] In 1858 this category contained the Chancellor, six university officials, and four canons of Christ Church who were not professors. In 1874, it contained the Chancellor, five university officials, six public examiners who were not 'qualified by residence' and one canon of Christ Church who was not a professor. In 1900 it included the Chancellor, four university officials, twenty-six public examiners not 'qualified by residence' and one canon of Christ Church who was not a professor. All of the university officials included in this category were non-resident.

[6] This figure is not the same as that for 'Fellows' in Appendix 3, above, p. 288. There were eighty on that chart since one fellow did not teach in his own or any other college but was a lecturer for a public hall, while four college tutors who were fellows were still BAs and, therefore, not eligible to vote in Congregation.

[7] The major reason for the discrepancy between this figure and the ninety-eight 'fellows engaged in educational work' in 1874 (see below, Appendix 8, p. 292) was the seventeen college tutorial fellows who were still BAs. There were also a few college tutorial fellows who, even though MAs, were not listed as 'qualified by residence' to vote in Congregation.

[8] The reasons for the discrepancy between this figure and the 137 'fellows engaged in educational work' in 1900 (see below, Appendix 8, p. 292) was that there were three tutorial fellows who were BAs and three more who, although MAs, still were not 'qualified by residence' to vote in Congregation. One of the latter was qualified to vote as a public examiner.

[9] The reasons for the discrepancy between this figure and the forty-four 'non-fellows' who were college teachers and 'other official teachers' on Appendix 3, above, p. 288 were that the forty-four included (1) five heads of public halls and one head of a private hall, (2) two college lecturers and one hall lecturer who, though MAs, were not included in the published list as 'qualified by residence' to vote in Congregation.

[10] This figure differs from the fifty-three non-fellows engaged as college teachers (thirty-three) and other official teachers (twenty), in 1900 (see below, Appendix 8, p. 292) since there were two lecturers who were BAs, three lecturers who, although MAs, were not listed as 'qualified by residence' to vote in Congregation, and two heads of halls who were counted as teachers on that list.

[11] There were actually 110 tutorial fellows but this figure does not include nine of them. Four were still BAs and five, though MAs, were not 'qualified by residence' to vote in Congregation.

APPENDIX 5: *Hypothetical Membership in Congregation — 1858*
(if persons not engaged in official academic work were removed)

		no.	%
I.	Heads of Colleges or Halls	24	13%
II.	Professors	26	14%
III.	Fellows engaged as official tutors or lecturers	77	41%
IV.	Fellows holding other academic offices	34	18%
V.	Resident MAs engaged as official tutors or lecturers	14	8%
VI.	Miscellaneous	11	6%
VII.	Total	186	100%

[1] From the actual composition of Congregation in 1858 (see above, Appendix 4, pp. 289-90), forty-four fellows who were not college officers, fourteen chaplains, and forty-five resident MAs have been removed. (Items V, VII, and VIII in Appendix 4.)

APPENDIX 6: *Oxford Students 1814-1900*

		1814	1845	1858	1874	1888	1900
I.	Scholars	165	184	212	371	435	486
II.	Exhibitioners[1]	42	71	137	177	220	278
III.	Gentlemen-Commoners	132[2]	89	59	34	-	-
IV.	Commoners	615[2]	1024	1074	1825	2126	2327
V.	Total	954	1368	1482	2407	2781	3091

[1] Includes clerks, bible-clerks, and servitors.

[2] In 1814 Christ Church did not provide figures separating commoners from gentlemen-commoners among its 78 undergraduates not on the foundation. However, the importance of gentlemen-commoners throughout the first half of the nineteenth century can be safely assumed. In 1845 they comprised 33 of the 69 non-foundationers. I have decided to make the conservative assumption that the ratio was the same in 1814, yielding 33 gentlemen-commoners and 45 commoners. Mason and Bill's *Christ Church and Reform 1850-67* (Oxford, 1970), does not mention any significant change in the number of gentleman-commoners during the first half of the nineteenth century.

APPENDIX 7: Oxford Teaching Positions 1814-1900[1]

		1814	1845	1858	1874	1888	1900
I.	Colleges	41	61	89	149	196	208
	a. Fellowships	41	54	80	96	123	138
	b. Not Fellowships	-	7	9	53	79	70
II.	Other Official Positions[1]	9	10	12	30	22	37
III.	Total	50	71	101	179	218	245

[1] These figures differ in some cases from those in Appendix 3, above, p. 288 since, on this chart, one person may be counted several times if he taught for several colleges or halls.

APPENDIX 8: Fellows Engaged in Educational Work in Oxford 1814-1900

		1814	1845	1858	1874	1888	1900
I.	Teach only for their own college	41	54	79	80	108	111
II.	Teach for their own college and teach outside their college as well	-	-	--	10	9	18
III.	Teach only outside the college of which they are fellows	-	1	2	8	6	11
IV.	Total fellows engaged in educational work[1]	41	55	81	98	123	140
V.	Total college fellows[2]	461	458	438	315	244	243
VI.	Percentage of total number of fellows engaged in educational work in Oxford	9%	12%	18%	31%	50%	58%

[1] These totals exceed those for 'fellows' in Appendix 3, above, p. 288 since a few fellows who did no college teaching did teach for a hall, etc. In Appendix 3, they are included among the 'other official teachers'.

[2] Only those fellows who were BAs or above have been counted. All Souls has been excluded since it had virtually no students to teach.

APPENDIX 9: College External Income 1871-1903[1]

		1871	1883	1893	1903
I.	Gross External Receipts	270,600	300,000	284,500	318,200
II.	Total Expenses	60,900	80,300[2]	93,800[2]	110,200[2]
	a. Rates, Taxes, Insurance	9,000	15,200	16,500	25,000
	b. Repairs and Improvements	23,500	26,300	35,000	42,400
	c. Interest on Loans and Repayment	19,600	30,300	33,400	33,200
	d. Management	8,800	8,500	8,900	9,600
III.	Net External Income	209,700	219,700	190,700	208,000
IV.	Cleveland Commission's Predictions[3]	-	282,600	308,600	-

[1] All figures have been rounded to the nearest £100s.

[2] These sums are lower than those used by Price because I have excluded several items of expenditure which Price included (augumentation of benefices, donations to local schools, quit-rents, and leasee's annuities) since none of these items could be extracted from the Cleveland Commission's data.

[3] These predictions were actually for 1885 and 1895, rather than for 1883 and 1893. This tendency toward over-estimating the increase, however, is counter-balanced by the fact that the prospective increments for St. John's were not included in these totals. The commissioners were not able to understand that college's accounts sufficiently to use them for this purpose. The Commission was not willing to make any concrete estimates for any of the colleges beyond 1895, although they expected the upward trend to continue at least until the mid-twentieth century.

Sources: For 1871 statistics, see 'Synopsis of the Property, Income, and Expenditure of the College and Halls in the University of Oxford', Table B, pp. 200-1; and for the Cleveland Commission's predictions, see 'Report', p. 32; both in PP 1873, xxxvii, part i. For 1883, 1893, and 1903 statistics, see *Jour. of the Royal Stat. Soc.* lxiv (1904), Table VII, p. 610 and Table X, p. 616.

APPENDIX 10: Resident MAs Not Engaged
in Official Academic Work 1858–1900

	1858: no. (%)[1]	1874: no. (%)[1]	1881: no. (%)[1]	1900: no. (%)[1]
Clergymen	28 (8)	46 (14)	36 (10)	53 (10)
Physicians	1 (-)	4 (1)	4 (1)	8 (1)
Other Laymen	13 (4)	33 (10)	31 (9)	90 (17)
Total	37 (12)	83 (25)	71 (20)	151 (28)

[1] All percentages in parentheses refer to Congregation as a whole, not to the totals on this chart.

APPENDIX 11: Age of Oxford Teachers 1814–1900

	1814: % (no.) 100% = 50	1845: % (no.) 100% = 71	1874: % (no.) 100% = 140	1900: % (no.) 100% = 190
Under 30	24 (12)	33 (23)	42 (59)	12 (23)
30–5	34 (17)	38 (27)	27 (38)	20.5 (39)
36–40	20 (10)	8 (6)	11 (15)	19 (36)
41–5	10 (5)	7 (5)	10 (14)	14 (27)
46–50	2 (1)	4 (3)	6.5 (9)	10 (19)
Over 50	10 (5)	10 (7)	3.5 (5)	24.5 (46)

Sources

The major sources for this study have been the Bodleian Library's extensive collection of pamphlets, occasional writings, and documents generated by reform debates in nineteenth-century Oxford; the reports of the three major government commissions (1850-2, 1871-3, 1877-81); and the statute revisions made by the colleges and university after 1854. A full listing of this printed material as well as relevant secondary literature, with Bodleian shelf-numbers, can be found in E. H. Cordeaux and D. H. Merry, *A Bibliography of the Printed Works Relating to the University of Oxford* (Oxford, 1968). I have also consulted the following manuscripts in the college and university archives:

Balliol College, MS 493 (Autobiography of Sydney J. Cole, MA, MD (Oxon.)).

MS 445^c (Diary of Ernest Walker 1888-94).

Bodleian Library, MS Top. Oxon. c. 326, fols. 38-43 (rough draft of letter from A. B. Poynton of University College to the editor of the *Yale News*, 10 Nov. 1914, concerning 'the Effects of the War on Oxford').

MS Top. Oxon. d. 35 (St. Alban Hall 1855-61).

MS Top. Oxon. d. 66 (Univ. Business Papers 1825-36).

MSS Top. Oxon. d. 114-16, 182 (E. B. Nicolson's corresp. and letters).

MS Top. Oxon. d. 310 (letters of Sir William Anson, 1892-1913).

MS Top. Oxon. e. 100 (Minutes of the Meetings of the Committee appointed 1 June 1868 to consider the structure of Council, Congregation and Convocation).

MS Top. Oxon. e. 182 (A Journal of the Easter and Trinity Terms 1890 by Mrs. B. B. Batty).

MS Eng. lett. c. 55 (36) (W. W. Fowler to Percy Gardner, 24 Jan. 1915).

MS Eng. lett. c. 286 (Corresp. of Sir Graves C. Haughton relating to the election of Boden Professor of Sanskrit in 1832).

MS Eng. lett. e. 130, fols. 1-51 (letters of E. H. Plumptre of BNC 1845-6).

Christ Church, MS Estates 17 (Statutes of 1867).

Exeter College, MS Minutes of Educational Council 1856-1937.

Jesus College, MS Box 2, List 3, Item 1 (tutors reports, Lent Term, 1879).

Lincoln College, MSS Day Books 1805-81.

MSS Ledgers, A, 1-4 (1882-1920).

MSS Order Books, 1801-36, 1836-71, 1872-89, 1889-1912.

MS Pattison letters 1836-52.

Oriel College, MS ETC A1, B4 (Provost Hawkin's letters and memoranda).

MS ETC F16 (papers and legal opinions relating to C. L. Shadwell's retention of his fellowship, 1875).

MS College Memoranda 1856–61, II, F12.
Pusey House, MS Corresp. of H. P. Liddon and E. B. Pusey.
University Archives, MSS St. Edmund Hall 66/1–3, 67/1–20 (Diary of
    the Revd. John Hill, Vice-Principal of St. Edmund Hall 1812–51).
    MSS Pattison 128–30 (Mark Pattison's Diary 1843–77).
    MS Hyp. A. 70 (Register of the Vice-Chancellor's Court 1835–40).
    MSS W. P. 24 (6–7) (Hebdomadal Register 1841–54, 1954–66).
University College, MSS Concerning College Statutes and Pension
    Scheme (1872–84).
    MS Order Book 1837–77.
    MSS Minute Books, III, 1869–80; IV, 1880–7.
    MS Register, III, 1842–1914.
    MS Bursar's Notes, Vol. E, 1879.
    MSS Concerning Royal Commissions (19th C.).
    MSS Legal Opinions and Papers on Various Matters *c.* 1820–1900.
    MSS Misc. Papers on College Finance and Administration 1850–1900.
    MSS Bursar's Ledgers 1810–1920.
Worcester College, MSS letters of W. W. Hadow 1888–9.

Index